ARKANA

Don Juan, Mescalito and Modern Magic

Nevil Drury was educated in England and Australia where he now lives. He has a degree in anthropology and has written or co-authored fourteen books, including *The Shaman and the Magician, Inner Visions* and *The Occult Sourcebook* (published by Routledge & Kegan Paul). He has appeared on numerous television and radio programmes dealing with the potential of human consciousness and has given lectures and workshops at a number of major conferences. He divides his time between making television documentaries and writing.

Don Juan, Mescalito and Modern Magic

The mythology of inner space

Nevill Drury

ARKANA

London and New York

First published in 1978
ARKANA edition 1985
Reprinted 1986
ARKANA PAPERBACKS is an imprint of
Routledge & Kegan Paul Ltd

11 New Fetter Lane, London EC4P 4EE, England

29 West 35th Street, New York, NY 10001, USA

Typeset by Columns of Reading
Printed and bound in Great Britain by
Cox & Wyman Ltd, Reading

© Nevill Drury 1978

ISBN 1-85063-015-1

for Serge

Contents

Note to Readers

During the production stages of this book, a new work analysing Carlos Castaneda's books and the nature of his apprenticeship to don Juan, was published in America. The book, entitled *Castaneda's Journey* and authored by Richard de Mille, alleges that don Juan is a fiction and that Castaneda drew on a number of anthropological and philosophical sources in producing his material. De Mille cites the work of Peter Furst and Gordon Wasson in particular, as likely sources for Castaneda's shamanistic material and states his personal belief that Castaneda was awarded a Ph.D. degree from the University of California for what amounts to an imaginary ethnography.

At the time of writing Carlos Castaneda has not responded to de Mille's allegations but there is no doubt that the latter's critique will continue to raise serious questions about whether the magical apprenticeship ever took place. At the same time, de Mille is anxious to point out that even if the don Juan episodes did not actually occur, the incidents and details which they recount are largely factual albeit drawn from a number of sources. *The Teachings of Don Juan* and the subsequent volumes then loom as an ethnographic amalgam based largely on the Huichol Indians, with smatterings of Wittgenstein and possibly even C.S. Lewis thrown in for good measure!

The present book is a comparison of two magical world views – that proposed by don Juan and that found in contemporary Western magic – of the type practised in the Hermetic Order of the Golden Dawn. As a thematic study only, it cannot answer the question of Castaneda's authenticity but does seek to demonstrate parallel lines of thought in magical systems other than those of Mexico and near-by regions. In view of the doubts raised about Castaneda's originality these parallels might now assume an even greater significance than might have originally been the case.

May 1977

Acknowledgments

The author and publishers are grateful to the following for permission to quote from the works cited: Greenhouse Publications, Melbourne, for quotations from 'Frontiers of Consciousness', edited by Nevill Drury; The New American Library, Inc., for the poetry extract from 'High Priest' by Timothy Leary; University Books Inc. for quotations from 'Astral Projection' by Oliver Fox, published by permission of University Books Inc. (a division of Lyle Stuart Inc.), 120 Enterprise Avenue, Secaucus, New Jersey 07094, USA.

Introduction

We live in times of rapid technological change which demand a pace of existence that many cannot sustain. Within this framework certain things have initially gone by the board. As science increased its scope during the last century and proved that the seven days of creation were in fact vast epochs of geological time, it came to replace the more fundamentalist versions of the Christian creed upon which Western Civilization had been based. Science appeared to be an alternative, pragmatic arbiter of the laws of the universe.

However in our own way we find in a sense that science has failed too. Laws and rules of form and energy tend to be hard and impervious. They lack a human dimension. Man cannot accept that they alone decide his destiny. And so he has tended to retain his religious beliefs, and has in certain cases modified them with the advent of science. The most progressive followers of Christianity in the Victorian Church were often scientific innovators themselves, crying out to the populace to accept a more flexible and less dogmatic approach to their creed. At one time in the early nineteenth century both chairs of geology at Oxford and Cambridge for example were held by clerics who wished to combine religious and scientific understanding.

But elsewhere religion took more bizarre forms, and new faiths such as Christian Science, Theosophy, the Oahspe teachings, Mormonism and various forms of Christian spiritualism came into prominence.

Inherent in all this diversity, which first mushroomed around a hundred years or so ago, was the need for some type of authoritative opinion. When man felt that science was eroding his faith, he either turned to a more remote or modified teaching which had not yet come under attack, or else he became a humanist or atheist. Whatever happened, he was not able to stand still.

Recently Russian astronauts reported that God was not alive

1

and living on the moon, and this statement had an understandable cynicism associated with it. However, many people – and I feel especially young people – have felt that technology, and the scientific prowess which has been able to place man on the moon, is not enough either. Such knowledge and scientific know-how does not tell us much about man himself, and his place in the scheme of things. Science has not replaced the religious or mystical sense of awe and wonderment felt as man contemplates the vastness of the universe. A sense of mystery is not in itself an empirical item. It cannot be measured, and yet it exists.

Today, as in times past, man looks for a guru, a wise and spiritual teacher whose wisdom is unassailable, and who can lead him to the light.

We have had a number in the last few years: the Maharaji Mahesh Yogi to whom the Beatles and Mia Farrow turned for inner guidance; Meher Baba who died without uttering the cosmic mantra which would dissolve the universe; Guru Maharaj ji, the adolescent saviour incarnate. Others too: for those who wished to project the UFO phenomenon into a religion, Erich Von Daniken came with the message that God was an astronaut. The golden age of wisdom lay in the dim past, in an epoch beyond Atlantis shrouded in antediluvian glory. And the gods who had brought this wisdom on which man's cultural heritage and knowledge was founded were now returning in the UFOs in the last days of man. There is much of significance which has come to light as a result of the more level-headed scientific inquiry into the UFO phenomenon, but Von Daniken above all others represents the transformation of outer space mysteries into a religion. This, too, in a time when man first reached out towards the stars.

When all this is said and done, one major step in the history of contemporary religious movements *did* occur in the West in the 1960s. It had grown up partly out of the idea that science is based on what is known to occur. In the United States in particular, where oriental religious thought had begun to penetrate, the idea that one has to experience what one is to believe, became a point of commencement.

Under the influence of Vedanta and Buddhism, people went off and meditated, looking for the answers to life and meaning within themselves. Others, like Leary, Burroughs and Ginsburg got high on various hallucinogens and experienced new dimensions of being. Now whether or not this approach was embraced by the majority of upright Americans, which it wasn't, a new inroad had been made. It is what I would like to call the beginning of the approach to inner space. And this is the subject of this book.

The idea behind all ventures into inner space is that man can begin where he is, and by means of certain spiritual disciplines and insights, he can begin to be aware of his more spiritual side. In so doing, he loses the more animalian, aggressive and self-centred approach to his fellow humans and gains a new perspective.

Yoga has been the mainstay of the inner space development, and in general there has been very much a 'return to the East'.

However an interesting Western phenomenon occurred in the late 1960s and early 70s. A young academic wrote an unfolding account of how he had gained a new understanding of the world and its manifestations through the techniques of sorcery. He had been instructed over a decade or so by a Mexican shaman named don Juan. The academic in question, an anthropologist from UCLA named Carlos Castaneda, gave the impression from his books that don Juan was very much a wise and learned man. He was in tune with nature's mysteries and understood how to come to terms with her. He had in his grasp techniques for altering his consciousness so he could manipulate those mysteries. These were his system of magic.

Suddenly a new guru had been found in the West, and Carlos Castaneda, as the go-between, found himself elevated to the status of one of the god-figures of the psychedelic revolution. In an interview in 'Psychology Today', Castaneda told how it was alleged in California that he walked barefoot like Jesus and had no callouses. He was also 'supposed to be stoned most of the time', and had 'committed suicide and died in several different places'.

The episodes of don Juan may or may not be fictional, as some have remarked. They could be either a remarkable work of the imagination or thoroughly innovative anthropology. At present only Castaneda and perhaps a few close friends could be assured of the authenticity of his writings although the evidence does seem to be in favour of his account being true. His original thesis was screened thoroughly by his academic supervisors who insisted on his adding a tedious 'structural analysis' of don Juan's sorcery. Since fame only came later, it cannot be suggested that Castaneda was initially writing to deceive a gullible sub-culture. Also there are points of remarkable comparison between the don Juan sessions and shamanism in general throughout South and Central America as a study of the works of Peter Hurst, Michael Harner and others will show. Don Juan is not unique. He *is*, however, admirably documented. And as such, as I have indicated, he became one of a number of the gurus in the West.

Besides Castaneda, two other people, at least, have made an important contribution to the field we are discussing. The first of these was Timothy Leary, who despite his more extravagant outbursts in recent times, was one of the original, systematic pioneers of inner space. By 'systematic' I mean that he endeavoured to structure altered states of consciousness in such a way that they produced elevating, beneficial results. It may perhaps be argued that Leary did not fulfil his own promise. Be this as it may, we must not pass over his valuable correlation of 'The Tibetan Book of the Dead' with modes of hallucinogenic and mystical consciousness. What Leary was saying, and it continues to be important, was that anyone undertaking the inner voyage needs sign-posts. He needs to know what to expect. He needs to know the kind of effects his sacrament will produce. He must know whether to expect gods or demons, just as don Juan instructed Castaneda in the ways of Mescalito (the deity of the peyote cactus) and the Allies of the mushroom smoke and datura vine.

Leary noted that 'The Tibetan Book of the Dead' offered man a means for his own spiritual rebirth. Using it as a guide to levels of mystical awareness he would achieve new realizations, increased understanding and a new mode for living.

A neuro-physiologist named John Lilly meanwhile undertook experiments in sensory deprivation, and the conditioning of both hallucinogenic and non-hallucinogenic mystical states. In his key book 'The Centre of the Cyclone' he evolved the idea of different spaces within the subconscious which man could enter at will. These spaces varied in content and imagery according to his belief system, but whatever the case, by means of mystical frameworks, man could attain transcendental states of being by increasing his rapport with his subconscious.

Castaneda, Leary and Lilly have one thing in common. They describe approaches to the mind and its mysteries. Their accounts retain a sense of awe, and have understandably reached a wide audience in the counter culture and elsewhere because they fulfil a condition I mentioned earlier: they are both systematic and mystical in their orientation. *They are all centrally founded in what you and I can experience.*

Now a shaman, such as don Juan, is a person who attempts, in a state of trance or ecstasy, to explore the religious or magical imagery of his own mind. This imagery contains all the 'archetypes' of his own culture. When he flies through the inner sky of his subconsciousness he encounters a living mythology made up of all the gods and demons of his race. In a Mexican context, Castaneda found himself experiencing Mexican archetypes since these were associated with the cultural modes of thought which he was learning from his mentor. Having pursued Hinduism and Buddhism, Timothy Leary found himself describing and perceiving levels of inner space in a mostly Eastern context.

I would like to stress at this point, however, that there are, I believe, inherent *Western* programmes too (to use John Lilly's term). There are Western archetypes which constitute the basis of Western mythology, and folklore and legends. These presumably reinforce images in our subconscious minds with which we may possibly have the most all-encompassing sense of rapport were we to undertake the journey into inner space. I am suggesting that most of us have been brought up in what Castaneda himself calls the 'Western Intellectual Tradition' and that this is a product of the thoughts (and archetypes) of ancient Greece, Rome, Egypt, Scandinavia and Central Europe. These are the origins of our culture. The gods and demons associated with these origins and thought processes are deeply embedded in the minds of all of us.

My intention in this book is to compare Carlos Castaneda's exposition of don Juan's Mexican sorcery with other modes of shamanistic activity, and also with other approaches to inner space. But my essential aim is to show that there is a basically Western shamanism which uses Western symbols and is easily accessible. I refer to the magic of the Qabalah and the Tarot. It is my belief as others have intimated, that these two in fact are not only a Western shamanism but represent the *yoga of the West*.

Yoga is a mystical discipline which describes levels of awareness culminating in union with Godhead. The Qabalah is similarly a mystical framework for the transcendental expansion of consciousness. Its tenfold system of mysticism, based on the Sephiroth or levels of being upon the Tree of Life correlate both with the yogic system of Kundalini chakras, and also with John Lilly's frameworks based on the teachings of Gurdjieff, and it is possible to show that the Twenty-two Major Tarot Trumps embody a symbolism which constitutes a sequence of doorways to the mind which is both as far-reaching and illuminating as the mind levels described in 'The Tibetan Book of the Dead'.

As with don Juan the mode of inquiry into the Qabalah and the Tarot has brought forth a system of magic rather than religion. Magic in a sense is more pragmatic and less intuitive. It searches after results actively rather than pursuing a passive approach, and perhaps it is this aspect which has assisted in the revival of the 'occult sciences' in the present day. However, magic is a debased word and lacks the spiritual connotation of yoga. I hope in the following pages to rectify this impression.

Qabalistic magic provides a structure of the mind, a sequence of archetypes and a series of shamanistic doorways. Eventually after a maze of imagery, the magician finds himself entering similar spiritual inner spaces to those described in the East. Only his journey, not his goal, has been different.

In modern magical practice there are two polarities. One is towards *possession* and the other is towards *ecstasy*. In the first instance the practitioner employs certain ritual practices based perhaps on ancient Greek and Egyptian religious expressions to help himself identify with the image of a god. He hopes in so doing to be inflamed by the uplifting energies of that god-image. He hopes, in short, to become a god. In the second, the magician makes use of certain trance techniques which I will be describing, to project his mind out of the body as it were. The consciousness explores new realms of mind within a transcendental sphere which was not formerly within its mode of perception. It is this second approach which most clearly parallels the teachings of don Juan and which will occupy us at length in this book.

In a 1973 issue of 'Rolling Stone', David Saltman described how he went in search of don Juan in Mexico. He was looking for the *brujo* or 'man of knowledge' who had inspired Castaneda to new heights. He was looking for the guru. He found the town of Guadalajara teeming with practitioners of 'nefarious conjuration' but no one had heard of don Juan.

My point in drawing the comparisons I make in this book, is that it was not necessarily vital to go in search of the guru. With the Qabalah and the Tarot, David Saltman could have stayed home.

PART ONE

The Inner Mythology

CHAPTER 1
The Shaman and his Universe

In 1960 Carlos Castaneda, who was then a student at the University of California, took the first step towards the dissolution of his own intellectual universe. He was researching in the southwest on the Indian use of medicinal plants, and a friend introduced him to an old Yaqui Indian who was said to be an expert on the hallucinogen peyote.

The Indian, don Juan Matus, said he was a *brujo*, a term which connotes a sorcerer, or one who cures by means of magical techniques. Born in Sonora, Mexico, in 1891, he spoke Spanish 'remarkably well', but appeared at the first meeting to be unimpressed with Castaneda's self-confidence. He indicated however that Castaneda should come to see him subsequently, and an increasingly warm relationship developed as the young Brazilian academic entered into an 'apprenticeship' in sorcery.

Carlos Castaneda found many of don Juna's ideas and techniques strange and irrational. The world of the sorcerer contained mysterious, inexplicable forces that he was obliged not to question, but had to accept as a fact of life. The apprentice sorcerer would begin to 'see' whereas previously he had merely 'looked'. Eventually he would become a 'man of knowledge'.

According to Castaneda's exposition of don Juan's ideas, the world that we believe to be 'out there' is only one of a number of worlds. It is in reality a description of the relationship between objects that we have learnt to recognize as significant from birth, and which has been reinforced by language and the communication of mutually acceptable concepts. This world is not the same as the world of the sorcerer, for whereas ours tends to be based on the confidence of perception, the *brujo's* involves many 'intangibles'. His universe is a vast and continuing mystery which cannot be contained within rational categories and frameworks.

In order to transform one's perception from ordinary to magical reality, an 'unlearning' process has to occur. The apprentice must learn how to 'not do' what he has previously 'done'. He must learn how to transcend his previous frameworks and conceptual categories and for a moment freeze himself between the two universes, the 'real' and the 'magically real'. To use don Juan's expression, he must 'stop the world'. From this point he may begin to *see*, to acquire a knowledge and mastery of the variable and mysterious forces operating in the environment which most people close off from their everyday perception.

The *brujo* operates in sacred territory. He takes his stand on the point of ground where he feels strongest, and which embodies his magical identity: a place 'soaked with unforgettable memories, where powerful events have left their mark, a place where he has witnessed marvels, where secrets have been revealed to him; a place where he has stored his personal power . . .'.

He takes upon himself the role of the warrior against the forces of an unpredictable universe with the knowledge that death will eventually play the trump card. The *brujo* has at his command a knowledge of ritual postures and a sensitivity to his surroundings whereby he can defend himself against magical opponents. In any circumstance, he will never be caught with his guard down.

However, apart from these factors, the *brujo* has four enemies or deterrents within himself: fear; clarity; power; and old age.

As he learns, he becomes *afraid* while encountering the previously unknown. As his purpose thereby becomes a 'battlefield' he may acquire *clarity* of mind which conquers these fears, but which at the same time fosters the illusion that his knowledge is becoming *complete*. A man able to overcome such self-confidence will wield considerable *power*, but he may not yet have mastery over himself: 'The power he has seemingly conquered is in reality never his.' Finally the sorcerer must resist the onset of *old age* as best he can, for this will produce in him a 'desire to rest'. If he can overcome this fatiguing tendency he may then become a *man of knowledge*.

A man of knowledge is one who *sees*. 'Seeing' is a means of perception which may be brought about often, although not necessarily, by hallucinogenic drugs, among them mescalito (peyote), yerba del diablo (Jimson weed: datura) and humito (psilocybe mushrooms). Through these, the *brujo* could acquire an *ally*, who could in turn grant further power, and the ability to enter more readily into 'states of non-ordinary reality'. The *brujo* becomes able to see the 'fibres of light' and energy patterns emanating from people and other living organisms; to encounter the forces within the wind and water-hole, and isolate as visionary experiences, as if on film, the incidents of one's early life and their influence on the growth of the personality. Such knowledge enables the *brujo* to tighten his defences as a warrior. He knows himself, and has command over his physical vehicle. He can project his consciousness from his body into images of birds and animals thereby transforming into a myriad of shapes and forms while travelling in the 'spirit vision'.

And yet he will always remain in control, able to exert his will while *seeing*. Finally, aware that his 'death' will follow all his actions and decisions during life, he will remain neutral with the world, for death does not permit him to cling permanently to anything. The sorcerer must choose his 'strategy' in a kaleidoscopic and forever unpredictable universe which will eventually claim him, impartially, as its prey.

Considered within his cultural context, don Juan, the wizened old Yaqui Indian, is in many ways a unique personage, a stranger even among his own people. And yet despite Castaneda's refusal to categorize him within a 'cultural milieu', don Juan as a sorcerer and shaman remains part of a universal tradition. This tradition is that of the ecstatic; the priest or magician who can voluntarily leave his body under trance and explore other dimensions of consciousness. Such techniques find strong representation in South and Central America.

It is generally agreed that a shaman is one who by means of various drugs, hallucinogenic ointments or mental disciplines undertakes a journey away from his body. Sometimes it seems to be a purely 'three-dimensional' affair, not involving transcendental encounters with deities and spirit images from the recesses of the subconscious mind. An interesting case of this type was reported by Father Trilles who worked with the Pygmies of Equatorial Africa. Trilles on one occasion required the assistance of a native on a fishing trip in Gabon. The native explained that he was going to Aleva, normally four days' walk away, and would be unavailable. However he also added that he intended to be there the following day, since he had an important 'reunion' to attend. Father Trilles was puzzled by this discrepancy in time and distance but was assured by the native that he 'had his means'. Trilles then asked him to convey a message to a person named Esab' Ava requesting cartridges and powder for his own fishing trip.

Meanwhile he was allowed to be present during 'departure preparations' for the reunion. The native, who was clearly a sorcerer,[1]

> first smeared his body with a special mixture . . . then he lit a
> fire and walked around it, saying prayers to the spirits of the
> air and the guardian spirits of the magic brotherhood. He
> then fell into a state of ecstasy, showed the whites of his
> eyes, his skin became insensitive and his limbs rigid. It was
> ten o'clock the next day when he came out of his trance, and
> during that time Father Trilles had not left his side. When he
> awoke, the man gave some details about the reunion at
> which he had been present and then, without being asked,
> said:
> 'Your message has been carried out. Esab' Ava has been
> warned. He will set out this morning and will bring you the
> powder and the cartridges.'
> Three days later . . . Esab' Ava arrived at the village with
> the goods. . . .

In Castaneda's account there are similar references to smearing with a toxic paste that caused a dislocation of the consciousness from the body. We find similar practices among medieval witches travelling to the Sabbath in the trance condition, while their bodies remained behind.

Normally, however, the shamanistic venture involves a confrontation with deities and spirits which embody the practitioner's own mythical heritage. He may encounter those who fashioned the world in the Beginning and who remain now as archetypes or guardians of the people. Alternatively he may experience visions of terrifying beasts which personify the fears and dangers associated with the jungle or rock canyons.

And most frequently, and particularly in South America, we find that the shaman is a healer also. He is able, in the hallucinogenic state, to perceive the energy body of human beings; he can see inside the organism as if it were transparent. If a magical object – a dart or power stone – sent by a sorcerer has caused illness by lodging in the body of the victim, it is the shaman's function to discover and suck the offensive object out of its harmful position. If the patient has lost his 'soul', the shaman must follow it on the visionary journey and bring it back to safety where it cannot be ensnared.

Don Juan was not, by Castaneda's account, a healer, although he was widely familiar with the use of medicinal and herbal plants, used as an adjunct to his sorcery. However, under don Juan's mescalin preparation, Castaneda was able to see water coursing through the vessels of a dog, and currents of light energy in his mentor's face.

The *brujo* employs various shamanistic techniques in order to gain access to supernatural territory, a dimension where he is able to meet his spirit allies and Mescalito and to transform into bird or animal shapes, and where the 'rules' are somehow less precise and the concepts and categories applicable to normal reality, no longer relevant. Don Juan was also able to induce in Castaneda, hallucinogenically, a clairvoyant state which Michael Harner believes is also a characteristic of the shaman.

Several of these paranormal aspects: clairvoyance, the out-of-the-body experience, lycanthropy and trance, represent dealings on a plane of existence one phase removed from everyday perception. According to Mircea Eliade, it is the shaman's prerogative to move with free access from one dimension to another, 'from earth to the sky or from earth to the underworld. The shaman knows the mystery of the break-through in plane.'

Frequently linked with this we find the notion of a certain *sacred* location, whether it is a hole between the rocks, a mountain reaching towards the sky, or a bridge scaling the heavens.

All of these things are present in the Castaneda account: he begins his tuition under don Juan by finding a special *spot* on the floor and is unable to locate it rationally. This will be the position where he feels safest, where he is strong against prospective enemies.

Later he listens to the sound of the spirit-catcher in the chaparral. He hears the sounds of the crickets and birds too, each with its particular vibration, and he notices that the rhythms have become 'visual'. The entry into the magical world is through a hole in the sounds, through a funnel where he may meet the ally.

Finally Castaneda's initiation and encounter with a friendly, talking, luminous coyote occur on his own sacred location, the place where according to don Juan he will eventually 'die' symbolically. This is the magic mountain where he will also perform his last dance before moving on to the afterworld.

Special locations, magical paths of entry and sacred mountains are very much a part of the universal shamanistic tradition. According to Eliade, the Cosmic Tree, Bridge or Stairway, is a widely disseminated idea connected with belief in the direct communication with the sky.

Don Juan used peyote, datura and psilocybe mushrooms to induce mental states of 'non-ordinary reality'. 'In using a powerful hallucinogen', writes Harner, 'an individual is brought face to face with visions and experiences of an overwhelming nature tending strongly to reinforce his beliefs in the reality of the supernatural world . . . .' He found this to be so particularly among the Jivaro of Eastern Ecuador, whose initiation techniques he studied at length:[2]

> The Jivaro believe that the true determinants of life and death are normally invisible forces which can be seen and utilised only with the aid of hallucinogenic drugs. The normal waking life is explicitly viewed as 'false' or a 'lie' and it is firmly believed that truth about causality is to be found by entering the supernatural world, or what the Jivaro view as the 'real' world, for they feel that the events which take place within it underlie and are the basis for many of the surface manifestations and mysteries of daily life.

The variety and rich cultural application of hallucinogenic plants has been widely documented. The Banisteriopsis vine which can be used to make a trance-inducing beverage is found among the Indians of Rio Negro in Brazil, the Rio Putumayo in Eastern Colombia, and among many tribes in Ecuador and Peru. Among the headhunting Jivaro it is called natema, in Colombia yage, in Ecuador and Peru ayahuasca, and in Brazil caapi.

The sacramental use of hallucinogenic mushrooms, called by the Aztecs teonanacatl, or God's Flesh, is at least as old as AD 300. Schultes notes, in fact, that on the basis of so-called 'mushroom stones' found in archaeological remains of the highland Maya of Guatemala, and previously thought to be phallic objects, this date may extend even as far back as 1000 BC.[3]

At the present time a number of Indian tribes consume the sacred mushrooms as part of their shamanistic activity, among them the Mazatecs, Chinantecs, Zapotecs and Mixtecs, all of whom come from Oaxaca, a region close to the location of the Yaqui Indians and don Juan's personal dwelling in Sonora.

Both don Juan and Gordon Wasson, who first brought the

sacred mushroom to the attention of contemporary anthropology, agree that the plant sacraments continue to compete with orthodox Catholicism.

> When the Spanish conquerors first arrived in Mexico, the civilization of Europe had known nothing like these novel drugs of Mexico, at least not in recorded history. Similar miraculous powers were attributed, in a way, to the Elements in the Mass; and the Catholic Church in Mexico was quick to perceive this. . . . But belief in the divinity of the Sacrament called for an act of faith whereas *the Mexican plants spoke for themselves.*

According to Henry Munn who married the niece of a Mazatec shaman and shamaness, the psilocybe mushrooms open vistas of supernatural awareness, although there are also traps and dangers:[4]

> They walk through the mountains along their arduous paths on the different levels of being, climbing and descending in the sunlight and through the clouds; all around there are grottos and abysses, mysterious groves, places where live the *laa'*, the little people, mischievous dwarfs and gnomes. Rivers and wells are inhabited by spirits with powers of enchantment. At night in these altitudes, winds whirl up from the depths, rush out of the distance like monsters, and pass, tearing everything in their path with their fierce claws. Phantoms appear in the mists. There are persons with the evil eye. Existence in the world and with others is treacherous, perilous: unexpectedly something may happen to you, and that event, unless it is exorcised, can mark you for life. . . .

Among the other hallucinogens referred to in the don Juan/Castaneda dialogues are datura and peyote. According to Schultes, this genus has two New World focal centres of use: the American south-west (i.e. California, Arizona and New Mexico) and adjacent Mexico. Apart from the Jivaro already mentioned, and the Incas of Peru, beverages made from this plant are also used by the Chibcas and the witch-doctors of the highlands of Ecuador. It is particularly potent, for the intoxication 'is marked by an initial state of violence so furious that the partaker must be held down pending the arrival of the deep disturbed sleep during which visual hallucinations, interpreted as spirit visitations are experienced'.[5]

The Jivaro use the datura beverage only when visiting the sacred waterfalls in their immediate vicinity to obtain an *arutam* soul, or spirit helper. Extremely potent visions arise, and the propitiant has by his side a special assistant to ensure that no accidents occur. Then the 'allies' may appear:[6]

> Some of the most common arutam include a pair of giant jaguars fighting one another as they roll over and over towards the vision seeker, or two anacondas doing the same. Often the vision may simply be a single huge disembodied human head or a ball of fire drifting through the forest towards the arutam seeker. . . .

Don Juan himself continued to use datura (Jimson weed) although he found its effects unpredictable. His own 'benefactor', who had instructed him in the ways of sorcery, nevertheless had chosen it for his own ally, and found it most conducive to the acquisition of mystical powers. 'An Ally', says don Juan, 'is a power capable of carrying a man beyond the boundaries of himself.'[7]

Don Juan, however, reserved special reverence for peyote. Its archetypal deity, Mescalito, was greater than an ally for he could teach, whereas an ally only supplied *power*. Mescalito was, in his own right, a most impressive deity. According to Castaneda's vision of him:[8]

> his eyes were of the water I had just seen. They had the same enormous volume, the sparkling of gold and black. His head was pointed like a strawberry; his skin was green, dotted with innumerable warts. Except for the pointed shape, his head was exactly like the surface of the peyote plant. . . .

Under mescalin, the main activating agent in peyote, Aldous Huxley noticed similar transformations from plant to God-head:[9]

> I continued to look at the flowers and in their living light I seemed to detect the qualitative equivalent of breathing – but of a breathing without returns to a starting point, with no recurrent ebbs but only a repeated flow from beauty to heightened beauty, from deeper to ever deeper meaning. Words like Grace and Transfiguration came to my mind, and

this of course was what, among other things, they stood for.
My eyes travelled from the rose to the carnation, and from
that feathery incandescence to the smooth scrolls of sentient
amethyst which were the iris. The Beatific Vision, *Sat Chit
Ananda*, Being – Awareness – Bliss – for the first time I
understood precisely and completely what those prodigious
syllables referred to. . . .

It is these hallucinogens, often deified or consumed only under
special ritual conditions, which allow the trance magician, or
shaman, to undertake his mystical journey. We have accounts
which suggest that both the native user of these plants and the
white visitor also are able to encounter the mythical pantheons
and transcendental revelations of the people to whom they are
sacred.

In Peru, among the Cashinahua, Kenneth Kensinger saw the
nixi pae spirit people accompanied by brightly coloured snakes,
armadillos and singing frogs. When Michael Harner partook of
natema he found himself in a bizarre mythological dimension:[10]

I met bird-headed people as well as dragon-like creatures
who explained that they were the true gods of the World. I
enlisted the services of other spirit helpers in attempting to
fly through the far reaches of the Galaxy. . . .

He was witnessing a cosmic drama similar to that seen by the
Trukano shamans of Colombia:[11]

after a stage of undefined luminosity of moving forms and
colours, the vision begins to clear up and significant details
present themselves. The Milky Way appears and the distant
fertilizing reflection of the Sun. The first woman surges forth
from the waters of the river, and the first pair of ancestors is
formed. The supernatural Master of the Animals of the
jungle and waters is perceived, as are the gigantic prototypes
of the game animals, the origins of the plants – indeed the
origins of life itself. The origins of Evil also manifest
themselves, jaguars and serpents, the representatives of
illness, and the spirits of the jungle that lie in ambush for the
solitary hunter. At the same time their voices are heard, the
music of the mythic epoch is perceived, and the ancestors are
seen, dancing at the dawn of Creation.

The shaman, confronted with the spectacle of a transcendental cosmic drama, could well be expected to lose complete control of his perceptive faculties, and be overcome by awe. However, it is precisely his ability to remain composed, even in his mythological confrontations, which distinguishes him from the schizophrenic. As Eliade says, the shaman is a *technician of the sacred*. His mystical journey is subject to *will*.

The initial act of will is one of conscious projection into a dimension normally sealed from everyday consciousness. It is deep within the more universal levels of what Jung has called the Collective Unconscious that the shaman travels among the archetypal gods of his tribal heritage. Now, the act of projection is a very interesting discipline indeed. It is certainly a central technique of don Juan's sorcery, and its parallel to what has been called in the West 'astral projection' or 'astro-travelling' will be discussed subsequently.

Among the Iglulik Eskimos the master shaman extracts the 'soul' or consciousness of his pupil in sequence from the intestines, brain and eyes, and the apprentice begins to feel that he is able to perceive a new plane of existence through a newly found luminous fire that courses through his brain.

This technique, which is similar to one used by modern occultists, also has a parallel among the Selk'nam of Tierra del Fuego who describe the astral projection in beautifully metaphoric terms:[12]

> This power (i.e. of psychic vision) is depicted as an eye that leaves the witch doctor's body and travels in a straight line to the object in his view, while still remaining connected to the witch doctor. The eye distends like a sort of 'thread made of gum' (this is how the Indians expressed it): it is able to function from any side of the head like the eyes of a lobster, and may be withdrawn, like a snail's antennae.

In the same way that Castaneda is taught to imagine that his head (= consciousness) is undergoing transformation into the body or vehicle of a crow (to enable him to 'fly'), so, too, the modern ritual magician builds up an image before his eyes to which he will transfer consciousness. This frequently takes the form of a hooded man, since the details are relatively easy to visualize and characterize a suitable anonymity on the astral plane. But in all instances the act of *identification* is crucially important. 'Instead of hearing or seeing the rustling of leaves in the wind, instead of hearing a word', writes de Martino, the shaman *'becomes* the word itself. There is no longer any discrimination – the image cannot prevent itself from becoming the act.'[13] Often the magician now finds himself outside his body, which is visible beneath him in a state of trance. He seems however to be joined to it by a fine, silken chord and may ebb or flow away from it according to the direction of his will. It is this activity which the Fuegans have described so poetically, and which represents the first stage of the shaman's journey from one plane of being to another.

CHAPTER 2
Astral Projection
The pioneers

It is not easy to obtain information on trance techniques from South American Indian or other native shamans who have out-of-the-body experiences. The universe in which they find themselves is an alien one for us, one that does not easily square with either our own logical (or even mythical) conceptions, or present much common ground. Carlos Castaneda, who was with don Juan during a decade still had trouble understanding the implications of 'stopping the world' and *seeing*. He and Douglas Sharon,[1] apprenticed to a Peruvian folk-healer, represent two among very few detailed first-hand accounts of what a native sorcerer or *curandero* feels when he transports himself out of the body.

Now, fortunately, there is slightly more information available in another direction. In the field of contemporary ceremonial magic we find a number of excitingly parallel trance and ritual techniques, and these will be given special attention presently. However, the phenomenon of 'astral projection' – the separation of a type of fluidic 'spiritual' counterpart of the human body and the exploration of other dimensions of existence – has been widely commented upon in recent years. There exist very definite methods whereby one can go about causing these effects. Sometimes they enlist the use of drugs. Very often they do not. Usually they are techniques of mental control which enable a person to transfer his consciousness from its normal three-dimensional physical framework to a more rarified perceptive organism which appears in many ways much more 'convenient' and flexible. It enables a person to float around his room or up through the ceiling, and perhaps into the sky. He may visit a friend and later corroborate that what he had observed or heard from his friend was in fact true, and not the product of fantasy or wish-fulfilment. On other occasions, and these are equally if not more interesting, certain transcendental elements from the sub-conscious might appear as if in a self-contained form and would behave as if they were real and tangible, despite their imaginary

20

origin. The astral projectionist would thus find himself sometimes engaged in a confrontation with 'spiritual images' in a fantastic drama, sometimes enacting very powerful cosmic 'events' which impressed him deeply at the time as being equally as true and valid as the phenomena of everyday reality.

Thus there are really two types of out-of-the-body experiences. There are those in which quite normal imagery is perceived, and in which certain events occur as if one is in a privileged vantage point to behold them. One wishes to visit a certain location and suddenly finds oneself there, observing familiar people and a familiar environment. Sometimes, however, certain things will be occurring that are not part of routines, or were unexpected, and these can be checked later for validation. Sometimes these events may be seen as if from overhead, or from a point far removed but observed as if looking through a 'tunnel', as if the consciousness without the body has the special capacity to find itself in certain specified places, under will and command.

The second type of 'projection' involves what may be called a 'fantasy' or perhaps more appropriately a *phantasy* element. Things occur which are normally part of the world of mythology and fairy tales. The onlooker meets in his vision bizarre human and non-human entities from another plane normally associated with the world of nightmares or ancient legends. Sometimes he is overwhelmed or awed by what he sees and feels himself 'reborn' under the momentous profundity of what has been expressed symbolically before his eyes. Now it is the latter condition which more approaches the universe of the shaman or mystical sorcerer. However, it is possible for both real and imaginary components to fuse in the out-of-the-body experience, for they represent a continuum of polarities and not a division of type.

To my knowledge there have been three outstanding pioneers of research into the more pragmatic techniques of astral projection and we will consider these first. Their names: Sylvan Muldoon; Oliver Fox (the pseudonym for Hugh Callaway) and Robert A. Monroe.

Sylvan Muldoon, who is best known for his book 'The Projection of the Astral Body' first published in 1929, began experiencing unusual psychic dissociation from the age of twelve. His mother was very interested in spiritualism and decided on one occasion to visit a camp of the Mississippi Valley Spiritualist Association at Clinton in Iowa. It was here, while also suffering from a state of ill-health, that Sylvan first experienced 'astral projection'.

He was in a state of half sleep at the time, a condition which seems on other evidence to be characteristic. He felt himself to have fallen into a 'silent, dark and feelingless condition'. It seemed to him that he was 'adhering' to the bed on which he rested. Gradually however, as he relaxed, he felt a new freedom except for a slight tension at the back of his head.[2]

> I took a step, when the pressure increased for an interval and threw my body out at an acute angle. I managed to turn around. There were two of me! I was beginning to believe myself insane. There was another 'me' lying quietly upon the bed! It was difficult to convince myself that this was real, but consciousness would not allow me to doubt what I saw.
>
> My two identical bodies were joined by means of an elastic-like cable, one end of which was fastened to the *medulla oblongata* region of the astral counterpart, while the other end centred between the eyes.

Muldoon describes another classic instance, similar to his own, in which the person concerned – a doctor – felt a numbness creep through his limbs, and gradually began to 'lose control' of his body. Lights began to flash before his eyes and ringing sound echoed through his ears. The account continues:[3]

> it seemed for an instant as though I had become unconscious. When I came out of this state, I seemed to be walking in the air. No words can describe the clearness of mental vision. . . . I became conscious of being in a room and looking down on a body propped up in bed, which I recognized as my own. I cannot tell what strange feelings came over me! This body, to all extents and purposes looked to be dead. There was no indication of life about it, and yet here I was, apart from my body, with my mind thoroughly clear and alert.

Sylvan Muldoon considered the astral counterpart to be the real and animating body, and the normal physical body to be no more than a shell for the perceptive consciousness. It is an ancient view in fact, held by many early Greek and Egyptian philosophers and mystics. The Gnostics even regarded the physical body as tardy and evil by comparison with the soul of righteousness normally ensnared within. Muldoon writes:[4]

> The astral phantom is so much our self that we do not realize how bound up in it we are . . . it is our life, this astral body, and when it permanently severs from the physical body, that physical is of no account . . . this phantomous body . . . is the 'You' of the present . . . your consciousness, your animation. Without the astral body your physical anatomy would be but a crude mass of insensible material, lying inert.

The Gnostics, Hellenistic philosophers and Neoplatonists believed that on death, the 'soul' or consciousness would ascend through various mystical 'spheres' of existence, eventually finding its heaven at an appropriate level of 'purity'. On birth, it was this soul that would descend, thus animating the physical organism. All creative activity, the writing of poetry and music and the production of fine works of art, owed their inspiration to the highest level of genius or illumination which could be attained by the gifted 'translator' while within the framework of his senses.

Muldoon's idea is thus hardly original. However recent investigations into psychic research in Russia have also shown that this conception may not be purely fanciful supposition.[5]

For Muldoon the astral body is more *real* than the physical counterpart. It allows a wider range of vision and it opens up dimensions of being unsuspected in the normal waking consciousness. Muldoon's main method of 'separation' involved a process he called *dream control*. The astral projection phenomenon does in fact resemble dreaming in a number of ways, for it may be that the person finds himself enmeshed in a sequence of quickly flowing, changing images frequently relating to activities in his waking existence. However, it is the clarity and apparent realism of the out-of-the-body experience which seems to impress upon the mind of the person involved, that *that is no mere dream*. Something is occurring which seems to be *valid*; certain things are seen which either mirror events as they occur simultaneously 'elsewhere', or apparently hint of something yet to occur.

Celia Green, of the Institute of Psychophysical Research in Oxford, calls the activity where the dreamer is aware that he is in fact dreaming, the *lucid dream*. This does not refer to the clarity of the imagery itself, although this too is characteristic, but to the element of *consciousness within the dream*. The person finds himself in an unfamiliar location and realizes, rationally, that he is there.

Celia Green's lucid dream and Sylvan Muldoon's astral projection resemble each other in so far as both involve the element of consciousness where we might not have expected it to occur. Muldoon however encountered little of a jumbled, kaleidoscopic nature in the out-of-body state. His projection is a technique for extending perception beyond the bodily confines. It rests squarely on what seems to be a very fundamental principle, namely that if the subconscious becomes 'possessed of the idea to move the body and the physical body is incapacitated, the subconscious will move the astral body independent of the physical'.[6] Among all writers known for their experiments in projection activities we find a common insistence that the body must be relaxed and at rest. In trance phenomena, the body acquires a rigid, death-like insensitivity as all conscious activity is withdrawn from it under the will of the shaman.

Understandably, Muldoon used a method of 'dream control' because it involved *willing* the subconscious to produce appropriate symbols representing the separation of the mind from the body. Providing one could retain some conscious grasp of these 'subconscious' manifestations, a type of shift of perception was bound to occur. Muldoon thus attempted to retain a sense of wakefulness as his body approached the state of relaxation whereby he would normally fall asleep. At the same time he would attempt to formulate a dream under will. He felt that the dream should pertain to pleasant activities relating to *motion* – swimming, flying or riding in a balloon for example. Often he would imagine himself riding upwards in an elevator, his own favourite image. The elevator would ride easefully up to the top of a multistoried building. It would stop, and he would now, very conscious of all his physical movements, walk out of the elevator, look cautiously around and carefully observe his environment. Very deliberately he would re-enter the elevator and ride down to ground level again!

The full astral projection occurs, according to Muldoon, when the beholder is fully 'aware' of the dream, and it has become as credibly 'real' as normal waking consciousness. His body has been left behind meanwhile, and he *actually perceives that he is floating*.

Normally Muldoon would will to see people that he knew, and thus contain his exploration within fairly modest boundaries. He represents only the first stage of the shaman's achievement, as do most contemporary projectors who have explained their techniques. However, in the accounts of Oliver Fox and more particularly in those of Robert Monroe we begin to find 'visionary elements' in addition to the normal dual consciousness.

Oliver Fox's experiences with astral projection produced the first documented records of their type. Two of his articles, 'The Pineal Doorway' and 'Beyond the Pineal Door' appeared in the 'Occult Review' of 1920, although they were not expanded into book form until 1939, ten years after the publication of Sylvan Muldoon's book. There is a great deal of Theosophical romanticizing in Fox's writing. We find florid descriptions of astral meetings with spiritual Masters of exalted 'grades' and with 'Celestial Beings, the great shapes of dazzling flame whose beauty filled the soul with anguished longing'.[7]

However, to judge him by the naivety of certain details in his account of his projections, would be missing the point. In many ways he confirms the descriptions of his American counterpart Sylvan Muldoon, and their techniques overlap. He did make an effort to record his experiences as soon as possible after they had occurred, and he writes ingenuously about both his successes and failures.

His first out-of-the-body experience happened when he was only sixteen, in 1902:[8]

I dreamed that I was standing on the pavement outside my home. The sun was rising behind the Roman wall, and the waters of Bletchingden Bay were sparkling in the morning light. I could see the tall trees at the corner of the road and the top of the old grey tower beyond the Forty Steps. In the magic of the early sunshine the scene was beautiful enough even then. Now the pavement was not of the ordinary type, but consisted of small, bluish-grey rectangular stones with their long sides at right angles to the white kerb. I was about to enter the house when, on glancing casually at these stones, my attention became riveted by a passing strange phenomenon, so extraordinary that I could not believe my eyes – they had all changed their position in the night, and the long sides were now parallel to the kerb! Then the solution flashed upon me: though this glorious summer morning seemed as real as could be, I was *dreaming*!

With the realization of this fact, the quality of the dream changed in a manner very difficult to convey to one who has not had this experience. Instantly the vividness of life increased a hundredfold. Never had sea and sky and trees shone with such glamorous beauty; even the common-place houses seemed alive and mystically beautiful. Never had I felt so absolutely well, so clear-brained, so divinely powerful, so inexpressibly *free*!

Fox here makes the very interesting point, which actually characterizes his techniques, that in order to bring consciousness to one's dreams or visions, one has to realize an incongruity in what one is perceiving. In this instance the stones in the pavement were wrongly aligned, and the *awareness that this was so* transformed the experience remarkably, heightening his clarity of vision in every way.

On a much later occasion, in September 1930, he dreamed that he was walking towards a certain railway station. In search of some chocolate which he had hoped to purchase on the platform, he took a stroll and located a near-by shop open, remarkably enough, in the middle of the night. At the back of the shop there appeared to be a large conservatory. Fox noticed a dozen or so green parrots with orange-rimmed eyes looking curiously at him. Only much later in his dream did he 'realize' that this escapade was purely imaginary. However, it was this act of recognition which told him that he was 'travelling' in the dream or visionary state, and allowed him to make decisions when to curtail his experience and so on.

Oliver Fox called this phenomenon the 'Dream of Knowledge', for 'one had in it the knowledge that one was really dreaming'. He believed that whereas dreams normally lacked the 'critical faculty', it was both possible and necessary to arouse this function. A change in the quality of perception would then occur. It would be as if one were exploring *consciously* a dimension normally unconscious. This could lead, as in the Muldoon experiences, to a new type of *freedom*. One could travel under will, to visit various friends and locations, possibly with the hope of 'verification'.

Oliver Fox was keen on rendezvous with friends on the astral plane. They would agree to meet at fixed times to prove to each other that such occurrences were in fact 'real'. Frequently Fox would perceive people enshrouded in a mass of auric colours. On one occasion a friend had arranged beforehand to 'visit' Fox during the evening:[9]

> He appeared instantaneously, in an egg-shaped cloud of intense bluish-white light and stood by my bed, gravely regarding me. He was dressed in a white robe . . . and as my eyes recovered from the dazzling effects of his sudden appearance, I saw that inside the bluish white ovoid surrounding him were bands of colour – deep red, rose-red, violet, blue, sea-green and pale orange . . . the pale orange was centred around the head, shooting upwards from it in a widening conical ray until it reached the ceiling. . . .

Fox's description recalls illustrations of oval-shaped auric emanations, which can be found in Bishop Leadbeater's Theosophical books on clairvoyant vision.

For some time Oliver Fox believed that the method of the Dream of Knowledge was the only way to obtain an out-of-the-body experience. But on one occasion, while relaxing, he found himself able to leave his body at will without an 'intervening dream':[10]

> Lying on the sofa in the afternoon with my eyes closed, I suddenly found that I could see the pattern on the sofa-back. This told me that I was in the Trance Condition. I then left my body, by willing myself out of it, and experienced an extremely sudden transition to a beautiful unknown stretch of country. There I walked for some time over wild and charming ground beneath a bright blue sky in which were fleecy sunlit clouds. All too soon my body called me back and on my homeward flight I distinctly remember passing right through a horse and van which were standing in some unfamiliar street.

Fox now arrived at the same basic conclusion as Muldoon, namely that for an astral projection to occur, *one has to send the body asleep while the mind is kept awake.* A dream state was a pleasant precursor to such a condition, but not an essential. Relaxation of the body to the onset of trance and projection of the consciousness under will was also possible. Fox called this more direct method the Way of Self-induced Trance, or the *Pineal Door technique.* His account is both lyrical and to the point:[11]

> Having chosen his position the student should concentrate upon an imaginary trap-door within his brain. His breathing should be deep and rhythmical, his eyes closed, but rolled upwards and slightly squinting. Presently he will feel a numbness, starting at his feet and travelling up his legs until eventually it spreads all over the body. This numbness deepens into a sensation of muscular rigidity, which may become quite painful, especially in the muscles of the jaw, and there is a feeling of great pressure in the head. At this stage he will have the effect of being able to see through his closed eyelids, and the room will appear to be illuminated by a pale golden radiance. There may also be flashes of light, apparitions and (almost certainly) terrifying noises. . . .
>
> And now the student will be experiencing the very peculiar sensation of having two bodies: the painful physical one and, imprisoned within it, a fluidic body. He is ready for the next step, which is by a supreme effort of the will, to force this subtle vehicle through the imaginary trap-door in his brain. It will seem to him that his incorporeal self, which was coincident with its physical prison, now rushes up his body and becomes condensed in that pineal point within his brain and batters against the door, while the pale golden light increases to a blaze of glory and a veritable inferno of strange sounds assails his ears. If the attempt should fail, the sensations are reversed. The incorporeal self subsides and becomes again coincident with the physical body while the light dies down and the sounds diminish in violence.
>
> If the attempt succeeds, he will have the extraordinary sensation of passing through the door in his brain and hearing it 'click' behind him; but he will *not* seem to be out of his body yet. It will appear to him that his fluidic self has again subsided within his physical body; but the terrifying sounds and apparitions are no more, and the room is evenly illuminated by the pale golden radiance. There is a blessed sense of calm after the storm, and fear gives place to triumphant exultation; for the phase of terror, with its suggestions of coming death or madness, is over. He has passed through the Pineal Door. . . .
>
> Our student will still feel himself to be within his physical

body; but now he can get out of bed in leisurely fashion and walk away, *leaving his entranced body behind him on the bed.*

I have referred to Oliver Fox's Pineal Door technique in detail because, as I hope to make clear later on, it is this method which seems to be most often used by sorcerers and shamans and most definitely underlies the means by which Carlos Castaneda felt that his head had transformed into the form of a crow. For as Robert Monroe points out below, the astral plane seems to operate under the duress of the *will* and thought forms imposed upon it. *What one imagines oneself to be, one becomes.*

It is in such a way that the shaman partakes of the cosmic dream of his own mythical heritage. He transposes himself. He is one with it. In his visions, he merges with gods, conversing with them and learning from them. The sorcerer meanwhile metamorphoses into shapes and forms that will suit his purpose.

As I have indicated earlier, it is unusual for parapsychological research or ordinary astral projection experimentation to uncover elements of this sort. On one occasion, however, Oliver Fox seems to have projected into a mythological recess within his subconscious, although he did not fully understand it at the time:[12]

the ground collapsed beneath my feet and I was falling, with seemingly tremendous velocity, down a dark, narrow tunnel or shaft. This downward descent continued until I lost my time-sense and it seemed that I might have fallen for hours. . . . At last I came gently to rest. Blackness and silence; then, as one awakening from a heavy sleep, I became progressively aware of my surroundings.

My eyes seemed hopelessly out of focus: I could see only a blur of bright colours – red and yellow predominating. I was naked and bound to an X-shaped framework in a vertical position. Something was trickling down my bare flesh. It was blood from many wounds. I was burning and smarting all over. I could not see, because my sight had been almost destroyed by red-hot irons. Now the colours were moving. They might be the robes of men or women. Every second the pain became more acute, as though the anaesthetic were wearing off. My body seemed to be a mass of wounds and burns and hopelessly mutilated. It was very difficult now not to panic, despite my affirmations that my physical body was in bed at Wimbledon, and I wondered if I might be dying.

Then I heard a man's voice speaking close to my right ear – calm but with horrible insistence: '*Say* thou are Theseus!'

I seemed nearly past speech, but with a great effort I replied: 'I am *not* Theseus. I am Oliver Fox.'

This incident took Fox unawares. In his account he passes it off as an embodiment of his own vanity. He may not have known, as Jung was later to formulate so clearly, that the energies, potencies and symbols of the great myths are alive in all of us, although usually operative only in the depths of the Collective Unconscious. Any trance or shamanistic activity always has the capacity to open these channels, and once again the myths are re-enacted. Oliver Fox becomes Theseus, son of Aegeus the King of Athens and slayer of the Minotaur which periodically devoured seven youths and maidens offered in tribute to King Minos of Crete. In a transformation of roles, Fox as Theseus finds himself in agonies from his wounds. His wounds are real. The blood is real blood. His consciousness is so fully enmeshed in the mythological realm that to all extents and purposes his experiences are as true to life as in his normal everyday existence.

Why Fox should have found himself in the drama of Theseus rather than of other Greek heroes is in itself a psychoanalytic issue which cannot be resolved here. However, the important point for our purposes, is that the paths which the shaman follows, and the sequence of visions of deities which the ceremonial magician pursues, are not random. The way in which these encounters are *structured* assumes paramount importance, for otherwise the subconscious may transform itself into a Hell of chaos.

The early accounts of astral projection are thus more valuable for insights into techniques, rather than of the structure of the mind. In Fox's material in particular, a great proportion of his experience is on the subjective level, and in a sense cannot avoid being so.

More recently new promise of scientific analysis, at least, of the physiological functions of out-of-the-body experiences, has emerged. Robert Monroe, the most important perhaps of all the 'pioneers' has worked in co-operation with Dr Charles Tart, of the Department of Psychology at the University of California. Tart undertook experiments in which Monroe attempted to produce verifiable results while in the out-of-the-body state. One thing has already emerged however. Out-of-the-body experiences produce a wave pattern in the brain which resembles that associated with dreaming sleep, and rapid eye movements occur in both instances also. There is also an important difference: normally, according to Tart,[13] one does not begin to dream until after eighty or ninety minutes of sleep. Robert Monroe was apparently able, on the other hand, to project his consciousness out of his body almost instantaneously. Astral projection thus represents a very special type of mental activity.

Monroe's out-of-the-body experiences began unexpectedly in Virginia in the spring of 1958. He had been involved with experimentation into techniques of learning data while asleep, by means of a tape recorder. He believed that somehow this may have been related to what was to happen to him.

One afternoon he was lying quietly on the couch of his living room when he felt a 'warm light' upon his body and began involuntarily to 'vibrate' quite strongly. At the same time he found himself 'powerless to move' and felt as if he were trapped in a metal vice.

During the following months the same condition recurred several times. Monroe gradually discovered, however, that he could move his fingertips during the onset of 'vibrations' and found to his amazement that they were able to extend themselves and to 'feel' things beyond normal reach. It became apparent though, that his fingers were not feeling in the physical sense, for they were able to penetrate through normally solid surfaces.

Shortly afterwards a similar experience occurred except that Monroe now found himself extended and floating in his entirety, just below the surface of the ceiling in his room. Beneath him lay his immobile body on the bed. A sense of panic surged through his mind for it suddenly seemed certain that he had died. In desperation he hurriedly sought to return to his body.

These initial fears proved groundless, and gradually he acquired more confidence. He subsequently began to explore the perceptive dimensions opened up by the use of his 'Second Body'.

On several occasions, Monroe would 'travel' to see his friends, noting in particular their conversation, their clothes and activities and so on, so that on next meeting he could confirm whether what he had 'seen' had in fact occurred. Once, during September 1958, he 'located' a friend outside his house when he had assumed him to be sick in bed. Details of clothing, and the exact times that his friend had been unexpectedly out walking were later confirmed.

Later, in 1959, at around 8.30 a.m. Monroe 'observed' in his out-of-the-body vision, a young boy tossing a baseball in the air while strolling along. A sedan car and an unfamiliar, small electrically driven object now became apparent, and then what Monroe calls a 'shift' in his perception, occurred. He was now 'standing' near a table where a person was 'dealing' what appeared to be 'large white cards'.

Unaware on this occasion of the specific identities of the people in his 'vision', Monroe visited some friends, the Bahnsons, that evening. In the course of discussion it became clear that it was their son whom Monroe had 'seen' throwing and catching the baseball while on the way to school. The unfamiliar electrical object could also be explained. That morning Mr Bahnson had been loading a Van De Graff generator into his car at precisely the time in question. Monroe could not understand however the nature of the 'cards' he had seen 'dealt' onto a table. Mrs Bahnson now explained that for the first time in two years, because she had risen late that morning, she had brought the mail to the breakfast table. She was handing out letters (white cards) to the family to be opened!

To begin with, Monroe's out-of-the-body experiences, like those of Oliver Fox and Sylvan Muldoon, were realistic in the everyday sense. They contained little or no suggestion of what we have termed 'phantasy'. Monroe called the realm of 'real and living people' and events 'Locale I'. It contained no strange beings, environments or places. All situations where he was able to verify data that actually occurred 'at a distance', could be said to occur in Locale I.

A new plane of 'events' however began to make its presence felt, a much stranger place with broader horizons of possibility. Monroe describes it as 'an immensity whose bounds are unknown which has depth and dimension incomprehensible to the finite, conscious mind'. 'In this vastness', he writes, 'lie all of the aspects we attribute to heaven and hell': 'Locale II'.

In this place, like Locale I, time is *non-existent*, 'there is a sequence of events, a past and a future, but no cyclical separation.' Both continue to exist coterminously with 'now'. In Locale II, says Monroe, to *think* something is to *make it happen* and 'like attracts like'.[14] It seemed to be a dimension teeming with a myriad of forms and images originating from the minds of those who had had access in dreams, thought or death.

'Locale II', according to Monroe, 'is the *natural* environment of the Second Body.' Among its residents, 'those [who are] alive but asleep, or drugged and out of their Second Bodies, and quite probably those who are "dead" but still emotionally driven'. In this region, also, one meets 'all sorts of disjointed personalities and animate beings . . .'.[15]

It is Monroe's Locale II experiences which are of most interest to us here, and he himself regards them as the most significant, However, it is worth digressing briefly to consider Monroe's third category, 'Locale III', which contains aspects not reported in any other of the major accounts.

In this dimension a type of time-warp involving 'scientific inconsistencies' was experienced. People seemed to go about their business in much the same way as in Locale I, except that their technology was more 'fanciful'; a surrealistic mirror image of our own;[16]

> Careful examination of one of the locomotives that pulled a string of old-fashioned looking cars showed it to be driven by a steam engine. The cars appeared to be made of wood, the locomotives of metal but of a different shape to our now obsolete types. . .

and so on. Despite the fact that this terrain of the subconscious was a phase out of step with normal reality, Monroe found himself projecting into its routines and environment. He seemed on one occasion to have assumed the 'body' of a married man within the Locale in a process of 'reverse possession'.

However, it is in Locale II that Monroe seems to approach similar ground to that of the shaman and sorcerer. On one venture there he found himself penetrating a barrier, beyond which lay a 'gray-black hungry ocean', a torment of prospectively hostile image – from such as one might find at the bottom of the sea. 'Could this be the borders of Hell?' he asked, 'It is easy to conclude that a momentary penetration of this nearby layer would bring "demons and devils" to mind as the chief inhabitants. They seem subhuman, yet have the evident ability to act and think independently.'

Later Monroe considers, rather in line with the explanations of psychic states in 'The Tibetan Book of the Dead', that one's destination in the heaven or hell of Locale II seems to be grounded completely within the framework of your deepest *constant* (and perhaps non-conscious) motivations, emotions and personality drives. The most constant and strongest of these act as your 'homing' device when you enter this realm.

The idea of *planes* or *levels* of after-death existence, while known in the West, has never been a major part of Christian revelation. The concept that on death one finds oneself plunging into a potentially chaotic dream condition is Eastern in origin, and with it the notion that one must die correctly. Relaxed and controlled dying ensures that the consciousness of the deceased will not be overwhelmed by the demonic, negative imagery emanating from the negative side of the subconscious personality. Instead, when one is at ease with oneself, a sense of balance and self-control is maintained, and the more positive virtuous aspects of the spiritual side of man manifest first, allowing transcendence. In agreement with Monroe, our last thoughts while living are therefore said to determine where we find ourselves in the world of the immediate, after-death imagery.

Several of the Gnostic sects alluded to the emanations or levels of being between man and Godhead, through which the disembodied consciousness had to find its way, according to the spiritual attainment of the person concerned.

In more recent years, the Qabalah with its profound imagery of the Tree of Life, has been reformulated as an expression of similar levels of being. Around one hundred years ago, Eliphas Levi suggested that the Major Tarot Arcana, that is to say the twenty-two Tarot Trumps corresponding approximately to our modern 'court cards', equated with the Paths connecting the major levels of consciousness represented on the Tree. This means that in effect the Major Tarot cards represent *a sequence of visions*, which if experienced under will in a certain sequence, lead the way to successively higher levels of spiritual reality. Within modern Theosophical terminology we can say that certain of these cards provide a valid symbolic structure of the mind as it is revealed on the 'astral plane'.

Returning now to Robert Monroe, it is very interesting that he appears to have found himself more than once in a region of Locale II represented by the Tarot card *Judgment*. This is one of three Paths leading into the lower astral plane from Malkuth, which is the symbolic entry to the subconscious mind.[17]

Monroe writes that in this place he would invariably hear a signal like heraldic trumpets and all the denizens of the region would stop what they were doing. 'It is a Signal that He (or They) is coming through His Kingdom.' As He passes by everyone lies down in an act of complete submissiveness, and at the same time 'there is a roaring musical sound and a feeling of radiant, irresistible living force of ultimate power that peaks overhead and fades in the distance.'

Paul Foster Case's traditional rendition of the Tarot Card *Judgment* shows the angel Gabriel visible in a cloud of radiant light, holding and sounding upon a magnificent trumpet. Naked human figures below present themselves in adoration: 'the man is self consciousness, the woman subconsciousness, and the child the regenerated personality. . . .'

Case continues:[18]

> The angel is the Divine Breath, or cosmic fire, yet he is obviously the angel Gabriel not only because he carries a trumpet, but also because Gabriel is the angel of the element of water, which is indicated by his blue robe.
>
> The action of heat upon water creates air, the substance of breath. Breath is specialized in sound, and the basis of sound is sevenfold . . . and 'sound is the instrument of final liberation'. . . . In the standard Tarot symbolism, only the male is submissive in his gestures, for the female and child hold their hands upwards 'to receive the influence of the angel in (their) outstretched hands'.

In this respect Monroe's account differs slightly.

Case's concluding remarks are however especially relevant to Monroe's own feelings about the scope of Locale II:[19]

> The card shows the sixth stage of spiritual unfoldenment, in which *personal consciousness is on the verge of blending with the universal*. At this stage the adept realizes that *his personal existence is nothing but the manifestation of the relationship between self-consciousness and subconsciousness*. He sees, too, that self-consciousness and subconsciousness are not themselves personal, but are really *modes of universal consciousness*.

Monroe seems from his account to have made the first steps

towards exploration of the numinous imagery of the deeper recesses of the mind. This is also the sacred territory of the shaman and it is interesting to compare the following statement from Monroe with the reference to the extraction of the soul and the incursion of light among the Iglulik Eskimos, referred to in the last chapter.[20]

> As I lay there with the vibrations strong in the dark, the special darkness I could 'see' with my closed eyes, the darkness grew brighter in one spot, as if clouds were parting, rolling back and unfurling, and finally a white ray of light came through from somewhere above my head.

CHAPTER 3
Further Considerations

Nothing, perhaps, would seem less likely than for a Mexican or South American Indian who had partaken of a hallucinogenic beverage or psychotropic mushrooms to be undertaking essentially the same sort of task as a Virginia businessman in a parapsychologist's laboratory. But their experiences are substantially similar.

When entering the trance state, Robert Monroe would relax his body in order to maintain the balance between sleep and waking consciousness, in much the same manner as Oliver Fox. He would fix his attention on a single image while gradually losing the awareness of the rest of his body. At this stage the 'vibrational state' would commence and he would direct these vibrations into a 'ring of force', channelling them all into his head. He now imagined these currents of force running along the periphery of the body down to the toes and back up to the head. Waves of energy would sweep rhythmically throughout his body.

Again, thought control and will become all-important. Monroe writes that he now attempted to activate the limbs of his Second Body in turn, until he was ready to 'lift out' in his entirety. He found it most helpful to focus upon a person or location at the same time, since this would give a definite direction to the projection.

Monroe's technique, which Oliver Fox calls the Pineal Door method, is also central to modern Western magic of the type practised by members of the Hermetic Order of the Golden Dawn, the Fraternity of Inner Light and other such Qabalistic groups.

These magicians employed what is known as the Middle Pillar technique. This activated the central nervous system as the projector imagined the descent of radiant white light from a position just above his head, down through his spine to the feet. The light energy found its course through what are termed in yoga the chakras, although in the Qabalah these take a slightly modified form. In modern Western magic there are five: above the

37

crown of the head (white); in the neck (mauve); above the solar plexus (golden yellow); level with the genital region (purple); and finally, in the feet (composite colours: russet, citrine, olive and black). Once the light had reached its nadir it was then channelled up around the body to the head again, in an act of symbolic containment. The practitioner now imagined a vortex forcing his consciousness upwards from the feet and through his body in stages. Progressively, the lower parts of the body would become inert, and finally only the head would remain 'awake'.

The crucial stage had now been reached – the borderland area between sleep, and lucid dreaming or astral projection. The act of transfer was all-important. In such an instance Monroe would focus on his destination, willing himself to 'be there'. In magical practice, which approaches the shamanistic situation rather more completely, a mental image would be held in the mind to determine the qualities of the particular vision into which the person would project his consciousness.

In Western magic, the medieval alchemical division of the elements into fire, earth, air and water is still meaningfully employed and the following symbols are used in projection:

Blue circle	Air
Yellow square	Earth
Red triangle	Fire
Silver crescent	Water

(Sometimes also an Indigo egg   Spirit)

These so called 'Tattvic' symbols give structure to what could otherwise prove to be a chaotic venture into the kaleidoscopic imagery of the subconscious. The magician is in effect issuing a directive to his subconscious that he is focusing *only upon certain paths of entry* and only wants to experience *certain things*. He meditates upon the symbol at the crucial 'last stage' described above and imagines himself passing through the after-image or complementary colour.[1]

The following is an account from the 'magical record' of 'Soror Vestigia' of the Golden Dawn (Mrs Mathers, the wife of Samuel McGregor Mathers, one of the founders of the Order and translator of the medieval 'Zohar'). Her focusing symbol had been the crescent of water combined with the indigo egg of spirit:[2]

A wide expanse of water with many reflections of bright light, and occasionally glimpses of rainbow colours [*were*] appearing. When divine and other names were pronounced, elementals of the mermaid and merman type [*would*] appear, but few of the other elemental forms. These water forms were extremely changeable, one moment appearing as solid mermaids and mermen, the next melting into foam.

Raising myself by means of the highest symbols I had been taught, and vibrating the names of Water, I rose until the Water vanished, and instead I beheld a mighty world or globe, with its dimensions and divisions of Gods, Angels, elementals and demons – the whole universe of Water.... I called on HCOMA and there appeared standing before me a mighty Archangel, with four wings, robed in glistening white and crowned. In one hand, the right, he held a species of trident, and in the left a Cup filled to the brim with an essence [*which*] poured down below on either side.

Modern occultists use the term 'skrying' for this type of activity. In essence it resembles the shamanistic journey into the hinterland of the subconscious. Archetypal figures, elemental demons and unusual transcendental imagery manifest as attributes pertaining to the original focusing symbol used in the meditation. The vision, and its resident pantheon, is of fire, air, earth or water accordingly.

In such instances the magician feels that he has entered a new plane of existence. His entire range of perceptions has altered. He finds himself in a dimension which will alter and transform itself according to his will. Robert Monroe similarly found himself able to change his form while in an out-of-the-body state. As several writers have suggested, such transformations could provide the basis for werewolf beliefs and other tales and legends, involving lycanthropy.

Carlos Castaneda's transformation into a crow now assumes special significance as part of the shamanistic technique of astral projection. He had smoked psilocybe mushrooms with don Juan, and Castaneda felt possessed of 'extraordinary clarity'. Don Juan told him that his body was going to disappear and eventually *only his head would remain*. In order to 'fly' in the spirit vision Castaneda would have to metamorphose into a suitable form: from his chin would come legs, from his neck the bird's tail.

Wings would emerge from his cheekbones: ('he said they had to be extremely long, as long as I could stretch them, otherwise I would not be able to fly. He told me the wings were coming out and were long and beautiful, and that I had to flap them until they were real wings').[3]

Castaneda had to reduce the bulk of his head 'by winking' and learn how to 'see' like a crow. A strong beak would form between his eyes, and then the transformation would be complete.

On a later occasion, having mastered the fundamentals of visualization, Castaneda prepared to 'fly'.[4]

I remember I 'extended my wings and flew'. I felt alone, cutting through the air, painfully moving straight ahead. . . . I saw a field with an infinite variety of lights. The lights moved and flickered and changed their luminosity. They were almost like colours, their intensity dazzled me. . . .

The last scene I remembered was three silvery birds. They radiated a shiny, metallic light, almost like stainless steel, but intense and moving and alive. I liked them. We flew together.

The mushroom smoke had transported Castaneda into the dimension of mind where whatever he could imagine, he would become. As such he needed a mental image which could safely house his projected consciousness. Don Juan had told him that a crow was essentially an anonymous bird; it could go anywhere without attracting attention. Larger creatures would take too much of one's energy in the transformation. Smaller creatures could be attacked by predators.

Don Juan also told Castaneda that when he died he would become the crow, and would fly with the other silver birds – *his emissaries* – that he had seen in his vision.

The trance and visionary state thus prepares us for our after-death existence. The 'roles' and 'transformations' are of a similar order, for they help us charter the Heavens and Hells of the subconscious. We have noted that several astral projectionists felt they were 'dying', for they could sometimes see their immobile bodies lying rigidly beneath them. On one occasion Oliver Fox felt himself 'locked out', and unable to return, although this proved to be untrue. At the same time his out-of-the-body experiences convinced him of his immortality.

Charles Tart writes:[5]

The person feels that he has directly experienced being alive and conscious without his physical body, and thereby knows that he possesses some kind of soul that will survive bodily death. [Quite properly, he went on to say] This does not logically follow, for even if the out-of-the-body experience is more than just an interesting dream or hallucination, it was still occurring while the physical body was alive and functioning and therefore may depend on the physical body.

The philosopher C.J. Ducasse has made much the same point. However, it is also fair to point out that the Russian developments in psi-research tend to suggest that the physical organism is dependent on its energy prototype, and not the other way around. One projectionist, Yram (the pseudonym of the French writer Marcel Louis Forhan), actually experienced the sensation of having a series of astral bodies rather like the layers of an onion, and each appropriate to a certain locale: 'Everything happens', he wrote, 'as if we had a series of different bodies boxed one in the other by means of a more reduced dimension. As the conscious will penetrates into new dimensions it uses a corresponding body.'[6] So it might be, despite the caution of Ducasse and Tart, that the parallel between astral projection and death has not been erroneously drawn. It may yet be shown that the Body of Light is capable of separate existence.

The death-comparison has been made by both those who use hallucinogens to achieve the out-of-the-body state, and those who do it 'naturally'.

Dr Claudio Naranjo, a psychotherapist working in Santiago, Chile, conducted several experiments with thirty-five volunteers who took mescalin and LSD. The aim was to examine cross-culturally the types of experiences that resulted. Within this sampling eight persons 'experienced visions or feelings of their own death'. Their comments suggest the characteristic astral separation: 'If I was going to leave the body, that didn't worry me. I knew that I existed in essence. . .'; 'I saw my own death, with anguish . . . I could see my face, once more from the outside and very close. . .'.[7] Another subject experienced sensations of flight just like Castaneda had done. However, whereas Castaneda had found the flight exhausting, this person found it exhilarating:[8]

I was turning into a winged being. I then stretched my wings and felt extreme freedom and expansion. . . . I felt my wings grow above the earth, with its extended wings beyond its limits, reaching infinity . . . the air passing through my body gave my breathing a special rhythm, a rhythm of flying which expressed not only the movement but the joy.

We have other accounts which suggest that the 'naturally induced' out-of-the-body experience does not differ from that brought about by hallucinogenic influence, except of course for the increased potency of subconscious imagery which may appear.

In 1959 a young writer from New York, Daniel Breslaw, took part with thirteen others in a medically supervised psilocybin experiment at Harvard. He was soon plunged into a mosaic of swirling colours and sounds. Forced to answer regular questions in a dialogue with his doctor, he found himself considering the nature of the relationship between mind and body:[9]

> Body? I glance down at my body, amazed that it is there. But is it there? True, something is lying on the bed, but something else is sitting on a chair taking its blood pressure. And I seem to have no more relation to the one than to the other. But it is suddenly important to decide which one is *really me*, for I recall from my pre-psychotic days the fact that one of them has taken a drug. But which one? Impossible to say. . . .

Another writer, Colin Turnbull, a professional anthropologist, has written a short account of how on a visit to Banares Hindu University in India he was entertained by some students to a treat of soft-drinks and sweets. He did not realize at the time that the sweets contained *bhang*, a mild form of Indian hemp.

'On leaving the restaurant', he writes, 'the effects of the drug became more marked. I was in perfect consciousness and could think clearly; my speech was somewhat blurred, and my vision was clear but wavering. The major effect at that time was that I had lost my sense of touch. . . .'[10]

Nevertheless he found his way across the city by bicycle to another location where he had intended to go, the ashram of Sri Anandamai. The ashram was superbly located beside the Ganges and the crowd of devotees provided a warm and friendly atmosphere. The river seemed to transfer into a 'holy living deity' and he began to be lulled into deep relaxation while pondering on it. Meanwhile he gradually became aware that he was floating in the air above the terrace of the Anandamai ashram; he was able quite easily to see woods on the other side of the Ganges as if from an aerial position. There was no awareness of his body and he felt 'he had no use for it any longer'. He was 'entirely free'. He experienced a soaring effect and found himself drifting through cloud formations. Passing above them he could discern the peaks of the Himalayas in the distance:[11]

I stayed there for a long time, looking at the craggy, icy cliffs, coming closer and closer. With no conscious act of volition I went down below and saw the forest-covered foot-hills, with rivers of clear water running through rocky gorges. I followed one of these until I came to the frozen source of the Ganges, a black cavern at the foot of a glacier, belching forth the icy water. I travelled over the glacier and up into the pass that leads to one of western Tibet's trade routes. The whole of this time there was no sign of human life, yet the whole world around me seemed to be more full of life than it ever had been before, and full of these qualities that the Hindu scriptures proclaim to be highest of all – truth, goodness and beauty.

We see from these accounts that hallucinogens can cause out-of-the-body experiences to occur, both with and without an incursion of subconscious imagery. The visionary content of the 'journey' seems to depend more on whether the person has precipitated an onrush of hallucinations and altered perceptions, either by means of his own mental condition (perhaps of doubt and uncertainty), or by more positive skrying techniques.

An interesting account of a non-hallucinogenic astral journey which begins normally but later acquires transcendental visionary qualities occurs in classical Greek literature. It concerns a certain Aristeas from the island of Proconnesus, who was able, from the account of Pliny and others, to fly from his body in the form of a bird. Maximus of Tyre writes:[12]

There was a man of Proconnesus whose body would lie alive, yes, but with only the dimmest flicker of life and in a state very near to death; while his soul would issue from it and wander in the sky like a bird, surveying all beneath; land, sea, rivers, cities, nations of mankind and occurrences and creatures of all sorts. Then returning into and raising up its body, which it treated like an instrument it would relate the various things it had seen and heard in various places.

Aristeas was known for his ability to fall into deep, death-like trance. On his most famous journey, which is described in the 'Arimaspea', Aristeas flies astrally over Scythia and near-by river regions noting details of the nomadic settlers there. His account provided 'essentially true'[13] information of a region not previously charted by Aristeas' Greek contemporaries. At this stage Aristeas' perception in the out-of-the-body state has not been altered or distorted by elements of subconscious phantasy. However we are told that on his journey he is possessed by Apollo, and soon he embarks on a mythical venture involving a golden treasure guarded by griffins and later stolen by a tribe of gnome-like creatures, the Arimaspi. The griffins are 'elementals' of the sun and Aristeas travels in cohorts with Apollo beyond the cold mountain slopes of eternal winter.

On a more pragmatic level we find that when Oliver Fox took chloroform it enhanced rather than negated the out-of-the-body effect:[14]

> it seemed to me that I shot up to the stars, and that a shining silver thread connected my celestial self with my physical body. Dual consciousness was very pronounced. When I spoke, it seemed to me that my words travelled down the thread and were then spoken by my physical self; but the process was simultaneous, and I could feel myself among the stars and on the sofa at one and the same time.

It was under the effects of a similar anaesthetic that Sir Winston Churchill had the following mystical experience during treatment for a minor operation:[15]

> The sanctum is occupied by alien powers. I see the absolute truth and explanation of things, but something is left out which upsets the whole, so by a large sweep of the mind I have to see a greater truth and a more complete explanation, which comprises the erring element. Nevertheless, there is still something left out. So we have to take a still wider sweep. . . . The process continues inexorably. Depth beyond depth of unendurable truth opens.

A drug or anaesthetic does not necessarily invalidate the

mystical experience, and may in certain circumstances enhance it. Writing of the very potent hallucinogen LSD-25, Sidney Cohen claims it to be 'like a trigger, not only in the way it releases chemical activities that proceed long after the drug has been eliminated. . . . It also seems to trigger a depth charge into the unconscious processes. The direction that the explosion will take is the result of factors *other than the drug*.'[16]

The following case of a drug-induced mystical experience, quoted by Dr Raynor Johnson who is well known for his books on religion, is highly interesting because in it a certain motif occurs that may be found in Oliver Fox's non-drug astral projections, and also in the account of don Juan.

On this occasion, a certain university professor (*not* Professor R.C. Zaehner!) took as a preparation a 30/70 carbon dioxide/oxygen mixture thereby altering the amount of oxygen in the blood in the same way that deep yogic breathing does. He saw a bright white light at the end of a tunnel, but was unable to reach it before the effects wore off. He then took 100 micrograms of LSD to heighten the perception. He had periods of 'hilarious laughter' and was then overcome by a 'rapid succession of beautifully coloured images – fantastically beautiful and brilliant. Some looked like jewels, others were gorgeous sprays of vivid colour, still others were in the form of geometrical designs.'

Subsequently, he began to feel himself separating from his body until it was as if his detached 'mind' was 'floating in faintly blue, and vast, space, congruent with ordinary three-dimensional space, and yet somehow off in another dimension'. At the same time he became aware of a friend on the same plane and a *God-like Presence*. The light which had previously been vivid at the end of the tunnel became apparent again, and he began to soar upwards toward it:[17]

> I was supported and enveloped by a pinkish cloud of light, and I knew this was the source of all love and beauty and goodness. I was filled with boundless, indescribable joy; enraptured with beauty, electrified with the currents of love pouring through me.

The motif in this account which seems to me to be especially important is *the tunnel*. A tunnel is an inroad to another dimension. It may be the entrance to a hidden place or even in don Juan's usage 'the crack between the worlds'. Within Eliade's terminology it is a device by means of which we transcend the planes.

In Oliver Fox's astral records we also find the tunnel image appearing. It is down such a shaft that he fell when transforming into the mythological role of Theseus. On another occasion it became the means by which he attempted to focus his will in a definite direction:[18]

> it seemed to me there was a sort of hole or break formed in the continuity of the astral matter; and through this, in the distance – as though viewed through a very long tunnel – I could see something indistinct which may have been an entrance to a temple, with a statue still further showing through it. . . .

Unfortunately Fox now experienced a shift of imagery and found himself in an unfamiliar location. Again he concentrated, and the tunnel once more came to view. However he was unable to enter it. His trance was broken – 'I rushed back to my body and awoke.'

While seeking a spirit-ally with don Juan, Carlos Castaneda, too, experienced the rift in plane. Don Juan was vibrating his special 'spirit catcher'. A piercing wail rent the air, seemingly in high pitched rhythmic unison with the already-existing noises of the birds and rustling leaves. Castaneda felt caught up in a wonderful universe of sound. However, it now seemed that 'The timing of each sound was a unit in the overall pattern of sounds. Thus the spaces or pauses in between sounds were, if I paid attention to them, holes in a structure.'[19]

Don Juan continued to create his eerie vibration and Castaneda perceived a 'huge hole in the sound structure' against the backdrop of low verdant hills. The hole began to entrance him, and he felt drawn to it. Suddenly magical contact was made: 'all sounds stopped; the two large holes (which had previously been superimposed) seemed to light up and next I was looking again at the plowed field; *the Ally was standing there.*'[20]

We will now examine more closely the magical universe of don Juan, and its associated techniques of sorcery and *paths of entry*.

CHAPTER 4
Comparisons
Two systems of magic

The magician has access to different planes of perception. In mythological terms these are often represented metaphorically or diagramatically in a cosmic system as levels. It is interesting that both don Genaro, don Juan's colleague in sorcery, and the Qabalistic Tree of Life – which is the basis of modern Western magic – refer to *ten levels of consciousness*. However, what is more important, perhaps, is that in the magical universe we invariably find a grading structure of symbolic levels and entities, which renders it easier for man to grasp as a whole. A sense of order appears essential.

In the account of don Juan, and elsewhere, we find this structuring principle assumes great significance. There are only certain ways in which one can meet the Ally, or Mescalito; there are specific locations where the shaman will perform 'at his best' and others where he might lose his 'balance'. Only certain instruments or power objects may be used, and these are sacred and treated reverently because of their ability to allow contact with the deity.

Finally, and perhaps most importantly, there are specific techniques of controlling the physical and mental processes which ensure that the magician is always in control. If he invokes a spirit-entity, he must ensure that it is always under his grasp, for otherwise it will conquer and possess the shaman. The magician must be forever alert, a 'warrior' awake to the world and his techniques of correct posture, and correct 'projection' through certain doorways of perception rather than others, ensure that the journey into the sacred realms of the mind, and whatever events may occur in the physical dimension, are subject to his will alone. Don Juan says: 'Will is what makes you invulnerable. Will is what sends a sorcerer through a wall; through space, to the moon if he wants. . . .

SPECIAL LOCATIONS/RITUAL POSTURES

As an apprentice sorcerer, Carlos Castaneda's first requirement was to find a special 'spot' on the floor inside don Juan's house. This location could not be identified rationally but only through intuition. After some initial disappointments in not being able to find the spot, Castaneda felt suddenly threatened in his task, possibly by don Juan himself; something seemed to be pushing against his stomach. Castaneda found himself adopting an unusual and spontaneous posture in defence. On another occasion, Castaneda was taught the 'fighting form', used in warding off an attack by malevolent spirit-entities. With his arms hunched up protecting his solar plexus, the 'centre' of his balance and power, the sorcerer had to stamp his foot and emit shrieking yells. Although his face was tucked close into his chest, and he did not actually observe the aggressor, it remained nevertheless an act of obstinate defiance, for he would never yield.

In modern Qabalistic magic we find the same concept of the special location. Often this place was a formalized dwelling, a room or building converted into a temple with full ritual paraphernalia, and permanent markings around the magical circle in the centre of the floor. The Hermetic Order of the Golden Dawn had such temples in London, Weston Super Mare, Edinburgh and Paris, and derivative societies continue in a similar, if less publicized way.

However, the temple is in itself only a symbol. Like a church, it is for its practitioners a sacred place. It is the meeting ground of man and transcendental forces invoked from a higher plane of being. It is a place where the atmosphere has been charged with potent Qabalistic mantras and where a type of shell of will and aspiration encloses the members in their ritual operations. Undoubtedly much of this is subjective, and relevant primarily to those involved in the magical operation. However, the metaphorical nature of the temple is a crucial aspect. In a modern city a sense of anonymity is desirable to avoid unwanted sensationalism. It enables the magician to proceed beyond his routine personality and roles. Don Juan advised Carlos Castaneda in much the same way: 'If you have no personal history, no explanations are needed; nobody is angry or disillusioned with your acts. And above all no one pins you down with their thoughts.'[1] From this it emerges that the temple is the anonymous meeting place of those upon the path of magical transformation. *But it is also a symbol of man himself.* Man, according to mystical tradition, mirrors the universe, and the temple will contain all the ritual enactments of the great mythological dramas which are in themselves related to energy vortexes deep in the subconscious mind. In the temple, man is able to unleash before himself the ceremonially expressed cosmic themes leading to his own illumination and spiritual rebirth. And his colleagues will portray the figures of the great pantheons, especially of ancient Egypt and Greece, and Zoroastrian Persia, as the mysteries take on a three-dimensional incarnate reality.

It follows though, that man may in one sense take the temple with him wherever he goes. Aleister Crowley and Victor Neuburg took it with them to the top of an Algerian mountain, to invoke the tenth of the Thirty Aethers of Dr John Dee, the spirit entity Choronzon.[2]

The temple in essence is nothing other than the location of the magical encounter. However, as we have indicated, the magician himself must remain in control of what he invokes, for this is what he wishes to become. If he invokes Taphthartharath, in a ritual assigned to Hod upon the Tree of Life, it is because he wishes to enhance his powers of intellect and creative, rational thinking. The entities he will encounter in the visionary state are embodiments, anthropormorphic precipitations, of these aspirations. If he invokes deities sacred to Netzach, it will be to develop the love of nature and art and the more intangible aspects which complement Hod. Now in such circumstances, control ensures that the magician will integrate these transcendental potencies into the fabric of his own personality. They will become a part of him in an active, positive way. A lack of control means that in a very real sense, he is 'possessed' or taken over by a negative, distorted aspect of these levels of subliminal energy. For this reason he develops certain 'controls' which do not so much constrict as focus the energies which are being utilized. Like don Juan and Castaneda, he has a special 'spot' and this is the centre of his magical circle. The circle defines the scope of his activity. It is very obviously, a symbol of containment. What is invoked causes a transformational effect only upon those within the circle itself. Beyond the circle lies chaos and non-integration. In his rituals, the Qabalist will 'banish' the potentially demonic or interfering aspects of his subconscious mind to the periphery of his mental activity. His will remains centred on the integrative and positive side of the work at hand. The circle thus allows a distancing effect, albeit an imaginative one, which distinguishes very clearly for the practitioner the polarities of good and evil, white and black, positive and negative, transcendental and debased. His aspirations will tend towards the development of the god in man or the animal in man, which I believe to be supremely expressed in the symbolism of the androgynous Gnostic god, Abraxas. Within such a magical area, upon sacred ground wherever it may be, the magician, like don Juan feels most 'at home'. It is the place where he will begin 'to see', where a new vision will be unfolded before his eyes. Where the learning of a new, magical description of the universe begins. In Western ritual, the occultist assumes the 'god-form' so that he can feel and live the realities expressed in the symbolism which the deity personifies. At Eleusis, the Neophytes watched a sacred drama which expressed the theme of cyclic life and death. Persephone, the daughter of Demeter and symbol of the living grain in the wheat field, was on the one hand ripe and fruitful at the peak of the harvest and, on the other, liable like all living things to the forces of destruction and decay. Thus she was snatched down into Hades, where in the cyclic rotation of the seasons she was forced to spend half her days.

In the Golden Dawn, the magician followed a path of development based on the structure of the Tree of Life. The initial rituals were ritual dramas associated with the levels of consciousness: *Malkuth; Yesod, Hod* and *Netzach*. In classical mythology the deities ascribed to these Sephirah were Persephone, Diana, Mercury and Venus, although much of the Golden Dawn usage, in line with founder McGregor Mather's eclectic tastes, was more far reaching and all-encompassing. Other pantheons, including the Persian, Egyptian and Chaldean, and expressing the same realities, were drawn upon.

Ideally, magical man learns from the archetypes in the same way that don Juan learned from his 'protector' Mescalito. In so far as he aspires to enter a mystical universe he attempts to see things as the gods would see them. He aspires to be like them, to incarnate their abstract qualities. In his rituals he *becomes* them because under will the imaginative metamorphosis is able to occur. A spiritual energy pervades his whole being. His identity is transformed. He is wiser and more knowledgeable than before, for he has left the shackles of his limited ego-based personality below in favour of a more transcendental direction. Accordingly, his actions become ritualized along traditionally 'sacred' lines. His conception of the god follows the pattern of description in the myths themselves or else the visual representation found in archaeological stelae, murals or decorative motifs. He will make appropriate instruments and wear certain garments to reinforce the sense of identification. When he is 'banishing' beyond the confines of his circle, he will perhaps use the powerful god-form of Horus, the hawk-headed Egyptian god who extends his hands before him in strength as he enters the Underworld to redeem his father Osiris. It is interesting indeed that this god form, which is used in the Banishing Ritual of the Hexagram,[3] resembles in type a spontaneous action which Castaneda found himself employing as a defence when threatened. He suddenly assumed a ritual posture which no one had taught him: *his arms were extended outwards before him, his fingers 'contracted like a claw'*.

Don Juan had also evolved another ritual posture to be used 'upon the "favourable spot" and this was his fighting form'. It was to be used in a situation of crisis, when one was being attacked. Castaneda writes: 'It consisted of clapping the calf and thigh of my right leg and stomping my left foot in a kind of dance. . . .' If the onslaught became too oppressive the magician could hurl a 'power object' accompanying it by a 'war cry, a yell that had the property of directing the object to its mark'. Such an activity ensures that the magician, in a very real sense retains his identity and is not overcome by externalised 'spirit-forces'.

MAGICAL ENTITIES

The shaman has within his magical universe means of contacting the Ally, and Mescalito. The Ally is on the one hand a type of latent force within the hallucinogen itself. It would seem that different anthropomorphic forms appear to different people although within a myriad of specific possibilities, the 'little smoke' was said to be 'masculine', and could be relied upon. Don Juan felt that the Ally of the Jimson weed (datura) was characteristically feminine: in his terms inconstant, and unpredictable. Nevertheless it was up to the 'brujo' to use the powers of the Ally as he best saw fit. In its effect the Ally was essentially neutral; the sorcery employing it however could be for good or evil. While the best means of contacting the Ally was through the hallucinatory plant, the Ally was in a sense beyond it: 'The smoke takes you to where the Ally is, and when you become one with the Ally you don't ever have to smoke again. From then on you can summon your Ally at will and do anything you want.' The Ally could be found near special places, in the water hole, or on top of one's initiatory mountain. He is called for the confrontation. Then comes the show of strength: 'When a man is facing the Ally, the giver of secrets, he has to muster up all his courage and grab it before it grabs him or chase it before it chases him. The chase must be relentless and then comes the struggle. The man must wrestle the spirit to the ground and keep it there until it gives him power.'

There was a greater force than one's Ally however. Whereas the Ally gave the sorcerer vital energy, Mescalito, the god of the peyote cactus, was able to teach. Like the Ally he would appear to different men in different forms. Don Juan knew that Castaneda had been designated as his special 'chosen' pupil and successor by the way in which Mescalito 'played' with Castaneda in the form of a dog. However Mescalito was an ambivalent deity and could illuminate one man while terrifying another. He could take the 'brujo' 'through the sky', and appeared to exist distinct from the observer, that is to say, 'outside people'. For those accustomed to his ways, though, he appeared as a light or as a man. For don Juan he had special significance as an equivalent and alternative to the more orthodox 'Protectors' of the Yaqui: Jesus Christ, the Virgin Mary, and the 'little virgin of Guadalupe'. Like these, Mescalito was a revered teacher and friend in the ways of knowledge.

In the dawn-time of man, when he first found himself enmeshed in the forces of nature, it must have seemed to him that in order for crops to grow, or for animals to be trapped, the gods had to be placated. Some of the gods were of a local nature; of a near-by stream, of a grove of trees, of a mountain top or of a special water-hole where animals would come to drink. Others of the gods, the more remote ones, dwelt high in the sky, far removed from man's immediate environment. Often, in comparative religion, we find that the deity who was supposed to have originated the universe is far from man; he has withdrawn as it were, and assigned the roles of spiritual maintenance of the cosmos to lesser gods. In Greek mythology, Kronos, the Source of All, assumes much less importance than Zeus who is the Father of the immediate world. In the Qabalah the highest point of creation is 'neutral' in polarity; it contains both male and female potencies. Below, we find specifically the Great Father (Chokmah level) and the Great Mother (Binah level) and lower still the personifications of the vengeful god, and the merciful god which more appropriately summarized for the Jews the practicalities and qualities of their tribal deity Yahweh. Man visualizes above himself a hierarchy of potencies greater than his own capacity. His pantheon is a representation of how he sees the universe, how its forces affect him personally, and which values and aspects are most significantly differentiated in his culture.

The pantheon of don Juan is and needs to be a restricted one. He remains a thoroughly pragmatic sorcerer. He has little concern with the afterlife (which for many societies reveals a vast array of gods) other than to infer that Castaneda's soul will one day wing its way off to the Other World in league with the silver crows.

For don Juan the most important deities were Mescalito, who as we have said equated for him with Christ and the Virgin Mary as a type of 'Protector' and 'Teacher', and of a lesser order, the Ally associated with each of the other hallucinogens.

Both the Ally and Mescalito could appear to the beholder in a variety of forms. Within Castaneda's account they are anthropomorphic – the easiest form in which one can behold what is essentially abstract and undefined. As Jung notes in 'Man and His Symbols', myths and dreams invariably involve humanized forms. It is not the 'essence' of the sun that is important but the Sun God hero himself. Not the subjective 'quality of the moonlight' but the Moon Goddess in all her splendour.

The Ally bestows power, and Mescalito teaches. Mescalito in fact appeared very much to have a separate existence. (Jung calls this the apparent 'autonomy of the archetypes'). He would teach the *brujo* a special song which was for him alone. Later it could be used as a means of contacting the deity, for it represented a personal link, or bond. Initially, Mescalito spoke to Castaneda: 'I heard him talking to me. At first his voice was like the soft rustle of a light breeze. Then I heard it as music – as a melody of voices – and I "knew" it was saying, "What do you want?" '

Later, while taking part in a peyote ceremony, Castaneda was 'given' two songs by Mescalito: 'I sang feverishly until I could no longer voice the words. I felt as if my songs were inside my body, shaking me uncontrollably.' He had been told by don Juan always to keep the songs a secret since they represented in one sense Castaneda's own magical identity. They were now a part of his very *being*. When he sang the special invocatory song, Mescalito would emerge from the peyote plants in an aura of bright, blue light. Castaneda would sing reverently before him; 'There was a sound of flutes, or of wind, a familiar musical vibration.' Confronting his Protector, Castaneda asked about the nature of his own personality and its deficiencies, and he asked his own magical name; 'He looked at me, elongated his mouth like a trumpet until it reached my ear, and then told me.'

Within Castaneda's account, he had not yet come to terms with the Ally. The fight for mastery had not yet occurred, even though on the sacred mountain he had had a magical encounter with a special type of spirit entity – the 'luminous coyote'. Castaneda had however caught a glimpse of the Ally. Following the ritual of the water-hole, the Ally had taken the form of a Mexican peasant. The landscape in which he had appeared seemed to be 'superimposed' on the actual landscape of the chaparral. Don Juan regarded Castaneda as unready for a full confrontation. 'To meet an Ally', he had told his pupil, 'a man must be a spotless warrior or the Ally may turn against him and destroy him.'

The Qabalistic magician has also to be fully on guard for his encounters, and unlike don Juan's system, the magical universe in the West is highly structured. There are many more divisions of 'powers' and 'potencies', a greater number of differentiated forms and beings whom he may encounter on different levels of the astral plane, even within the 'mythology' of the one esoteric framework: the Qabalah.

The ancient Qabalists postulated a broad, tenfold division of the universe, according to what seemed to them to be the unfolding of the act of creation. The Divine Energy slowly precipitated itself downwards into form in a zigzag path known as the 'Lightning Flash'. Now although Judaism is monotheistic, each of the levels stands metaphorically by itself, while connected to all other regions of the Tree of Life by inference. Thus whereas the Greeks, Romans and ancient Egyptians had pantheons of apparently distinct deities, the Qabalists preferred to refer to *aspects* of the One God.

Below the Trinity (made up of the Neutral Origin, *Kether*, the Crown; the Great Father *Chokmah*; and the Great Mother *Binah*) lay the lower, more accessible levels of the Tree of Life. *Chesed* and *Geburah* represented different polarities, Mercy and Severity, of the Tribal Father-deity, a lower form than Chokmah. Beneath this level of the 'Demiurge' (or Father of the tangible universe) lay hope for man in the form of the symbol of rebirth, the Divine Son (*Tiphareth*). If man could ascend from his lowly station even as far as this level of consciousness he would begin to realize his sacred origin, shrouded from his perception since the 'Fall'. Still lower on the Tree lay levels of being representing love and nature; the rational intellect; the moon and the sexual instincts, and finally the entrance to the subconscious, *Malkuth* the kingdom.

These ten levels of awareness in the universe of man's potential, define in a broad sense his exploratory domain. Below the Trinity 'which is above *form* per se, and therefore devoid of 'imagery', the mystic and magician has as his territory certain levels of his own subconscious mind, with all its mythological contents. It is up to him to conquer and bring within his reach the loftier reaches of his spiritual personality and aspirations. In his Qabalistic mysticism, he had in fact invented an early form of psychotherapy. Full conquest of the Tree of Life would ensure a total integration of all aspects of his being at a transcendental level of much greater awareness.

As if to make progress a long and tedious business, the Qabalists divided each of the ten levels (Sephiroth) into 'Worlds'. Thus within each Sephirah were different levels again. The most 'spiritual' was said to take the God-name. Since a single God-*image* could not be given in a tenfold monotheistic system, different 'names' were ascribed instead. These are really like mantras or vibrationary levels. The Magician puts himself in touch with specific levels of consciousness when he utters the God-name, in the same way that special names were the bond or connection between Castaneda and Mescalito.

Beneath the level of the God-name or mantra, was the form of the archangel. Raphael, Gabriel, Michael and Sandolphon, for example, represent the archangels of the sun, the moon, mercury and the four elements (earth). These spiritual energies, too, are invoked by their *names*.

At a lower level still according to the Qabalists, and within each sphere of consciousness, were the ordinary angels and the planetary energies or 'mundane chakras'.

It would be a mistake to dismiss these constructs as 'merely imaginary' or 'fictitious'. They represent an elaborate meta-phorical framework of the energies of the Judaic subconscious. Each culture imposes its own 'programme' to use an expression of John Lilly's. The hierarchy of spirit-entities merely represents grades and directions enabling the mystical ascent of man to be orderly and manageable in an astral domain liable itself, at any time, to plunge into the negative forms of Chaos and Hell. Thus when the Qabalist ventures onto the astral plane he arms himself with the names of God. He aligns his aspirations with the positive aspects of creation, in an effort to rise above the negative and evil side of things. Unlike the black magician who aims to become more bestial (through identification with the Devil or Goat deity), he wishes to become *more transcendentally aware, more God-like*.

We have previously used the word 'archetype' to describe the core image or 'meaning' of a god in a particular pantheon. It is thus an *anthropomorphic symbol pertaining to a certain level of the mind*. As described in the first part of this book, the role of both the shaman and magician is an *encounter with the archetypes*.

Mescalito has a rather similar function for don Juan, as Dionysus and Bacchus – gods of ecstasy and wine – had for the ancient Greeks. Mescalito is the deity associated with an hallucinogenic plant, and he is also the Protector during the time when the magician finds himself 'outside himself' on his astral wanderings. In Castaneda's instance this 'separate reality' was brought about initially by the dissociating effects of the drug. On another occasion, when he had 'flown' under hallucinatory impetus, he had wanted to know where his body had gone. It is clear that either a drug, or the mental disciplines of astral projection referred to earlier, or both, may assist in the exploration of the land of the archetypal gods.

Now whereas Mescalito appears to resemble a 'god-level' of consciousness (in this case the spiritual aspect of a sacramental plant), the Ally is clearly of a lesser order of being. He does not 'teach', to use don Juan's expression, he merely bestows *power*. This power is gained by mastery of the subconscious; through a knowledge of the forces and forms which the mind can make in transformation.

In Qabalistic magic, when a practitioner projects 'astrally' through a symbol appropriate to one of the elements, it is tantamount to an instruction to the subconscious that certain images and not others should appear in a vision. If he has chosen the symbol for earth, he will see earth spirits and they will give him information about the more material side of his personality, albeit in a visionary, symbolic form. Don Juan's Allies seem more to resemble this type of entity. Castaneda describes how the Ally appeared at the other end of a visionary 'tunnel' which had become apparent under hallucinogenic influence. The magician, in astral flight, uses similar techniques of 'penetrating the planes'.

Don Juan assured Castaneda that he would have to be thoroughly prepared for his meeting with the Ally. He had to retain dominance at all times.

In magical practice, the practitioner makes symbolic gestures which are 'appropriate' to his level of contact. If the spirit entity 'responds correctly', the magician knows he is safe, and that his astral venture will be mystically 'authentic'. The following vision of the elements Earth and Fire combined by Soror Vestigia, comes from the magical records of the Order of Golden Dawn, and shows how on the astral journey, the occultist would take the initial precaution of 'testing' the guide. The Neophyte and Philosophus Signs mentioned below, refer to specific ritual grades upon the Tree of Life:[4]

> No fire is to be seen, but the type of land is volcanic. Hill and mountains, hot air, and sunny light. Using a Pentacle, and calling on the Earth Names, I see before me a species of Angelic King Elemental. *On testing him, I find that he gives me the Neophyte Saluting Sign, and the Philosophus (Fire) Sign. He bows low to the symbols that I give him, and says that he is willing to show me some of the working of that plane.* He has a beautiful face, somewhat of the Fire type, yet sweet in expression. He wears a Golden Crown, and a fiery red cloak, opening on a yellow tunic, over which being a shirt of mail. In his right hand he bears a wand, the lower end or handle being shaped somewhat as the Pentacle implement, and the staff and upper end being as the Fire Wand. In his left hand (but this I do not clearly see) he bears a Fire Wand; I think that the right hand points upwards and the left downwards, and is a symbol to invoke forces. Little figures of the gnome type come at his call. When commanded some broke the rocky parts of the Mountain with

pick-axes which they carry. Others appear to dig in the ground. In breaking off these rocky pieces, there fall away little bits of bright metal or copper. Some of these Gnomes collected the bits of metal and carried them away in little wallets slung by a baldrick from their shoulders. We followed them and came to some mountainous peaks. From these peaks issued some large and fierce, some hardly perceivable, fires. Into cauldrons or bowls placed above these fires, the collected pieces of metal were placed. I was told that this was a lengthy process, but asked that I might see the result of what appeared to be a gradual melting of this metal. I was then shown some bowls containing liquid gold, but not I imagine, very pure metal. I again followed my guide, the Angelic King Elemental Ruler, who gave me his name as Atapa, and followed by some gnomes bearing the bowl of liquid gold, we came, after passing through many subterranean passages cut in the mountains, to a huge cavern of immense breadth and height. It was like a Palace cut out of the rock. We passed through rudely cut passages until we reached a large central hall, at the end of which was a Dais on which were seated the King and Queen, the courtier gnomes standing around. This Hall seemed lighted by torches, and at intervals were roughly cut pillars. The Gnomes who accompanied us presented to the King and Queen their gold. These latter commanded their attendants to remove this to another apartment. I asked the King and Queen for a further explanation, and they, appointing substitutes in their absence, retire to an inner chamber which appeared more elevated than the rest. The architecture here seemed to be of a different kind. This small hall had several sides, each with a door, draped by a large curtain. In the centre of the Hall was a large tripod receiver containing some of the liquid gold such as that we had brought with us. The King and Queen who had before worn the colours of Earth now donned, he the red, and she the white garments. They then with their Earth-Fire Wands invoked and joined their wands over the Tripod. There appeared in the air above, a figure such as Atapa, he who had brought me here. He, extending his wand, and invoking, caused to appear from each door a figure of a planetary or zodiacal nature. These each in turn held out his wand over the gold, using some sigil which I can but dimly follow. The gold each time appearing to undergo a change. When these last figures have retired again behind the curtains, the King and Queen used a species of ladle and compressed together the gold, making it into solid shapes and placing one of these at each of the curtained doors. Some gold still remained in the bowl. The King and Queen departed, and it seemed to me that I saw a figure again appear from behind each curtain and draw away the pieces of gold.

Soror Vestigia combined her elemental symbols well. Fire (masculine) and earth (feminine) constitute a stabilizing, balancing effect. From her vision she comes to understand symbolically the transformation of the 'base metal' of undeveloped man into the 'gold' of illumination, in a process resembling the language of alchemy. The king and queen represent a unity, enhanced by the addition of all the planetary figures which circle the sun (= gold, and spiritual rebirth). The monarchs overlord the gnomes, representing earth, but have wands of fire, again showing the union of opposites.

It emerges from this account that in magical astral projection, the Ally is the one who first appears, and who will be the guide on the visionary journey. He must first be 'mastered' in an act of identification for otherwise he could lead the magician astray. In effect he could uncover a type of unconscious 'chaos' which could lead to severe mental unbalance. However the magicians of the Golden Dawn used certain 'controls' at all levels of their investigations. These controls resemble the state of mental alertness which don Juan calls the Way of the Warrior. The assault on the unconscious will be into unknown regions of the mind, but nevertheless the magician must trust his armaments: 'Our lot as men is to learn', says don Juan 'and one goes to knowledge as one goes to war . . . with fear, with respect, aware that one is going to war, and with absolute confidence in oneself . . .'[5]

ASTRAL TRANSFORMATIONS

The potential of the 'brujo' is hampered essentially by only one thing: the scope of his imagination. Before him lies the territory of his subconscious mind with all its interacting imagery, subject to sudden change and transformation. The sorcerer may 'fly' as a crow, like Castaneda did, or as La Catalina (don Juan's magical 'foe') in the form of a blackbird. One could adopt the vehicle of an eagle to soar to great heights like don Genaro. Given that the crucial transfer of consciousness had been achieved it was entirely up to the magician to choose and change his astral form under will. Accordingly he could use images appropriate to his form of travel. On one occasion Castaneda sat looking at the surface of a pool of water. Bubbles arose within his vision and don Juan advised his apprentice to board one of the bubbles and let it carry him ('a "brujo" uses the water to move'). Castaneda was able to merge his consciousness with the image. He found that he became the bubble. However, he had to beware of being 'carried off' by the water to the extent where the sense of discipline and control was lost. If the spirit of the water-hole succeeded in enticing Castaneda away, don Juan would never be able to bring him back.

A similar function was involved in the act of 'not-doing' which referred to unlearning previously assumed roles and descriptions used to define 'reality'. In order to enter the magical universe the candidate had to give equal status to both physically real and imagined objects. According to don Juan a useful exercise for the 'brujo' to practise was an action whereby one felt oneself to be pushing and pulling an imaginary object. Eventually the object would become 'heavy' impeding the free movement of the hand. In such a way the apprentice in sorcery would come to doubt his own notions of physical causality in the real world, and would understand that the only crucial factor was will. What was willed to be true, would come to be, perceptually. In the same way, in the realm of the imagination, the sorcerer would never be trapped on his astral journey if he could 'imagine himself into' an appropriate vehicle to escape the pitfalls. Don Juan favoured the form of a crow because as a species of bird, it was untroubled by others, and would not be attacked by predators:

> *I learned to become a crow because these birds are the most effective of all. No other birds bother them, except perhaps larger, hungry eagles, but crows fly in groups and can defend themselves. Men don't bother crows either, and that is an important point. Any man can distinguish a large eagle, especially an unusual eagle, or any other large, unusual bird,*

but who cares about a crow? A crow is safe. It is ideal in size and nature. It can go safely into any place without attracting attention.

There was thus no risk of an 'astral attack'. However, by the same token, a magician operating on this plane might surprise unawares an opponent who had not planned his symbolic defences so carefully. In an extended projection, according to don Juan, 'a "brujo" can move a thousand miles in one second to see what is going on. He can deliver a blow to his enemies long distances away.'

Usually a hallucinogen was employed to enable the sorcerer to 'see' in the astral light. With Devil's Weed, said don Juan, 'a man can soar through the air to see what is going on at any place he chooses.' Sometimes the toxic substances were rubbed over the skin to produce the out-of-the-body effect. With hallucinogenic paste on his skin Castaneda felt a sensation of flying rapidly through the air: 'I enjoyed such freedom, and swiftness as I have never known before.'

Under such conditions human beings appeared translucent and vibrant: they seemed to consist of fibres of light, enmeshing the body outline in a web of fine threads reaching from the head to the navel. Thus each man looked like an 'egg' of energy fibres, his arms and legs glowing like 'luminous bristles, bursting out in all directions'. Long tenuous fibres which reached out into the immediate environment appeared to exhibit a stabilizing factor. Through them a man could retain his sense of balance.

There are several techniques of astral projection in the West, some of which are variants on those described by Sylvan Muldoon, Oliver Fox and Robert Monroe. Ritual magicians usually refer to the act of projection of consciousness as 'rising on the planes' since it is used in conjunction with the 'mythological' framework of the Tree of Life. Basically the act of projection entails imagining something into 'reality'. The magician meditates upon a single image. Perhaps it is a symbol of the elements – a doorway through which to pass – or perhaps it is an image of a man like himself which he will try imaginatively to 'occupy'. Projection occurs when the image becomes equally as real to the observer as in his normal perception. Something occurs to make his normal body seem to be only an outer vestige. Perhaps it starts to fall to pieces and he finds himself 'reconstituting' on a new level.

Normally the magician activates what are known in the East as 'chakras' and which align on the 'Middle Pillar' in the Qabalah. Man is said traditionally to be made in the image of God; he is the microcosm and reflection of the universal creative process. Thus the Tree of Life is within himself:

He imagines radiant white light descending from above his head and vibrates the mantra *Eheieh* (pronounced EeeHeeYeh).

The light now descends to his throat, and is imagined to radiate forth in the form of mauve light: *Jehovah Elohim* (Ye-h-waa Eloheeem).

Descending further, it reaches the region of the heart and solar plexus. It has now transformed to golden yellow light: *Jehovah Aloah Va Daath* (Ye-ho-waaa Aloaaa Vaaa Daaath).

From the heart, down to the region of the genitals. From yellow into radiant purple: *Shaddai El Chai* (Shai-Dai-El-Haii).

Finally, the light reaches the feet and the colours of earth, russet, citrine, black and olive are visualised: *Adonai Ha Aretz* (Aadohnaiii Haaa Aaaretz).

The magician now imagines white light streaming down his left side, beneath the feet, and up his right side to the top of the head. He then visualizes a similar band of light energy travelling from his head along his nose, down the chest, once again beneath the feet, and up past the back of his legs to the head. In his mind he has enclosed his body, which may be lying horizontally or seated meditatively in a chair. His breathing is deep and regular. He imagines that the boundaries of light define a translucent container which is in reality his consciousness. It now seems to him that the container is filling up, perhaps with liquid, and that the amount of unoccupied space left in the container represents his extent of consciousness. At first his legs 'fill' and he is aware of his body only above the knees. Then the level rises and he remains 'aware' of only his chest. Soon the only conscious part of his body remaining is his head, for the rest has fallen into trance and is to all extents and purposes 'inert'. It is at this stage that the act of projection occurs. A rapid vibrationary sensation occurs and the magician begins to lift away from himself. He may experience the sense of duality, seeing his body inactive below while he appears to hover in a semi-illuminated 'darkness'. He may begin to encounter aspects of his subconscious imagery and will be able to subjugate or enhance these imaginatively by his command. Should he find himself unpleasantly threatened by negative images or potentially hostile forms, he will surround himself with a 'mental defence'. Perhaps this will take the form of a sphere or shell, a variation in effect, upon the magical circle as a means of 'distancing' unwanted visionary forms. In an act of strength and well-being he will vibrate an appropriate mantra or God-name. He finds himself operating in a changing, flaccid and elastic environment. Thought images seem to become hazily real. The perceptive surroundings change according to one's thoughts, and *one becomes what one is imagined to be*.

It is in this condition, that the magician begins to *see*. He has opened up new visionary channels into the recesses of his mind. In one way he has learned to mistrust his normal understanding of reality, learning now that reality is only where one's consciousness is located. At this stage his mind and body seem far apart. He may be flying in the form of a crow, he may be exploring textures, sounds, tastes, colours that had never been quite as accessible before. His projection may appear to be essentially three-dimensional; that is to say it coincides with his normal environment seen from a new vantage point (Monroe's Locale I), or, it may be an entry into the phantasy dream-time of the subconscious (Monroe's Locale II).

It is in this condition that the South American Indians undertake their trance-healing since the physical body seems luminous and translucent. The cause of illness appears as a type of psychic blot which the healer is able immediately to locate and remove 'under will'.

Finally, he may encounter a sequence of archetypal deities, if he wills himself into an appropriate location to do so. The English occultist Aleister Crowley, who believed that his teachings embodied the new doctrine of Horus, frequently imagined himself in the astral form of a hawk. Like don Juan and Castaneda, he would attempt to fly upwards to new levels of visionary awareness.

At this point we must consider the idea that 'reality' is merely a description of effects in a given locale. Sometimes a shift of awareness occurs and it is necessary to implement a new description of what is perceived. Such is the case when the magician makes the transition from the 'real world' to the transcendental one. It is this effect which don Juan appeared to be alluding to when he said that Castaneda must train to *see* rather than *look*. Don Juan said to him: 'For me the world is weird because it is stupendous, awesome, mysterious, unfathomable; my interest has been to convince you that you must assume responsibility for being here, in this marvellous desert, in this marvellous time. . . .'[6] On certain occasions the parallel universes move closer together. It is the task of the *brujo* to understand their relationship, and how, by various means he may have access from one plane of 'reality' to another.

CHAPTER 5
Towards a Framework for Inner Space

According to Castaneda, both the world of normality, and the magical universe are 'descriptions'. From an early age we are raised to observe only certain things in our environment as meaningful. We give these things names, and our language is thus built around communicating sounds and concepts which we agree upon as a basis to begin with.

It is known that ideas which do not have a word tag soon lose prominence in the process of communication. Ideas and language are mutually reinforcing. Thus we come to depend on our description of the world, regarding it as the only 'reality'. Castaneda insists that this is not in fact the case. His contact with don Juan meant that he gradually lost his certainty about his own concepts of normality, and learnt a new description of the world. That is to say, he came to regard new things as meaningful; talking to plants before eating them, paying closer attention to the mysterious forces in the wind and night; adopting ritual postures in his role as a 'warrior', acting as if each move was his last. These were all things that in his normal life as a city dweller would have seemed absurd to him before. They would have appeared to have no rationale, no logic. There could be no sense of cause and effect arising from these actions within his logical and intellectual framework of what was 'true'.

Castaneda believes that don Juan used hallucinogens to shatter his self-assuredness, his clinical and closed view of the environment. They introduced him to new visionary realities. On occasions his mind and body seemed to part directions. He encountered strange beings like Mescalito and the Ally; he learnt that one could be magically attacked by a sorceress like La Catalina who was able to project her consciousness into a myriad of different forms. He watched don Genaro, a friend of don Juan's, balancing precariously on tiny rocks high up in a lofty waterfall, maintaining superb control, as he was later told, by means of fine tentacles of force issuing from his solar plexus.

These tentacles could grip the surroundings, steadying his actions and allowing control.

Don Genaro was in fact employing in a very unusual way, the stabilizing forces of the solar plexus chakra, which is familiar to practitioners of both yoga and Qabalistic magic, but at the time Castaneda found his perception forcing doubt and realization simultaneously upon him. He literally could not believe his eyes. Don Juan told him then that he should learn to perceive not only with the eyes but with his whole body: 'According to sorcery, this burden on the eyes is unnecessary. We know with the total body. . . . The problem in sorcery is to tune and trim your body to make it a good receptor. . . . The body is an awareness and must be treated impeccably.'

Earlier we quoted Mircea Eliade's idea that the shaman is one who *breaks through in plane*, who is able to gain access to parallel realities. Each of these, Castaneda would say, is only a description, or to use Talcott Parsons's phrase, a 'gloss'. He defines a gloss as a 'total system of perception and language'. It seemed to him that as he learnt the techniques of sorcery, he was undoing one description or plane of reality, and reconstituting another. For this reason Castaneda says, 'I say he [i.e. don Juan] was reglossing me and he says he was deglossing me. By teaching me sorcery he gave me a new set of glosses, a new language and a new way of seeing the world.' The use of peyote, the mushroom smoke and datura 'created a gap in my system of glosses'; 'They destroyed my dogmatic certainty'.[1]

Over a number of years Castaneda learnt how to control his dream images and how to project his mind beyond its normal confines into dimensions he had never conceived of before. He learnt that ritual behaviour, communication with plants and animals, and the alertness of the warrior, confer power. And more far-reaching than this, the philosophy and application of the magical view of reality bestows a new set of meanings . . . a richer and more poetic sense of causality in the world.

If some people have found the imagery of the astral plane so enticing that they would never want to return to normal consciousness, this is not so for Castaneda. The warrior takes his place in the world with full knowledge of all the far-reaching possibilities. He does not and cannot shirk his responsibilities. Thus although the lessons have been learned, in a sense, by transcendence, the application is that one comes back to use this magical knowledge in the normal world.

Castaneda says: 'It has been this element of engagement in the world that has kept me following the path which don Juan showed me. There is no need to transcend the world. Everything we need to know is right in front of us, if we pay attention.'

He has perhaps forgotten his own apprenticeship in part here, because it is clear from his account that the magician has first to achieve the breakthrough, he has to *stop the world*, before he can apprehend the 'separate reality'. His initial transcendence allows him *thereafter* to see the world with magically dual vision. His perceptions are reinforced by the discovery that his former description of the world was inadequate.

Castaneda's account is one of the most illuminating and far-reaching descriptions of the exploration of inner space and the consequences of 'magical' awareness that we have. It is not, despite its unique qualities, the first. We referred earlier to the pioneers of astral projection and the Qabalists of the Golden Dawn who were undertaking activities quite similar in some ways, although with varying degrees of significance. Those who went the furthest had a 'description' or framework, such as the Tree of Life with which to work. More recently, with the revival of interest in oriental religion and mysticism, and the initial impetus of psychedelic drugs in the United States in the mid-1960s, we find that 'modern shamanism', if we can use that term to describe the psychedelic voyage, initially took an Eastern direction.

The pioneers of the psychedelic revolution, among them Timothy Leary, Ralph Metzner and Richard Alpert, the triumvirate of Harvard PhDs, found themselves adopting Buddhist and Hindu frameworks for inner space. Later it was apparent that a number of 'descriptions' or 'glosses' of these dimensions are available to us in the holy and esoteric texts of both East and West. The teachings of Gurdjieff and the Qabalistic Tarot, among others, acquire new relevance in this context.

However, we must return to the first rumblings at Harvard University, and the first mystical experimentation with the psychedelics. Leary and his colleagues sought to clarify how the impulses, currents of energy, and subtleties of form, which distinguish different aspects of the inner voyage, could make it for some a terrifying immersion in an ocean of paranoic images and for others, a revelation.

Leary took seven of the sacred mushrooms in a Spanish-style villa in Cuernavaca in August 1960. A friend of his, Gerhat Braun, an 'anthropologist-historian-linguist' from the University of Mexico had discovered that the mushrooms revered by the Aztecs, and used on special ceremonial occasions, still grew on the volcanic slopes near Mexico City. A peasant woman had undertaken to get some.

The *hongos* made Leary slightly nauseous at first, and his face began to tingle. Soon his vision was awash with wafty hallu-cinatory impressions:[2]

> Starting back to terrace
>   My walk has changed
>   Rubber legs
>   Room is full of water
>   Under water
>   Floating
>   Floating in air-sea
> Room
>   Terrace
>   People
>   All
> Under
> Water
>   BUT NO WORDS CAN DESCRIBE. . . .

Like Huxley he began to discover a profound richness in the kaleidoscopic imagery unfolding before his eyes, a new brilliance.[3]

Mosaics flaming colour Muzo emerald, Burma rubies
Ceylon Sapphire,
Mosaics lighted from within, glowing, moving, changing,
Hundred reptiles, jewel encrusted. . . .

He now began to ponder on his own life-force, his bloodstream, his pulsing arteries. The organic basis of all creativity over-whelmed him. His body contained a myriad universes; his cell tissue seemed to hold the secret of life and energy.

Leary was perceiving the motions of the universe at the atomic and subatomic levels. Finite imagery had been left far behind. He was witnessing the tides and motions of energy and form in their most profoundly elementary and essential phases of manifestation. The experience was quintessentially *religious*:[4] 'I came back a changed man. You are never the same after you have had that one flash glimpse down the cellular time tunnel. You are never the same after you have had the veil drawn.'

It was this initiatory experience which led Leary towards a systematic exploration of inner space. He gathered his friends for the journey. It seemed to him that a new chapter in the development of human thought was beginning: the quest for greater consciousness. There had been visionaries before, but they had been isolated individuals. Now a *movement* was underway. The earlier mystics and seers were forerunners and could act as guides:[5]

> We did sense that we were not alone. The quest for internal freedom, for the elixir of life, for the draught of immortal revelation was not new. We were part of an ancient and honorable fellowship which had pursued this journey since the dawn of recorded history. We began to read the accounts of early trippers – Dante, Hesse, Rene Daumal, Tolkien, Homer, Blake, George Fox, Swedenborg, Bosch, and the explorers from the Orient – Tantrics, Sufis, Bauls, Gnostics, Hermetics, Sivits, Saddhus . . . no, we were not alone.

During the autumn and winter of 1960, Leary spent most of his spare time studying the hallucinogenic qualities of psychotropic mushrooms. By day he continued to deliver lectures on clinical psychology at the Harvard Graduate School.

One of his students, a man who seemed to Leary at the time to be rather academic and 'ivory towerish' in his attitudes, but nevertheless brilliant at his work, was Ralph Metzner. Metzner said he wanted to experiment with psilocybin on prison inmates, to provide them with an experience which would change the course of their lives. There was no way in which they could predict the outcome, or the reaction of either inmates or wardens. But perhaps it could lead to new methods of integration and rehabilitation. It seemed an incredible idea so they tried it. There began what was to be a series of prison sessions and at first they weren't entirely successful. Leary on one occasion found himself viewing one of the inmates, a Polish embezzler, with acute distrust. Someone put on a jazz record, alleviating the tension and everyone relaxed. However the mood ebbed and flowed. Leary writes: 'There were high points and low points, ecstasies and terror.'

There were more sessions. Some of the convicts were able to leave on parole. Mild-mannered and changed men, they were sometimes, on Leary's admission, unable to cope with society pressures. However, the prison and its psychiatric unit had become, in certain measure, a 'spiritual centre'. It was a step forwards to a new understanding.

The prison sessions inspired Leary towards a sense of brotherhood. He had found communication, albeit uneasy, with men of quite a different ilk from him. The psilocybin had unshackled the psychiatric doctor-inmate-warden roles, they were 'all men at one . . . all two-billion year old seed centres pulsing together'. But the effect was not enduring. 'As time slowly froze we were reborn in the old costumes and picked up the tired games. We weren't yet ready to act on our revelation.'

It took an eccentric Englishman, Michael Hollingshead, to point out the next stage along the way. Hollingshead as it turned out was a 'medium aged' writer-cum-yogic practitioner who devised plots for his novels with a semi-autobiographical basis. At first Hollingshead seemed rambling and vacillatory to Leary. However he had a trenchant interest in the psychedelics. He had taken LSD, the most potent of all hallucinogens in the terms of dose, quantity, and urged Leary to do so. Leary refrained. LSD was a chemical, synthesized in a laboratory, whereas the mushrooms had a natural and even a cultural basis. They grew in the ground. And the Aztecs regarded them as holy.

Hollingshead insisted that LSD was of overwhelming 'religious' significance, paling psilocybin by comparison. Leary was eventually won over. Together with a group of friends, he and Hollingshead consumed a dose early in December 1961. Once again he found himself falling into an eddy of transforming shapes and forms. On reflection he thought of his role as father of his children. Had he been living a sham existence based merely on a routine form of parental devotion? Suddenly he seemed to be surrounded with death and falsity. Amid the confusion, what could be said to be *real*? He considered the structures and patterns of society: cultivation of crops, cities, invasions, migrations, moral codes, laws, but eventually these too seemed illusory as a basis for *being*. They were merely constructs and episodes of man, they did not identify his origins. He now found himself falling inwards. Beyond structure, into energy: 'nothing existed except whirring vibrations, and each illusory form was simply a different frequency. . . .' His perception seemed reduced to a primal level. Then, as the effects began to wear off, he experienced a terrible sense of loss. He had been to the heart of an energy vortex. 'Why had we lost it?' he asked. 'Why were we being reborn?' 'In these silly leather bodies with these trivial little cheese-board minds?'

Leary had reached a level of consciousness which for the first time had seemed to define a sense of reality and being-ness. He had never reached this level before. He had never been to the core. Why couldn't it be more accessible?

Meanwhile he continued to explore other hallucinogens as a means of entry to these states of realization. He partook of DMT with Richard Alpert and discussed it with Alan Watts, and with William Burroughs who had also chronicled at length the effects of *yage'* in the South American jungle. He began to ponder whether the visions of the mystics and seers of the past had a biochemical origin. Was he entering the same 'psychic spaces' of mind as Jacob Boehme, Blake and St John of the Cross had before him? Leary meanwhile received some inkling from an unexpected source.

The new development came to be called the 'Good Friday experiment', and once again owed its impetus to the enthusiasm of a Harvard student – this time Walter Pahnke, young and eager, with a medical degree and a Divinity qualification from the Midwest already under his belt and currently undertaking PhD studies in the philosophy of religion. Pahnke wanted to pin down the visionary experience within experimental parameters. Twenty theological students could be assembled in a church setting. Some would be given psilocybin and others would remain as the 'control group'. There would be organ music, prayer and a sermon; all the normal things in a Protestant service in fact, and it would be interesting to see whether anyone found themselves expanding consciousness in a transcendental, mystical direction. Leary thought Pahnke's suggestion was outrageous, but the student insisted. He had a medical degree, and would undertake 'psychiatric interviews to screen out pre-psychotics'. The volunteers would be carefully chosen, and the experiment would proceed in the respectable presence of Dr Walter Huston Clark, a visiting theological scholar to Harvard, and Dean Howard Thurman of the Boston University Chapel.

The experiment took place on Good Friday 1962 in the Chapel at Boston University. Some of the students were given psilocybin, the active component in the sacred mushrooms of Mexico which Leary himself regarded as sacramental. Others were given a placebo, nicotinic acid, which produced pleasant side effects but which was not hallucinatory. None of the participants knew who had received what.

I have mentioned Pahnke's own analysis of the results of the experiment in Appendix A of this book. In short however, it was found that those students who had taken the psychedelic, experienced mystical heights of quite a different order and intensity from those who had only taken the placebo. This did not in itself offer proof that a person ingesting psychedelic substances would necessarily have a mystical experience. It is evident from the literature that often they do not. However, the Good Friday session did seem to show that within a 'religious context' any expansion of consciousness could take a mystical direction. Leary writes: 'Our studies, naturalistic and experimental, thus demonstrate that if the expectation, preparation, and setting are spiritual, an intense mystical or revelatory experience can be expected in from 40 to 90 per cent of subjects.'[6]

When man ascends to the lofty heights of spiritual consciousness during a mystical illumination, his personality undergoes transformation. His new vision allows him to see the limitations of his ego-based human frameworks – his jealousies, fears, guilt, insecurities and so on – as if from a new more far-reaching vantage point. On his return to 'normal' consciousness, if he is able, he will bring some of his unifying spiritual knowledge down into incarnation. It will assimilate with and hopefully remould the earlier and more limited personality which existed prior to the voyage into inner space.

It is meaningful therefore to speak of mystical consciousness as a *rebirth* for those who pursue the path of transformation. Not only will they *change*, but the more negative non-integrated aspects of one's being are subsumed in favour of more positive, integrating characteristics. Jung called this process *individuation*, or making oneself *whole*. The shamans or ecstatics go on an inner journey and have encounters with their tribal ancestors or mythical archetypes. Often the shaman is 'taken to pieces' by the god figure and 'reassembled', as it were. In one account from Siberia, the shaman visits the mighty iron-forging deity, in the heavens, and is reshaped on the anvil into a mighty magician capable of superhuman power and insight.

'Flights of the soul' are common in the mystical literature of many cultures and on a less transcendental level constitute the mechanics of 'astral projection'. Don Juan remains both a great shaman and a great teacher, for he has integrated his knowledge of the 'separate reality' or magical dimension, into his normal faculties of perception. This does not produce schizophrenia so much as a more sensitivized, less routine-dominated world-view incorporating a wider vision.

The East is the direction of new light by day, and it is symbolically appropriate that Timothy Leary and his colleagues Ralph Metzner and Richard Alpert should have sought a Buddhist framework for the drug-orientated mystical illumination. They needed an appropriate guide, a well-charted basis for structuring the ego-death and spiritual-rebirth sequence on the psychedelic journey.

They chose as their model the 'Bardo Thodol' or 'The Tibetan Book of the Dead', translated into English by W.Y. Evans-Wentz. Aldous Huxley, a practising Buddhist, had prized this Mahayana text and had alluded to it in his pioneering book on mescalin, 'The Doors of Perception'.

Quite rightly, Leary and his colleagues stressed that the 'Bardo Thodol' was really addressed to the living, that is to say those who had necessarily to face the inevitability of death. On the one hand a sequence of post-mortem visions was described; the successive 'Bardo' phases of consciousness in between separate incarnations. Leary noted however that these descriptions were in fact an esoteric guide to mind expansion as well as a manual from which Tibetan priests read to those near death. The Bardo levels were realms of consciousness with which one could familiarize oneself prior to the final post-mortem separation of mind and body.

The psychedelics allow visionary projections and wanderings on the 'astral plane'. The out-of-the-body imagery takes different shapes and forms according to the mental attitudes of the person concerned, for he is projecting into the recesses of his mind, a universe of sensory impressions. He may liberate himself from the more constricting aspects of his make-up or he may become enmeshed in a hell world of negative personality traits. During such projection, as we have mentioned earlier, he is undertaking a journey rather like *dying*. Those who have written pioneering accounts of astral flight have described it in these terms. Some of those who had out-of-the-body experiences during Claudio

Naranjo's experimental drug sessions also referred to it in this way. And as Leary and his colleagues point out, 'The Tibetan Book of the Dead', also, relates 'dying' to the projection of the faculties of perception.

The 'Bardo Thodol' begins with the loftiest experience of all: the Clear Light of Illumination, experienced as the beholder loses his own ego in favour of the Void. This is a state of transcendent equilibrium and knowledge, of well-being and Unity with All. It is a state of sublime Liberation from the constrictions of the sensory world.

If this state of being cannot be maintained there dawns the Secondary Clear Light. This occurs at a primal mystical level where the beholder is illuminated in an ecstasy of what Leary calls *wave energy flow*; 'the individual becomes aware that he is part of and surrounded by a charged field of energy, which seems almost electrical.' If he rides with the flow he may sustain this consciousness. But should he attempt to control it, this in itself indicates an act of ego, reflective of *duality*, that is to say, the sense of oneself *distinct* from the surroundings. The flow of energy associated with the experience of Unity and the heights of Kundalini ebbs away. The individual begins to fall into lower levels of mind, called in 'The Tibetan Book of the Dead' the Chonyid Bardo, or karmic hallucinatory stages.

This Bardo equates with what Qabalistic magicians refer to as the 'Higher' astral plane, whereas the initial Bardo relates to the state of mystical aweness and Unity above the Abyss on the Tree of Life. In the second Bardo, writes Leary, 'strange sounds, weird sights and disturbed visions may occur. These can awe, frighten and terrify unless one is prepared. . . .' The answer is to remain composed and neutral before these mental events. Rationalizations are traps for the unwary. It is characteristic that don Juan was unable to provide Castaneda with 'logical' constructs relating to this level of consciousness.

In the second Bardo, 'any and every shape – human, divine, diabolical, heroic, evil, animal, thing – which the human brain conjured up or the past life recalls, can present itself to consciousness; shapes and forms and sounds whirling by end-lessly.'

'The underlying solution – repeated again and again – is to recognise that your brain is producing the visions. They do not exist. Nothing exists except as your consciousness gives it life.'

It was in this phase that the Tibetans believed they would encounter the Seven Peaceful Deities and the Seven Visions of the Wrathful Deities incorporating fifty-eight embodiments of the human personality couched within traditional, culturally delineated forms and shapes. These, together with lower grades of forces and potencies constitute the Tibetan pantheon. Evans-Wentz writes:[7]

> the chief deities themselves are the embodiments of universal divine forces, with which the deceased is inseparably related, for through him, as being the microcosm of the macrocosm, penetrate all impulses and forces, good and bad alike. Samanta-Bhadra, the All-Good, thus personifies Reality, the Primordial Clear Light of the Unborn, Unshaped *Dharma-Kaya*. Vairochana is the Originator of all phenomena, the Cause of all Causes. As the Universal Father, Vairochana manifests or spreads forth as seed, or semen, all things; his *shakti*, the Mother of Great Space, is the Universal Womb into which the seed falls and evolves as the world-systems. Vajra-Sattva symbolizes Immutability. Ratna-Sambhava is the Beautifier, the Source of all Beauty in the Universe. Amitabha is Infinite Compassion and Love Divine, the *Christos*. Amogha-Siddhi is the personification of Almighty Power or Omnipotence. And the minor deities, heroes, *dakinis* (or 'fairies') goddesses, lords of death, *rakshasas*, demons, spirits, and all others, correspond to definite human thoughts, passions and impulses, high and low, human and sub-human and super-human, in *karmic* form, as they take shape from the seeds of thought forming in the percipient's consciousness-content.

The third phase or *Sidpa Bardo*, is the period of 're-entry', the descent from the heights of the Here and Now. The return to the familiar environment. A person able to bring full knowledge of spiritual Unity down to his temporal existence would be an avatar or saint. Below this level there would be various levels of inspirational attainment ranging from greater than normal human perception, down to the lowest forms of animal consciousness manifest (or re-awakened) in man.

Since the dimensions of mind which the beholder finds himself in are directly related to his ability to retain control over thought and not be 'captured' by its imagery, it is important that during the 're-entry', the will should be focused as much as possible on integrated spiritual values rather than symbols of the ego.

Otherwise, the individual may find himself enmeshed in Judgement visions relating to Karma associated with his personality; debased sexual fantasies, or other projections of neurosis.

To summarize the essential teaching of the 'Bardo Thodol': The Great Liberation is achieved by ego-loss or 'death of the ego'; this state may be achieved in the first Bardo of the Clear Light, or by transcending the images of deities in the second Bardo. Below these levels, the ego gains more and more strength, and seeks 'rebirth' in the world of the senses where it is able to assert itself once more as dominant. Most of us, says Leary, are doomed to return to 'normality' after the journey. However, training for these levels of consciousness allows greater familiarity with the most sacred realms of mind. Eventually the choice for Liberation will be taken.

Since the height of the psychedelic revolution and the publication of the 'Bardo Thodol' commentary, the ways of Leary, Alpert and Metzner parted somewhat. Leary found himself becoming a scapegoat for political distrust of psychedelics, and in recent years has lived the unfortunate life of a jail-escapee-cum-hunted-man on the basis of an initial charge of possessing less than an ounce of marijuana.[8]

Richard Alpert went to India, initially to discover what the holy men could make of LSD. A Californian named Bhagwan Dass took Alpert to his guru, in the foothills of the Himalayas. Subsequently Alpert showed his sacrament to the Maharaji. The holy man consumed Alpert's entire stock – 900 micrograms – and was totally unaffected! Someone explained to Alpert that the sage operated in a mental space called *sahaj samadhi* which was not dependent on sources of stimulation deriving from the biophysical level.

Alpert had found a higher source of spiritual authority than he had anticipated. The Maharaji allowed Alpert to stay, providing him with a teacher, and the former Harvard professor now became Baba Ram Dass.

Dass says 'the only thing you have to offer to another human being ever, is your own state of being.' He remains a Westerner, if only by heritage, and has found his main role, if it is possible to isolate such an activity, in communicating the spiritual truths of

Indian Yoga to Western audiences. A transcript of his excellent lectures for the Menninger Foundation, Topeka, Kansas, was published in 1973 in a book entitled 'Doing your Own Being'.

Ralph Metzner meanwhile began the lengthy task of comparing all the major accessible frameworks for the exploration of inner space. Following his experiences at Harvard with Leary and Alpert, he spent several years pursuing various schools of mystical thought and psychotherapy. These included the teachings of Gurdjieff and Wilhelm Reich, encounter groups and Gestalt therapy. He says that he found most of these avenues of thought 'valuable in some ways, but limited'. In 1970 he completed a book which compares some of the mystical systems he found most useful in charting the geography of inner space. This work, entitled 'Maps of Consciousness' provided outlines of the 'I Ching', Tantra, Tarot, Alchemy, Astrology, and a new development called Actualism, based on *Agni Yoga* and incorporating the methods of Russell and Carol Schofield. Metzner agreed with Leary that the old subject-object duality was outmoded in the field of scientific observation. A scientist, particularly one dealing with intangibles like thought processes and altered states of consciousness, had to be prepared to enter his own experiments and be his own testing ground. As a researcher, himself, into patterns of human evolutionary development at 'growth centres' in the United States, Metzner has been inclined to disregard existing behavioural models in psychology in favour of self-development systems outlined in various forms of mysticism. He writes:[9]

> The esoteric psychological schools as well as some of the oriental ones, have maintained the knowledge of the Higher, Immortal Self, the Krishna-consciousness, or Christ-consciousness, which is the teacher-knower within who can guide the person's evolutionary growth towards individuality. Concepts of what is 'normal', or 'right' or 'should be' are all image-obstructions to our receptive perception of what actually is; which can only be learned by listening-looking-sensing within. . . .

In the 'I Ching', Metzner found an 'interesting matrix of change, that fuses the positive and negative energies' in the interplay between yang and yin. Usually, the 'I Ching' is used as a divinatory oracle. Forty-nine yarrow stalks are taken and the heap divided in a certain way to produce alignments on a 'hexagram' pattern which can be interpreted according to a body of traditional meanings. The 'I Ching' seems to operate upon laws of balance, and since man is the microcosm, there is a correspondence between internal tuition (used in divinatory interpretation) and external events in the world itself (the macrocosm). Man may therefore use the oracle to determine appropriate courses of action at a given time.

Metzner is interested in astrology for much the same reasons. In particular, what he terms 'the linkage between planetary and other cosmic cycles on the one hand and processes on earth, particularly in man, on the other' concerns him most. It is thus not planetary influences per se which should be considered but the symbolism of their movements in the heavens describing cycles and 'geophysical rhythms' affecting man in the form of accident proneness, incidence of disease, human fertility and so on. In addition, relevant insights are acquired into the individual personality facets which allow the self-inquiring experimenter to recognize character traits he may 'work with or through'. He should view them in this way rather than 'obstacles in the form of *faults* given at birth'. What Metzner is saying in effect, if we may paraphrase words of his friend Baba Ram Dass, is that we begin with the *here and now*. Whatever is our lot is our starting point. It is no use blaming planetary alignments for deficiencies in personality. One begins with the combination one is assigned.

In his chapter on Tantra, the yoga of sexual energy, Metzner pursued further a direction begun with Leary and Alpert in their psychedelic adaptation of the 'Bardo Thodol'. Particular emphasis has been laid in this branch of yoga upon *yantras*, geometrical diagrams used for visualization processes; *mantras*, specially conceived rhythmic utterances designed to modify consciousness in a certain way, and *mudras*, special postures and gestures, especially of the upper limbs, which enabled 'transformations of bodily experience through the channelling of energies' to occur. Tantra seeks to unite in man his opposite polarities – the male and female characteristics which Jung had alluded to in the form of his *animus/anima* theory (the idea that men and women have complementary sexual forces active within the unconscious). The supreme state of bliss is a Unity above opposites, and means of raising the Kundalini to this level had intrigued Metzner since his original study of Bardo states of consciousness. The Kundalini, as a union of opposites in itself, constituted the mystical axis of man.

Upon it lay certain chakras, 'the points in which psychic forces and bodily functions merge into each other or penetrate each other'. Two encapsulating lines of force or *nadis* were said to operate around the central nervous system or axis (sushumna): *Ida*, the negatively charged lunar current, and *pingala*, the positive and masculine current. The special value of this knowledge in Metzner's view was that 'part of the esoteric practice of the Tantric psychologists undoubtedly consisted of increasing one's awareness of the psycho-physical field by amplifying energy flow through the *nadis*.'[10] Another point of importance was that some experimenters with psychedelics seemed to be arousing Kundalini without fortifying the body by *Hatha Yoga* techniques in the customary way employed by Tantrics.

Actualism, a school of thought based on *Agni Yoga*, or 'union by fire', like Tantra, also involves the roles of opposite polarities and the channelling of energy. The 'fire' is itself the *inner* fire, 'which brings light into darkened areas of consciousness and the consuming fire aspect is used to burn out obstructions to the fire flow of energy from inner sources'. Russell Schofield stresses that knowledge of the higher recesses of consciousness is not by itself enough. The practitioner has to learn to eliminate 'psychic residues' preventing man from acting in full capacity as an energy transformer. *Agni Yoga* offers a discipline for burning out by 'inner fire', unwanted blockages in the energy channels. According to Metzner, the god Siva originally symbolized a destructive force which was able to strip away such excrescences to allow the inner light to shine forth. In Actualism the same principle applies:

> We gradually learn . . . to channel, direct, focus, concentrate energy flow into and throughout our own energy systems, then to exterior energy systems. This starts the awakening process – awakening the created energy systems to the creator within them – the teacher-knower within, the physician within etc. – all the many aspects of the creator.

The process of mastery is long and gradual, but the end result is a meditative tool as potent as a laser beam, within the inner dimension. Metzner compares it with the Tarot card of the Tower struck by lightning which shows 'the laser light of Jupiter Fulminans striking the structure and throwing off the false images of self which fall like dead men from the tower'. The uniting principle underlying the whole school of *Agni Yoga* is that the false outer shells of man are discarded in favour of the Actual Self. This equates to a large extent with a concept in transcendental magic which we shall consider presently, namely that of the Higher Self, and the True Will. For Aleister Crowley, who was in his own right a Tantric occultist, this had much the same meaning as the Actual Self does for Metzner: 'Upon reaching the goal of wholeness within, one is capable of knowing and carrying out the purpose for which he entered in as a God-Child upon the creative venture of the Father-Mother-Creator-God of this macro-cosmos.'[11]

Actualism thus enables us to realize a profound sense of unity in being and purpose within the cosmos. It is this aspect in fact which runs through all of Metzner's compared systems (including the Tarot and alchemy). The 'I Ching', astrology, Tantra and Agni Yoga all involve a thorough understanding of polarities and opposites, of cycles and energy-flow through what another writer, John Lilly, has termed the human *bio-computer*. And it is to Lilly that we must now turn, as one of the other major contributors to the recent literature on inner space.

Like Leary, Alpert and Metzner, John Lilly brought a thorough scientific training to bear in his initial researches into altered states of consciousness. Like them he has adopted mystical systems for defining states of spiritual perception rather than biophysical explanations of causality. He begins with what is known and concedes the last word to what is unknown. This remains the only possibility. Man is only now beginning to scratch away at the surface of infinity.

Lilly was originally trained as a psychoanalyst and neurophysiologist, and undertook some valuable work on communications between man and dolphins. This led to two books, 'Man and Dolphin' and 'The Mind of the Dolphin', before his acute awareness of the sensitivity and intelligence of dolphins caused him to have ethical objections to further clinical research on them. He adopted the position that it is preferable for a scientist to be his own guinea-pig before inflicting himself on his subjects.

From the start Lilly has been challenged by the potential of human consciousness. A few years after gaining his doctorate from the University of Pennsylvania he decided to test the idea that a person remains awake because he is bombarded with sensory stimuli. He took himself off to what he calls a 'solitude-isolation-confinement' tank at the Institute of Mental Health in

Bethesda, Maryland. His idea was to enter an environment where sensory input was minimized as far as was humanly possible, and see what happened. Wearing a special latex rubber mask fitted with breathing apparatus, Lilly floated naked in quiet solitude and darkness, in water heated to a constant 93°F, the temperature at which one is neither hot nor cold. In the darkness Lilly felt as if he were floating in a gravity-free dimension. He discovered that the brain compensates for the reduction of sensory stimulation by producing a marked degree of heightened *inner* awareness. 'I went through dream-like states, trance-like states, mystical states', he writes. 'In all of these states I was totally intact.' He remained simultaneously aware of his floating body and the nature of the experiment.

This inquiry into sensory deprivation was Lilly's first scientific contact with mystical reality. It seemed to him that under these conditions the brain or 'bio-computer' released a particular 'programme' of sensory experiences. The programme would be directly related to one's concepts and beliefs, that is to say, one would only perceive things within grasp of the imagination. A person with narrow conceptual confines would find himself in a barren, constricting 'space' when his mind-contents were shown to him.

Lilly found that, potentially, sensory deprivation states offered tremendous *freedom*. External reality had been shut out. He could programme a mental journey to any place which his imagination could conceive (we have found similarities to this approach in the records of the pioneering astral projectionists). His choice of programme would take him to various 'spaces' or states of consciousness of varying transcendental attainment.

During the early 1960s Lilly took LSD for the first time, and found that he was also capable of entering mystical dimensions by this means. He had been raised as a devout Catholic in his youth and knew full well that on death the pure soul winged its way to God. Now, years later, while listening to Beethoven's Ninth Symphony under hallucinatory influence, Lilly found himself experiencing a similar 'flight of soul'. He saw angelic beings and an aged patriarchal God seated on His throne. The programmed learning from his youth had been re-activated by the drug! 'Later', says Lilly, 'I was to realize that the limits of one's beliefs set the limits of the experiences.'

Sometimes on his inner journeys Lilly contacted entities he calls his 'two guides'. He resists describing these beings, beyond indicating that they represent a particular type of direction and knowledge applicable only to his own wanderings on the astral planes. On occasions they appeared to epitomize his higher self talking down to the more constricted personality – showing the way to more integrated being. At other times they took the form of karmic conscience, reminding Lilly that he had commitments to his friends and family and could not be an inner-planes drop-out without dire consequences.

We find the concept of the *guide* in Qabalistic magic too, as we indicated in the vision of Fire and Earth. The guide is either anthropomorphic or else appears as a friendly 'presence'. Lilly was unable to locate the origin of his guides either as contents of his own mind or as entities from other universes or time-warps. He nevertheless regarded them as indispensable: 'it is essential to have something, someone, ahead . . . setting the goals of where you are going.'

As mentioned earlier, magical projection and shamanism both employ 'protective techniques' to ensure safety on the inner planes. By comparison caution is lacking in the accounts of Leary and Baba Ram Dass, and to a lesser extent, in Metzner. For Lilly, however, it is the framework or programme itself that is the safeguard, for the experience which follows is a direct consequence of the programme. It is up to us to rid it of flaws. Now the flaws may be very potent indeed – what Lilly calls 'self-destruct' organisms that in a way declare war on other parts of the human bio-computer. These may be activated by the drug and may in extreme instances override the instinct for survival. Myths and legends abound with accounts of such demonic 'temptations' and 'possession' and it is in this light that these tales have real, cautionary value. Within Lilly's framework 'possession' is nothing other than getting trapped in a 'negative space' and finding oneself unable to escape its binding and terrifying imagery.

Lilly thus trusts more to correct 'metaprogramming' as he calls it, than faith, say, in a guru. The devotees surrounding a holy man, for Lilly, resemble the scientist who is unwilling to experiment upon himself. Both avoid a central, critical role. Both are too dependent on others. According to Lilly, we begin *now* with what we have. Our set of beliefs are our programme. Eventually we will transcend those beliefs at the 'limits of creative imagination'. Beyond that is only Samahdi, Unity, the end of individuality and the beginning of Infinity.

Like Castaneda, Lilly began from a 'safe place', a point of reference. Lilly's was the dark and silent void of the water tank – 'absolute zero point' – a place 'out of the body, out of the universe as we know it'. Before him were endless planes of possibility barred only by limits of the imagination.

On one occasion Lilly found himself in a space which he called the *cosmic computer*. It seemed to him that he was a very small and insignificant part of *someone else's* macro-computer, in rather the same way that Jorge Luis Borges writes of an individual 'dreamed' into reality by the power of another person's imagination.[12] Lilly sensed tremendous waves of energy, of the same intensity as those described as pertaining to the Bardo of the Secondary Clear Light. However, there was no sense of well-being or order. He found himself in total terror, in a whirlpool of swirling, meaningless energy – a loveless cosmic dance with 'no human value'.

Afterwards Lilly thought over his conceptions of the origin of the physical universe, which had been formulated during his scientific training. There had been no room here for mystical trance elements, or doctrines of love and meaning. His negative Bardo vision showed that a new programme was necessary. He had failed to acknowledge the energies of the Godhead working through him.

Subsequently Lilly had discussions with Alan Watts about Eastern mysticism. At the Esalen Institute at Big Sur, California, he talked over the merits of Gestalt therapy with Fritz Perls and Ida Rolf. Here too he met Baba Ram Dass, back from India.

Dass introduced him to certain yogic techniques and the sutras of Patanjali. A major upshot of this was that Lilly perceived that if he wished to find Union with the Infinity of the Void, he would have to stand back from both the programmer and the programme. He would have to see his results and frameworks in a new light, for the twofold division of see-er and seen could no longer apply in a state of absolute *Unity*. He came to write: 'Beyond transcendence is an infinite variety of unknowns. . . . Beyond these unknowns, now unknown is *full complete Truth*.'

This means that even when we hold to a set of beliefs, they must always remain open-ended, for they cannot hope to encompass the transcendent unknown and contain it within finite expressions and concepts.

With Oscar Ichazo, the Chilean mystic who has a meditative

school in Africa, he discussed negative spaces. It would be most appropriate for the person seeking full mystical consciousness to have an automatic means of escaping the negative faculties of the inner planes of mind. Metzner had learned a laser-beam technique of fire yoga for burning out these obstacles to Unity. Lilly calls the process he learned the 'burning of Karma'. A high degree of concentration is called for. The negative qualities are seized upon and ruthlessly exhumed in transcendentally negative spaces, where they will never again exert any influence. No longer will they register on the map of inner consciousness.

Ichazo's system is based on the teachings of Gurdjieff and focuses on degrees of spiritual awakening in man. In an interview in 'Psychology Today', Ichazo claimed that one of his major aims was to destroy ego-dominated thoughts. When the ego or a society reaps the full hell they have sown in their quest for false security and status, they come to the point of collapse and rebirth. The collapse comes at the moment when the ego games are completely exposed and understood; illusion is shattered, subjectivity is destroyed, karma is burned. For Ichazo the decline of society brings with it the first moment of enlightenment. Its roles and programmes are suspended. The only thing left is the *first Satori*.

Lilly had come to him for an alternative to current scientific conceptual frameworks, and at a time when drug hysteria in the United States made worth-while research into LSD impossible. It was Ichazo who provided Lilly with a structure of the positive and negative states of consciousness from Satori through to anti-Satori. Like archetypal images, these vibrational levels according to Lilly are 'definitely part of our human heritage' and are 'available to most of us'.

In Table 5.1 (see pp. 86-7) I have summarised the main divisions according to Gurdjieff/Ichazo/Lilly. Beside them are the corresponding chakras according to both the Kundalini yoga, and Qabalistic systems. They are fruitful grounds for comparison.

John Lilly would probably agree that his system, as well as the others are 'programmes' rather than absolutes. They help us to conceive of a progressive awakening of the consciousness. We move from the lowest levels of bio-computer awareness through to the most Universal non-ego directions of Being.

Lilly has also ascribed certain metaphorical positions on the body (which microcosmically equals the universe) to levels of mind. In Eastern mysticism these are the chakras, which

Rammurti Mishra calls 'neuro-hormonal mechanisms'. They are centres of psychic energy, and are activated in turn during the raising of the Kundalini. The Qabalists know them by a different name. They are the Sephiroth on the so called Middle Pillar, the Western equivalent of Sushumna.

Each of the 'programmes' has a different emphasis, and this relates partly to the way in which the body is divided into spiritual zones.

Yogic lotus posture is not much used in Western magic, and thus we find that the lowest chakra in yoga (the genitals) is only the second lowest in the Qabalah. The magician often sits in a posture resembling the seated Egyptian god-kings and thus his final contact with the earth is his feet. Lilly also has a chakra corresponding with the feet; it is the starting point, the beginning of the mystical ascent. The cross-legged yogi however begins to raise Kundalini from his reproductive area. The currents of male and female energy twisting like a caduceus around the central Sushumna pillar lead towards the birth of new being. Finally the grand fertilization will occur as his consciousness merges with Godhead in a blissful ego-less Union.

The Qabalists regard the genital chakra as the basis of both the sex instinct and the animal consciousness. It is this level of inspiration which is the basis for lunar worship, witchcraft and worship of the Horned God. The loftier reaches of consciousness are associated with the more spiritual or transcendental aspects of the 'soul'. In the Qabalah, there is no equivalent of the Buddha level in the head or the Manipura level in the lower belly. Again, whereas both Kundalini yoga and Qabalah have a chakra in the neck, Lilly has omitted it from his system.

This does not mean that one system is superior to another or 'more truthful'. They are all programmes in their own right. We choose one and follow its path. All genuine systems, all valid roads in the terrain of inner space, lead to the same place. Some merely mark the milestones at different points. What is more important is that the mystical quest is made intelligible, and *that we know where we are when we arrive at any particular point on the inward journey.*

TABLE 5.1 Chakra levels

LILLY/GURDJIEFF LEVEL OF CONSCIOUSNESS	DESCRIPTION	YOGA	QABALAH
+ 3 Classical Satori	Death of the ego Consciousness transforms itself to a Universal level Union with the Godhead (*Chakra:* above head)	*Sahararam*	*Kether*
+ 6 Buddha Consciousness	Ego-consciousness reduced to a very small point Direct communication at the level of Essence Astral projection/encounters with spiritual beings (*Chakra:* head)	*Ajna*	
– – – – – – – – – –		– – – *Visudha* – – –	– – – *Daath* (*Chakra:* neck)

Level	State	Description	Sephiroth / Chakra
+ 12	Christ Consciousness	Cosmic love and Divine grace Joy in the company of others Perception of the aura (*Chakra*: centre of chest)	*Tiphareth* *Anahata*
+ 24	'the basic professional state'	Control of the bio-computer Ability to act knowledgeably and freely within certain 'programmes' (*Chakra*: lower belly)	*Manipura* *Svadhisthana* (*Chakra*: lumbar region) —*Yesod* (*Chakra*: genitals) *Muladhara*
+ 48	Normal Consciousness	Rational behaviour Openness and 'neutrality' receptivity in human interaction	*Malkuth* (*Chakra*: feet)

PART TWO

The Qabalah Revisited

CHAPTER 6
Christianity, Magic and Science

I

It may seem unlikely that the detailed and far-reaching models of inner space proposed by people like Timothy Leary, Ralph Metzner and John Lilly were not the first, and in fact had an important precursor some seventy years earlier.

Leary turned to Hinduism as Huxley had found new insights in Mahayana Buddhism. Lilly meanwhile adopted Ichazo's Gurdjieff models of consciousness. Why had they taken these directions? The answer, it seems to me, is that the psychedelic phase in America grew up partly as a result of disillusionment with Christianity, which as a devotional religion has tended to stress faith rather than experience. When a person meditates or ingests an hallucinogenic substance things may occur inwardly which impress him as spiritually profound. The Eastern religions have had more to say about levels of consciousness than Christianity or orthodox Islam, and thus it is not surprising that the parallel development of interest in psychedelics and in oriental thought has been, and certainly was in the early 1960s, mutually reinforcing.

The historical antecedent I have referred to above was the Hermetic Order of the Golden Dawn, a group of Masons practising ceremonial Qabalistic magic based on the symbol of the Tree of Life. Its members were either non-Christian, or sought in the Qabalah, a more profound alternative to the then-existing fundamentalist Christianity. Like John Lilly's attempt in his book 'The Human Bio-computer' to provide scientific models for the religious experience, so too did the Golden Dawn emerge at a time when the debate between orthodox religion and science was at its peak. This period of philosophical crisis in Victorian England has considerable relevance to the present time, and I should like to discuss the setting which gave rise to the first systematic exploration of inner space in the West. It is interesting that this debate had its basis in the interpretation of symbolism. Funda-

91

mentalist diehards clung closely to their holy texts as an explanation of the cosmos, while scientists began, in the early nineteenth century to erode the belief that the universe came into being, as written, during the Seven Days of Creation.

CHRISTIANITY VERSUS SCIENCE

The historian, Owen Chadwick, writes:[1]

between 1820 and 1840 geology became the science of the day. It captured popular imagination ... the first step of the advance demanded time; time on a scale unknown; vistas of unimagined time while the strata of rocks were formed and embraced their fossils. They met the calculation of Archbishop Usher, placed in the margins of the King James (Bible) that God created the world in 4004 B.C. ... geologists demanded millions of years of time.

As early as 1820 however noted clergymen, such as Reverend William Buckland who was to hold the Chair of Geology at Oxford, were proclaiming the symbolic nature of the Genesis chronology. In his inaugural lecture he said that the 'days of Creation' were epochs of unspecified length and not days of twenty-four hours. He was further inclined to view the chronological statements concerning the Flood as metaphorical. Old Testament theorizers had calculated that Noah's forty days and nights of rain began to fall on Sunday, 7 December 2347 BC! Sir Charles Lyell now put forward considerable evidence to show that the biblical time period was insufficient since fossil evidence indicated a flood catastrophe ranging over an extended period. Buckland accepted Lyell's evidence.

However, in 1844 William Cockburn, Dean of York and one of Buckland's notable adversaries, condemned both him and Oxford University for 'leading a movement away from orthodoxy to atheism'.

Chadwick writes:[2]

The opinions of leading Christian divines quickly changed during the late thirties and early forties. ... By 1844 the gap between educated theology and popular theology was widening. Popular opinion conceived geology to be somehow dangerous to scripture ... the people accepted the recent origin of the world and man, and therefore regarded scientists with suspicion and prejudice.

In this year Robert Chambers, an amateur geologist and encyclopaedist published 'Vestiges of the Natural History of Creation' which claimed that all the species of the world ascended by transmutation from lower to higher. Man had evolved from lower forms. In selling over 23,000 copies in eleven British editions it offered the public the first popular history of the prehistoric world. It correspondingly eroded the beliefs of the comparatively unsophisticated adherents of the Christian Church. Even Lord Tennyson, who read 'Vestiges' had his faith in man's origins shattered by 'dragons tearing each other in the slime, nature red in tooth and claw, shrieking against his creed' (i.e. of the Divine Creation of Man)

> Antagonism between religion and science had reached popular non-philosophical minds only in the sense that one or the other was instantly known to be wrong. ... As science gained converts, the Churches in England sought to tighten their dogmatic authority. At the same time they met new ideas which threatened their dogmas and authority at source. The historical method could not leave the Bible a document exempt from anatomising. Geology forced more educated people to jettison their axioms about the origin and age of the world.[3]

P.T. Marsh in his book 'The Victorian Church in Decline' writes that the publication of Darwin's 'Origin of Species' in 1859:[4]

> began a twenty year period of some of the most intense criticism of Christianity in England's history. Few of the critics' concepts were new! Evolution had been in the intellectual atmosphere for half a century. What was new was the painstaking experimentation and building up of documented proof which appropriated the name 'science' ....
>
> Acts of faith seemed more difficult now, and were also wanting among clerics themselves. The Church of England had many dissenting intellectuals and 'no person or tribunal or assembly could pronounce a decision effectively binding

on the consciences of all churchmen. As a result the voice of the Church was often the voice of internal controversy. Fear of schism within the Church paralysed its leadership. So did the increasing fear that the faith of the Church might not be able to retain its present adherents let alone make headway against the sceptical.

In the later years, certain of the more flexible clerics attempted to reconcile their faith with the tenets of science. A.P. Stanley, the Dean of Westminster, who gave the funeral sermon for Sir Charles Lyell in 1875, continued the view proposed by Buckland in the 1840s. Having quoted Genesis 1: 2, he said:[5]

> The language, however poetic, childlike, parabolical and unscientific yet impresses upon us the principle in the moral and the material world, that the law of the Divine operation is the gradual, peaceful progressive development of discord into harmony, of confusion into order, of darkness into light.
>
> It is now certain that the vast epochs demanded by scientific observation are incompatible both with the six thousand years of the Mosaic chronology, and the six days of the Mosaic Creation. No one now infers from the Psalms that 'The earth is set so fast that it cannot be moved' or that the sun actually 'comes forth as a bridegroom from his chamber' or that 'The morning stars sang' with an audible voice at the dawn of the Creation. To insist on these details as historical or scientific is as contrary to the style and character of the sacred books themselves as it is to the undoubted facts of science.

However in the popular mind it continued to be a case of *either* Christianity *or* science. Meanwhile, in the same year as the above address Madame Blavatsky announced the birth, in New York, of the Theosophical Society. Its major aim was to bring Indian thought, Hinduism in particular, to a Western audience, as an alternative to Christianity, but under the pretext of universalizing religion. And her 'Secret Doctrine' was said to provide a 'synthesis of science, religion and philosophy'.

It was within the London Theosophical circles, that the Hermetic Order of the Golden Dawn first came into existence. The founder, Dr Wynn Westcott intended that the new Order could offer its practitioners an even more systematic and anciently derived exposition of the so called 'mystery teachings' than Theosophy. Unlike Theosophy, the Golden Dawn was based squarely upon the Qabalah and the 'Western cultural tradition'.

Its inception may be thus explained in terms of what it could offer its adherents in the wake of the Christianity versus science debate.

As an alternative to Christianity

1 A detailed account of the symbolism of the Genesis account of Creation which appeared to be beyond scientific reproach (QBL – Qabalah – means 'from mouth to ear' and the original esoteric commentaries on Genesis were said to precede the written word).

2 An account of how man could become god-like by eventually encountering and embodying in a visionary state the archetype of rebirth, universalized beyond the figure of Jesus Christ to include other resurrected deities such as Osiris.

3 A teaching which did not require faith, but progress through self effort, and which began with man, rather than with God.

In sympathy with science

4 A strong emphasis on evolution towards a higher state of being in keeping with Darwin and current theories of progress.

5 A systematic doctrine of 'laws' said to embrace the whole manifested Universe, but not in conflict with known principles of Science.

Beyond both existing Christianity and science

6 A system of techniques which not only embraced the existing facts of Science but which offered adherents the next stage of evolution in advance, namely *the god-man*.

7 Techniques for exploring consciousness not yet evolved by psychology.

8 A gathering together of esoteric religious teachings which potentially embraced every major pantheon of deities which had ever existed in a far-reaching and systematic scheme of mystical knowledge.

II

These were impressive claims and, as we shall see, they attracted an impressive and diverse membership. However, as with all large institutions, religious or otherwise, we encounter problems of authority and power. The Golden Dawn suffered rather badly in this respect, and it is my intention to show how, despite the fact that the Order was short-lived in its usefulness, certain things may be salvaged. Most importantly of all, we find the first pragmatic system in the West for exploring inner space.

Throughout history there have been a number of mystical *systems* which described levels of reality between man and the divine Godhead – Gnosticism, the Neoplatonic 'Chaldean Oracles', medieval alchemical mysticism and so on, all with their 'emanations' and levels of purity – but there is no indication that these frameworks were applied as pragmatic maps of consciousness in the way that we have been considering. What does seem more evident is that for the ancient Greeks, Romans and Egyptians, whose thoughts and beliefs came together in a whirling eddy of eclectic ideas at the same time as Christianity was born, *the gods were entities in their own right*. Man respected and feared the gods. They were masters of destiny. On occasions, by the use of ritual, the gods could be made to bend to the will of man. However, there was no concept that the gods were forces and potencies within the mind of man; no notion that man had at the deepest levels of his mind personifications of the great 'archetypal' experiences, to use Jung's term.

It took a single man, Samuel Liddell McGregor Mathers to tie together some of the strands. It was he who borrowed from ancient Hellenistic, Gnostic, Persian and Egyptian sources actually to write, as authentically as possible, the rituals of the Golden Dawn and its higher grades. His aim was to draw upon the great pantheons, which embody the figureheads of man's aspirations and awe, and structure them into a workable meditative system. This system, which became the first 'modern' map of inner space was a means of exploring, as shamans do, the deities of the Western cultural heritage which lie as sacred images deep in our Collective Unconscious.

The system used in the Golden Dawn was a venture into the mind, a type of early psychoanalytic exploration whereby specific areas of consciousness were progressively revealed. By means of ritual and the activation of the imagination new inroads into the actual source areas of inspiration could be made. To penetrate into these realms was literally to bring consciousness into an area where it had not been before. Using the terminology and metaphors of medieval expression, Mathers re-shaped the body of ritual magic beliefs according to which the magus gradually 'conquers' the spirits (and demons) of his mind. They stand outside his circle; they obey his commands. They offer privileged information about their domain, when questioned. They may illuminate or possess man, according to his degree of control.

It would be a mistake to dismiss these concepts on their face value, as superstition, because they, like so many other profound images, are powerful through the use of metaphor. The spirits and angels, demons and elementals of fairy tales are all ways of expressing a structure of being. The structure is the mystic's ladder. It becomes easier for him to scale the heights of heaven when he can proceed a step at a time. Mathers wisely took the Tree of Life – 'levels of consciousness' – idea, and applying it as a basis, developed a body of rituals designed to re-activate the awareness of those parts of the mind symbolized by deities and spirits.

Man is imperfect, unintegrated. His animal nature is often evident. He is at the lowest rung of the ladder. His path upwards will consist of conquering his animal instincts, or at least, integrating them in their proper perspective, and then gradually shifting the balance in favour of a more spiritual emphasis. Thus he aspires to be like the gods; to see things from their viewpoint; to enlarge his consciousness to the point where it acquires a more universal understanding, and the narrow terrestrial limitations fall away. Eventually, as in the various forms of yoga and trans-cendental Buddhist mysticism, the ego is totally negated. Union with the formless, Absolute Energy, the sublime Godhead of Totality, occurs.

In actual historical fact this aim was not realized to the extent it might have been, by members of the Golden Dawn. As it turned out, losing one's ego was not the simple task it appeared, and some magicians, including Mathers, found themselves behaving like 'gods' without having first gained the complete spiritual awakening. Such a person finds his ego expanding rather than contracting. He imagines he has access to divine authority. His word is law. It is to these developments that we must first turn, before considering the Qabalistic framework for inner space which evolved.

CHAPTER 7
The Hermetic Order of the Golden Dawn
Ceremonial for the God-man

In 1887 Dr Wynn Westcott, a London coroner and Freemason, acquired a manuscript in cipher from a Dr Woodford. He in turn had discovered it among the papers of a deceased friend, formerly a member of an English Rosicrucian Society.

By means of an alchemical code, Westcott was able to transcribe the manuscript which yielded five Masonic rituals. Westcott then invited a friend, Samuel Mathers, to expand the material so that it could perhaps form the basis of a new Masonic Society. Westcott also claimed to have found among the leaves of the cipher manuscript the name and address of a certain Fraulein Anna Sprengel, said to be an eminent Rosicrucian adept. On her authority, and following a lengthy correspondence, Westcott announced in Masonic and Theosophical circles that he had been instructed to found an English branch of her German occult Order, calling it the Golden Dawn.

The most recent research into the history of the Society suggests that both the correspondence and the personage of Fraulein Sprengel were fictitious. Westcott concocted them in competition with Madame Blavatsky's esoteric school in the Theosophical Society. Blavatsky claimed to be inspired by Mahatmas, or Masters, living in Tibet, with whom she had psychic rapport.

The grades of the Hermetic Order of the Golden Dawn, for Masonry loved grades, were designed by Westcott to correlate with the Sephiroth or stages of mystical consciousness upon the Qabalistic Tree of Life. The five rituals contained in the cipher manuscript correlated with the Societas Rosicruciana in Anglia grades, and these were called by the imposing Latin names of Zelator, Theoricus, Practicus and Philosophus. There was also the so-called 'Neophyte grade', which properly speaking existed 'below' the actual positions on the Tree of Life.

Westcott, however, expanded the grade system so that it covered all of the stages of consciousness attainable upon the Tree of Life. Having called the first series of grades from Neophyte to

Philosophus, the *First Order* he compounded the *Second Order* of grades. These were called Adeptus Minor, Adeptus Major, Adeptus Exemptus, and included the sixth, fifth and fourth levels upon the Tree respectively.

Beyond this he conceived of a mystical Third Order which corresponded to the Sephiroth which lay above the Abyss in the esoteric, Jewish conception: those principles of the universe in fact which had been unaffected by the Fall of Man. This was the domain of special 'Secret Chiefs' and contact with their Divine Power was said to be only possible in a state of astral consciousness, which could be brought about mystically by 'rising on the planes' or by specific rituals designed to inflame the imagination.

Westcott established the Isis-Urania Temple of the Hermetic Order of the Golden Dawn in London in 1888, inviting Mathers and a masonic friend Dr Woodman to join with him as Chiefs of the new Temple. All too the grades of $7° = 4°$ which corresponded with the Sephiroth Chesed, the fourth emanation on the Tree of Life, equating mythologically with Jupiter. In this capacity they functioned by using secret mottoes, for on principle Golden Dawn members could only be allowed to know the mottoes of their peers and those with lower grades.

On the Tree of Life, there is said to be a 'Veil', Paroketh, between the sixth and seventh emanations. It is the bridge between old and new being. The sixth emanation, Tiphareth, represents the visionary state of consciousness where spiritual transformation or 'rebirth' occurs. Westcott, Mathers and Woodman therefore used different mottoes relevant to this grade, as visible signs that they were leaders of those who had not yet been fully initiated, that is, those with grades below the Veil of Paroketh. They were the leaders toward the Light.

The top three grades on the Tree of Life, were those of the 'Third Order', $8° = 3°$ (Magister Templi), $9° = 2°$ (Magus) and $10° = 1°$ (Ipsissimus) which were allegedly, or at least in Westcott's mind, the level of the 'Secret Chiefs' approximating to Madame Blavatsky's inspirational Mahatmas.

Westcott's system, like Masonry, was hierarchical and he was able to appeal to Fraulein Sprengel's illuminating and guiding authority in addition to that of the Secret Chiefs. Shortly after Sprengel's 'death' Westcott claimed that 'all the knowledge was safe with him', but his own dominance failed to endure. Following

Woodman's death in 1891, and Mathers's increasing importance as author of the elaborated rituals of the Golden Dawn, Westcott was forced into an administrative role of secondary importance. In 1892 Mathers claimed to have established a spiritual link with the Secret Chiefs enabling him to write rituals for the grades of the so-called Second Order from Sephirah six to four; Tiphareth/Adeptus Minor ($5° = 6°$); Geburah/Adeptus Major ($6° = 5°$) and Chesed/Adeptus Exemptus ($7° = 4°$) which he and Westcott already held in an honorary capacity. This situation however gave Mathers the spiritual edge, as 'communicant' of the higher grades, which he named the Rosae Rubae et Aurea Crucis (RR et AC): the Red Rose and the Cross of Gold. Meanwhile the Golden Dawn Temples continued to grow in number. In 1896 beside the Temple of Isis-Urania in London, there were Temples of Osiris in Weston-Super-Mare, Horus in Bradford, Amen-Ra in Edinburgh and Ahathoor in Paris. It was while Mathers was in absentia in Paris that the first power struggle occurred.

While translating a lengthy and important occult manuscript entitled 'The Sacred Magic of Abremelin the Mage', Mathers presided over the Ahathoor Temple and attempted to maintain dominance over the English temples simultaneously. A letter to Annie Horniman, a key member of the Isis-Urania Temple, who had queried the funding of Mathers's stay in Paris, reveals several aspects of Mathers's 'magical' personality and his appeal to 'occult authority'.

Prior to the establishment of the Vaults of the Adepts in Britannia (the First of the Golden Dawn in the Outer being therein actively working [wrote Mathers] it was found absolutely and imperatively necessary that there should be some eminent Member especially chosen to act as the link between the Secret Chiefs and the more external forms of the Order. It was requisite that such Member should be me, who, while having the necessary and peculiar educational basis of critical and profound occult archaeological knowledge should at the same time not only be ready and willing to devote himself in every sense to a blind and unreasoning obedience to those Secret Chiefs — to pledge himself for the fidelity of those to whom this Wisdom was to be communicated: to be one who would shrink neither from danger physical, astral or spiritual, from privation or hardship, nor from terrible personal and psychic responsibility . . . he must further pledge himself to obey in everything the commands of the aforesaid Secret Chiefs 'perinde ac cadaver' body and soul, without question and without argument whether their commands related to: Magical Action in the External World; or to Psychic Action in Other Worlds, or Planes, whether Angelic, Spiritual or Demonic, or to the Inner Administration of the Order to which so tremendous a knowledge was to be communicated.[1]

It is clear that belief in the 'Secret Chiefs' was a central doctrine maintaining Mathers's position as head of the hierarchy of graded G∴ D∴ members.

Mathers was unable to supply his followers with many details of the attributes of these spiritual entities:[2]

I do not even know their earthly names. I know them only by certain secret mottoes. I have *but very rarely* seen them in the physical body; and on such rare occasions *the rendez-vous was made astrally by them* at the time and place which had been astrally appointed beforehand.

For my part I believe them to be human and living upon this earth but possessing terrible superhuman powers.

The concept of physical personages whose inspirational levels lay above the Abyss was an impressive one, for it suggested that there were 'living gods' that could be contacted once one had reached the highest Sephirothic grades.

Florence Farr who conducted the splinter 'Sphere Group' within the G∴ D∴ itself believed her coterie to be controlled by a 'certain Egyptian astral form', and Dr R.W. Felkin, who founded the Order of the Stella Matutina after the London Temple deserted Mathers in 1900, continued to strive for contact with the Secret Chiefs. In 1902 he wrote to his colleagues: 'We beg to assure you that we are in entire sympathy with the view that if in fact the Order is without the guidance and inspiration of higher intelligences its rationale is gone.' It occurred, however, to certain members that it might be possible, by reverting to the original constitution, to re-establish a link with the Third Order.[3] Felkin plumped, in turn, for certain 'Sun Masters' and then for Ara Ben Shemesh whom he described as a 'discarnate Arab (with a) Temple in the Desert where the Sons of Fire live (who) are in personal communication with the Divine and are no longer bound in the flesh so that their material life is a matter of will'.

Aleister Crowley, whose magical philosophy I should like to discuss presently, broke from Mathers on communication with his own 'Secret Chief', Aiwaz. There is also evidence that Yeats believed in the existence of these transcendental entities, for, true to his Theosophical orientation, he referred in a pamphlet dated 1900, to 'the stream of lightning awakened in the Order, and the *Adepts of the Third Order* and of the Higher Degrees of the Second Order summoned to our help. . .'.

Such questions were predominantly of interest for those who had entered the Second and Inner Order of the Rose of Ruby and the Cross of Gold and who had taken the following pledge:

> I will from this day forward apply myself to the Great Work which is to purify and exalt my Spiritual nature, that within the Divine aid, I may at length attain to be more then human, and thus gradually raise and unite myself to my Higher and Divine Genius and that in this event I will not abuse the Great Power entrusted to me.

The early stages, however, were the lesser grades of the so-called 'Golden Dawn in the Outer', which are described in sequence.

The Neophyte grade was signified $0° = 0°$ and was, according to Francis King 'unquestionably the most important since it gave him not only a glimpse of the Light to be experienced in the future but a key, (albeit in an embryonic and undeveloped form) to the inner and hidden significance of the entire Order.'[4]

Dr Israel Regardie who first compiled the G∴ D∴ rituals for publication affirms this view in writing of their central theme:[5]

> If one idea more than any other is persistently stressed from the beginning that idea is the word *Light*. From the candidate's first reception in the Hall of the Neophytes when the Hierophant adjures him with these words, 'Child of Earth, long hast thou dwelt in darkness. Quit the night and seek the day', to the transfiguration in the (Second Order) Vault Ceremony, the whole system has as its objective the bringing down of the Light.

The aspirant was instructed in the 'First Knowledge Lecture' which gave details of the four elements of the Ancients (fire, earth, air and water) and the twelve signs of the Zodiac. It also correlated these signs with the elements so that Aries, Leo and Sagittarius were said to be fire signs; Taurus, Virgo and Capricorn, earth signs and so on. Some elementary Hebrew was also included in a table which provided the letter of the alphabet, its English equivalent, its name, and its meaning. Finally the elementary symbolism of the Sephiroth was included:

1   KETHER – The Crown
2   CHOKMAH – Wisdom
3   BINAH – Understanding
4   CHESED – Mercy
5   GEBURAH – Severity
6   TIPHARETH – Beauty
7   NETZACH – Victory
8   HOD – Glory
9   YESOD – The Foundation
10   MALKUTH – The Kingdom

On the practical side, the Neophyte was expected to know the Lesser Ritual of the Pentagram, an occult exercise designed to 'clear the air' of minor malevolent forces surrounding the magician during his ritual invocations.

Knowledge lectures provided as components of the Zelator (1° = 10°) grade included details of alchemical symbolism, the Order of Elemental Spirits (gnomes: earth; sylphs: air; undines: water; and salamanders: fire), and the link between the Sephiroth and the planets. In the latter case, each Sephirah had gods associated with it, which could be drawn from any of the great pantheons and charted as 'Correspondences'. The definitive work on this subject was made by Aleister Crowley in his book '777'.

The Theoricus (2° = 9°) was taught the Qabalistic division of the Soul or mystical consciousness into the three parts: *Neschamah* ('answering to the Three Supernals'); *Ruach* ('answering to the six Sephiroth from Chesed to Yesod, inclusive') and *Nephesch* ('the lowest answering to Malkuth'). It was said that *Neschamah* 'answers to the higher aspirations of the Soul', *Ruach* 'to the mind and reasoning powers' and *Nephesch* 'to the animal instincts'. They thus provided a structure for the spiritual evolution of man from a lowly bestial status, to that of a spiritual god-man.

The Knowledge Lecture for the Practicus Grade (3° = 8°) included details of certain ritual symbols and their meaning, among them 'the Cubical Cross' the Cup of Stolistes, and the Symbol of Mercury, these two being symbols which incorporated into their design certain of the Sephiroth. More important, though, was a table of the 'Attribution of the Tarot Trumps' which correlated the Tarot Trumps of the Major Arcana (that is to say the twenty-two 'court cards') with paths linking the ten Sephiroth. This produced a total meditative construct of the manifested cosmos which constituted a more detailed version of the Tree of Life.

This correlation was not a part of ancient Judaic thought and is believed to owe its origin solely to an idea of Eliphas Levi (Alphonse Louis Constant) who discussed the connection in a book published in 1856.

Mathers, under his ritual initials of SRMD (S Rhioghail Mo Dhream)[6] provided some notes on the elementary symbolism of the major Tarot Trumps from 'The Fool' who ironically through a twist of metaphor[7] equates with the First Sephirah, through to 'The Universe' which equated with the Tenth, Malkuth. Some remarkable statements drawn from the Zohar were also included. These incorporated an explanation of the symbolism of the Garden of Eden before and after the Fall.

Finally, the Knowledge of the Philosophus ($4° = 7°$) grade, which completed that given in the Outer Order of the Golden Dawn, was of an assorted nature, dealing mostly with what were referred to by the magicians themselves as god-names. The significance of these will become apparent later. ABBA was the mystical title of the Supernal Father, AIMA the Supernal Mother. Further details of the symbols linking alchemy and astrology, were also provided, and a list of the Qlippoth on the Tree of Life, that is to say the negative cosmic energies equating with the ten positive Sephiroth mentioned above. An example is Lilith, 'Queen of the Night and of Demons' who was an evil counterpart of Malkuth, the divine Daughter and who in Greek mythology equated with the evil aspect of Persephone, queen of the Underworld and embodiment of the harvest.

The candidate of the Mysteries was now on the 'border' of the Second Order, that of the Rosae Rubae et Aurea Crucis – the Red Rose and the Cross of Gold. A 'waiting period' of nine months was required, in which the magician could apply upon himself a type of psychotherapy, for he was encouraged to be rigidly self-analytical. Francis King has eloquently described this phase of self-development in his book 'Ritual Magic in England' (1971).

Such self-analysis was suitable at this stage because the magician was now mystically stationed in the Veil of Paroketh, an 'Abyss' of consciousness marking off those Sephiroth of the Tree beneath Tiphareth which contained the archetypes of spiritual rebirth. The magician was about to undergo a mystical transformation of personality.[8]

> In the Ceremony of the Grade of Adeptus Minor (Tiphareth) the candidate himself is Hodos Chamelionis, Lord of the Lights upon the Path of the Chameleon. He undergoes a symbolic burial and emergence in the Tomb of the Adepti identifying with Christian Rosenkreutz, the Rose and Cross of the Immortal Christ, and the risen Osiris. The tomb has seven sides representing the seven lower Sephiroth beneath the Supernal triad and the Seven 'Days' of Creation. It is situated symbolically in the centre of the Earth just as Tiphareth resides in the centre of the Tree of Life. The spiritual rebirth occurs after 'one hundred and twenty years' which are the ten Sephiroth multiplied by the twelve signs of the Zodiac, and it follows ritually the form of the myth of Osiris whereby the body of the slain King of Egypt is magically revitalised. The five earlier rites, and death upon the Elemental Cross, have prepared the candidate for his entry into the Tomb of the Sacred Mountain.

> Philosophus lies clothed with the symbols of the embalmed Osiris: the symbol of the Rosy Cross also rests upon his breast:

> Eternal One ... let the influence of thy Divine Ones descend upon his head, and teach him the value of self-sacrifice so that he shrink not in the hour of trial, but that thus his name may be written on high and that his Genius may stand in the presence of the Holy Ones, in that hour when the Son of Man is invoked before the Lord of Spirits and His Name in the presence of the Ancient of Days. It is written: 'If any man will come after Me, let him take up his cross, and deny himself, and follow Me.'

> Philosophus extends his arms so that his body forms a cross, the ritual expression of rebirth:

> Buried with that Light in a mystical death, rising again in a mystical resurrection. ... Quit then this Tomb, O

Aspirant, (whose arms have been earlier) crossed upon thy breast, bearing in thy right hand the Crook of Mercy, and in thy left the Scourge of Severity, the emblems of those Eternal Forces betwixt which the equilibrium of the universe dependeth; those forces whose reconciliation is the Key of Life, whose separation is evil and death....

The Aspirant, filled with light, now comes forth as Christ – Osiris, by day:

> 'I am the First and I am the Last. I am He that liveth and was dead, and behold! I am alive for evermore, and hold the Keys of Death and of Hell.... I am purified. I have passed through the Gates of Darkness into Light....'.
>
> 'I am the Sun in his rising. I have passed through the hour of cloud and of night.'
>
> 'I am Amoun, the Concealed One, the Opener of the Day. I am Osiris Onnophris, the Justified One.'
>
> 'I am the Lord of Life triumphant over Death.'

CHAPTER 8
Aleister Crowley and the Aeon of Horus

Aleister Crowley found himself having differences with McGregor Mathers, and was soon to point to his own source of spiritual authority. Despite his extravagances, however, he remains the most spectacular figure in the history of contemporary Western magic. Evicted from Cefalu in Sicily by Mussolini where he established an Abbey for practising ritual magic, constantly embroiled in legal disputes over the publication of Hermetic secrets, famous for his escapades with women, Crowley was known popularly during his own lifetime as the 'Great Beast'. Primarily this was due to his claim as the incarnate Anti-Christ which followed what he regarded as a spiritual illumination in Cairo in 1904. Throughout his life he involved himself in sexual escapades hoping that his partner would embody the person of the Great Whore of the Book of Revelations, the Beast's opposite number, and it was this which brought him public notoriety.

He was the major magical writer of his period, his work encompassing detailed studies of the Qabalah, Tarot card symbolism, Yogic and Tantric techniques of altering consciousness, and numerous diaries concerning his ritual results.

In his most central book on magical theory, 'Magick in Theory and Practice' (1929), Crowley outlined the basic philosophy underlying the entire venture which was essentially to make man god-like in both his vision and power.

A man who is doing his True Will has the inertia of the Universe to assist him.[1]

Man is ignorant of the nature of his own being and powers. Even his idea of his limitations is based on experience of the past and every step in his progress extends his empire. There is therefore no reason to assign theoretical limits to what he may be or what he may do.[2]

Man is capable of being and using, anything which he

108

perceives for everything that he perceives is in a certain sense a part of his being. He may thus subjugate the whole Universe of which he is conscious to his individual will.[3]

The Microcosm is an exact image of the Macrocosm; the Great Work is the raising of the whole man in perfect balance to the power of Infinity.[4]

There is a single main definition of the object of all magical Ritual. It is the uniting of the Microcosm with the Macrocosm. The Supreme and Complete Ritual is therefore the Invocation of the Holy Guardian Angel, or in the language of Mysticism, Union with God.[5]

In modern ritual magic the actors portray, and attempt to embody, in an act of imagination and will, the forms of deities from the Egyptian, Greek and 'Chaldean' pantheons. This occurs, as previously mentioned within an enclosed area, in the Temple which represents the manifested Universe.

Introduced to the Hermetic order of the Golden Dawn by a friend, Crowley soon grasped that those with the loftiest grades were able to wield profound 'spiritual authority' and claim rapport with Secret Chiefs emanating from higher planes of being. In 'Magick' he wrote: 'Every man is more or less aware that his individuality comprises several orders of existence.'[6] Magic was a means of transforming the consciousness under will, to allow union with these spiritual forces in the Cosmos. Accordingly, Crowley's rise through the preliminary grades of the G∴ D∴ was rapid.

He was initiated as a Neophyte on 18 December 1898. In December he took the grade of Zelator, and those of Theoricus and Practicus in the following two months, for he was keen to ascend through the Sephirothic grades as rapidly as possible.

He seems to have been keen also to emulate McGregor Mathers's attainment as a $7° = 4°$ for he was the first magician to attempt the lengthy six month Abremelin ritual which Mathers had translated from the French. Apart from allowing the magus the services of 316 spirit advisers it was also said to grant one communion with the Holy Guardian Angel, an embodiment in visionary form of one's higher spiritual self. Successful performance of this ritual would also allow Crowley to claim spiritual parity with Mathers. One of its immediate attractions for

Crowley was that it lay outside the strictly Christian tradition: Mathers wrote in his introduction to the work:[7]

> Considering the era in which our Author lived (the book was allegedly written in 1458), and the nation to which he belonged he appears to have been somewhat broad in his religious views; for not only does he insist that this Sacred system of Magic may be attained by anyone, whether Jew, Christian, Mohometan (sic) or Pagan.

According to Mathers, The Sacred Magic of Abremelin the Mage was based on the following conceptions:[8]

> a)   That the Good Spirits and Angelic Powers of Light are superior in power to the Fallen Spirits of Darkness.
> b)   That these latter as a punishment have been condemned to the service of the Initiates of the Magic of Light.
> c)   As a consequence of this doctrine, all ordinary material effects and phenomena are produced by the labour of the Evil Spirits under the command usually of the Good.
> d)   That consequently whenever the Evil Demons can escape from the control of the Good, there is no evil that they will not work by way of vengeance.
> e)   That therefore sooner than obey man, they will try to make him their servant, by inducing him to conclude Pacts and Agreements with them.
> f)   That to further this project, they will use every means that offers to obsess him.
> g)   That in order to become an Adept, therefore, and dominate them; the greatest possible firmness of will, purity of soul and intent, and power of self-control is necessary.
> h)   That this is only to be attained by self-abnegation on every plane.
> i)   That man, therefore, is the middle nature, and natural controller of the middle nature between the Angels and the Demons, and that therefore to each man is attached naturally both a Guardian Angel and a Malevolent Demon, and also certain Spirits that may become Familiars, so that with him it rests to give the victory unto the which he will.
> k)   That, therefore, in order to control and make service of the Lower and Evil, the knowledge of the Higher and Good is requisite (i.e. in the language of the Theosophy of the

present day, the knowledge of the Higher Self).

From this it results that the magnum opus propounded in this work is: by purity and self-denial to obtain the knowledge of and a conversation with one's Guardian Angel, so that thereby and thereafter we may obtain the right of using the Evil Spirits for our servants in all material matters.

This, then, is the system of the Secret Magic of Abramelin, the Mage, as taught by his disciple Abraham the Jew; and elaborated down to the smallest points.

During the Abremelin rituals, according to John Symonds, Crowley was seized with some spectacular visions:[9]

He saw Christ with the woman of Samaria, then himself crucified; he stood within the Divine Light with a crown of twelve stars upon his head; the earth opened for him to enter into its very centre, where he climbed the peak of a high mountain. Many dragons sprang upon him as he approached the Secret Sanctuary, but he overcame them all with a word.

This was an alchemical vision of his success in the Great Work. Crowley realised that he was born with all the talents required for a great magician.

Having attained the grade of Philosophus, Crowley approached Mathers, who was then living in Paris, for ritual entry into the Second Order, the Red Rose and the Cross of Gold. Under Mathers's supervision, Crowley was 'admitted to the Glory of Tiphareth', the Jungian archetype of rebirth. He was now an Adeptus Minor, $5° = 6°$. Having returned to England, Crowley challenged W.B. Yeats for leadership of the Golden Dawn. Yeats was unimpressed, regarding Crowley as an 'unspeakable mad person', and Crowley was in the short term, unsuccessful in his bid for supremacy. The dispute, however, caused a rift in the loyalties of the Golden Dawn membership since Crowley had been sent by Mathers, who, in turn, in a letter to Annie Horniman, had claimed a spiritual autocracy and infallibility over the Order as his right.

Unpredictably and apparently on pure impulse, Crowley suddenly withdrew from the dispute and embarked upon a series of travels through Mexico, the United States, Ceylon, and India, arriving finally at Cairo, which was to be a major milestone in the building of his new magical Universe.

On the 14 March 1904, in his room near the Boulak Museum in Cairo, Crowley performed a magical ceremony invoking the Egyptian deity Thoth, god of Wisdom. His wife appeared to him to be in a dazed, mediumistic state of mind, and four days later, when in a similar state of drowsiness announced that Horus was waiting for her husband. Crowley was not expecting such a statement from his wife, who according to his Diary, then led him to a near-by Museum which he had not previously visited. She pointed to a statue of Horus in the form of Ra-Hoor-Khuit and Crowley was amazed to find that the exhibit was number 666, the number of the Great Beast of the Book of Revelations. Crowley regarded this as a portent, and returned to his hotel where he invoked Horus:

> Strike, strike the master chord!
> Draw, draw the Flaming Sword!
> Crowning Child and Conquering Lord,
> Horus, avenger!

His wife continued to fall into a passive introspective state of mind and began to recite mediumistically. The resulting statements which were allegedly dictated by a semi-invisible Egyptian entity named Aiwass (or Aiwaz) were later called by Crowley the 'Book of the Law',[10] and became a turning point in his magical career. In the communication Crowley was instructed to drop the ceremonial magic as taught in the Golden Dawn and pursue the magic of sexual polarities instead.

'Now ye shall know that the chosen priest and apostle of infinite space is the prince-priest the Beast, and in his woman called the Scarlet Woman is all power given. They shall gather my children into their fold: they shall bring the Glory of the stars into the hearts of men.' Crowley identified with the Horus figure Ra-Hoor-Khuit whose statue he had seen in the Museum. He came to realize that Aiwaz equated with Hoor-paar-Kraat (or Harpocrates, the God of Silence) who was an entity whose origin lay above the Abyss. He had thus contacted a Secret Chief without the aid of Mathers.

In Egyptian mythology, the deities Nuit (Female – the Circle – passive) and Hadit (Male – the Point – active) were said to formulate by their union a divine child, Ra-Hoor-Khuit. This combination of the principles of Love and Will incarnated the 'magical equation known as the Law of Thelema'.[11] Thelema is the Greek word for Will (Crowley was an eclectic in his term-usage) and the main dictum of the 'Book of Law' is 'Do what thou Wilt, Love is the Law, Love under Will.' By this he meant that one should live according to the dictates of one's true Will, or Spiritual direction. His own destiny had been indicated clearly by the communication from Aiwaz. Kenneth Grant writes:[12]

> According to Crowley the true magical revival occurred in 1904, when an occult current of cosmic magnitude was initiated on the inner planes. Its focus was Aiwaz and it was transmitted through Crowley to the human plane. . . . The initiation of this occult current created a vortex, the birth pangs of a new Aeon, technically called an Equinox of the Gods. Such an event recurs at intervals of approximately 2000 years. Each such revival of magical power establishes a further link in the chain of humanity's evolution, which is but one phase only of the evolution of consciousness.

Crowley was the divine Child who was able to establish in mankind a consciousness of the union of Nuit and Hadit. Previously, according to Crowley there had been two Aeons, that of the Moon and that of the Sun. The first of these, the Aeon of Isis was the Matriarchal Age, characterized by the worship of lunar deities: 'the Virgin contains in herself the Principle of Growth. . . .' The second Aeon was that of Osiris, the Patriarchal Age, 'the formula of incarnating demi-gods or divine Kings, these must be slain and raised from the dead in one way or another.' Osiris and the resurrected Christ both belonged to this Aeon, and had now been superseded by the Aeon of Horus.

'With my Hawk's head (i.e. Horus) I peck at the eyes of Jesus as he hangs upon the Cross. I flap my wings in the face of Mohammed.' Other religions would fall too: 'With my claws I tear out the flesh of the Indian and the Buddhist, Mongol and Din. Bachlasti! Ompedha! I spit on your crapulous creeds.'

The Age of Horus was based upon the union of male and female polarities. In one sense this meant that the legendary symbol of the androgyne assumed special importance. A man had to cultivate his female polarity. In 'Magick in Theory and Practice', Crowley writes:[13]

> God is above sex, and to therefore neither man nor woman as such can be said fully to understand, much less to represent, God.

It is therefore incumbent on the male magician to cultivate those female virtues in which he is deficient, and this task he must of course accomplish without in any way impairing his virility.

However Crowley was also the Beast which the Book of Revelations had prophesied would be the hallmark of the new Age – in the 'Book of the Law', the Moon principle is rendered as Babalon, the Scarlet Woman. The Great Work or sacred Union, which would result in identification with Absolute Consciousness constituted the sexual union of the Great Beast with the Whore of Babalon: 'The Beast, as the embodiment of the Logos (which is Thelema, Will) symbolically and actually incarnates his Word each time a sacramental act of sexual congress occurs, i.e. each time love is made under Will.'[14]

Grant writes: 'In the Aeon of Horus, physical life is recognised as a sacrament. The sexual act of union for Crowley involved possession by the Highest Consciousness (namely, Aiwaz).'[15]

Crowley spent a large part of his life seeking out lovers and concubines who could act as his Divine Whore, but was frustrated in his attempts to find a suitable partner, although there were many who filled the role temporarily.

Crowley thus proposed a different form of magic to that offered in the Golden Dawn. Mathers had considered Osiris as a symbol of rebirth and had included references to that god in the Tiphareth ritual of the Second Order. Crowley claimed to go beyond this teaching, and as the new avatar, could offer to his followers a means of producing trancendent consciousness in them, by a sacrament of sex:[16]

In sexual congress each coition is a sacrament of peculiar virtue since it effects a transformation of consciousness through annihilation of apparent duality. To be radically effective the transformation must be also an initiation. Because of the sacramental nature of the act, each union must be magically directed . . . the ritual must be directed to the transfinite and non-individualised consciousness represented by Egyptian Nuit. . . . The earthly Nuit is Isis, the Scarlet Woman.

Crowley was able to supersede Mathers, however, not merely in terms of technique, but by virtue of his own magical significance as Lord of the new Aeon. Long reference is made by Crowley in his 'Confessions', to this.[17]

> I was told that 'The Equinox of the Gods had come', that is, a new epoch had begun. I was to formulate a link between the solar-spiritual force and mankind.
>
> Various considerations showed me that the Secret Chiefs of the Third Order (that is of the A∴ A∴ whose First and Second Orders were known as the G∴ D∴ and R.R. et A.C. respectively) had sent a messenger to confer upon me the position which Mathers had forfeited.

Crowley claimed that his teaching was at least equal to that of Moses or Buddha: Such men indeed formulate their transcendental conception of the Cosmos more or less clearly – the heart of their theory is that the problem of sorrow has been wrongly stated, owing to the superficial or incomplete data presented by normal human experience through the senses, and that it is possible for men, by virtue of some special training (from Asana to Ceremonial Magick) to develop in themselves a faculty superior to reason and immune from intellectual criticism, by the exercise of which the original problem of suffering is satisfactorily solved (in Buddhism, suffering and ignorance are synonymous).

Having had the communication from Aiwaz, Crowley was now 'messenger of the Lord of the Universe', and could 'speak with absolute authority'.[18] Thelema, he added

> implies not merely a new religion, but a new cosmology, a new philosophy, a new ethics. It co-ordinates the disconnected discoveries of science. Its scope is so vast that it is impossible even to hint at the universality of its application. . . . The Aeon of Horus, that of the Child is not merely a symbol of growth, but of complete moral independence and innocence. We may then expect the New Aeon to release mankind from its pretence of altruism, its obsession of fear and its consciousness of sin.

In a sense, Crowley was echoing the words of Freud, whom he admired. Freud held that there were three essential stages of growth in an individual: narcissism (self-centredness), dependence on the parents and maturity. Freud correlated these psychological stages with magical, religious and scientific belief. But Crowley's magic was no mere magic, it was an application of solar energy which embraced science, a 'means of communication based on the "highest mathematics" '.[19] As such it was a true liberation from the earlier maternal and paternal forms of magic and religion.

Crowley has the following note in his 'Confessions':[20]

> I wrote a formal letter to Mathers informing him that the Secret Chiefs had appointed me visible head of the Order, and declared a new Magical Formula. I did not expect or receive an answer. I declared war on Mathers accordingly.

When he founded his own Magical Order, the A∴ A∴ or Argentinum Astrum, Crowley used an amended form of the Golden Dawn grades and re-wrote Mathers's rituals, including some yogic and oriental material. He also published Mathers's secrets of the Second Order, the R.R. et A.C. in his magazine 'The Equinox' (1909). However, he did not include sexual magic in his Order until after his contact with a society practising it in Germany. This was Dr Karl Kellner's Brotherhood of Light which was known esoterically as the Order of the Temple of the East (Ordo Templi Orientis) a reference to 'the place of sunrise, the source of illumination'.[21]

This society claimed, in a 1912 edition of its journal 'Oriflamme' to possess 'the KEY which opens up all Masonic and Hermetic secrets, namely, the teaching of sexual magic, and this teaching explains, without exception, all the secrets of Nature, all the symbolism of Freemasonry and all systems of religion'.

The Ordo Templi Orientis had ten grades: the first six being ritually conferred and the seventh, eighth and ninth being concerned with sexual magic including masturbatory and hetero-sexual practices. The tenth grade, according to King, was 'administrative'. Later Crowley added an eleventh grade, which was concerned with homosexual magic in which one member played a female role according to his notion of polarities, and the development of female latencies. He used this rite with the English poet Victor Neuberg in the so called 'Paris Working', a lengthy shamanistic ritual invoking Hermes and Jupiter.

Crowley was invited to join the OTO in 1912 by Kellner's successor Theodor Reuss, entering at the ninth degree. He had unwittingly published their main secret in his 'Book of Lies', where in a chapter headed 'The Star Sapphire' he refers to the magic of sexual polarities disguised beneath the symbols of the rood (phallus) and the mystic rose (vagina). To draw Crowley within the net of Oriental Templars as they were also known, he was initiated in Berlin and installed as 'Supreme and Holy King of Ireland, Iona and all the Britains within the Sanctuary of the Gnosis', that is to say, Chief of the British subsidiary of the OTO, the Mysteria Mystica Maxima.

In England Crowley merged the MMM with his own A∴ A∴ as a preliminary to membership of the latter. The Ordo Templi Orientis still exists and is headed by Kenneth Grant who succeeded Crowley in 1946, a year before his death:[22]

> I received an initiated interpretation [writes Grant] of tantric methods relating to the Vama Marg, or Left Hand Path, which deals with the highly secret worship of the Primal Goddess or Devi – It is an Eastern version of rites involving a 'Scarlet Woman' or consecrated priestess, and its chief value ... lies in corroboration via ancient sources of the sexual magical techniques that Crowley habitually employed.

The A∴ A∴ initiated close to a hundred obscure followers of Crowley. Among the more impressive were Norman Mudd, Professor of Applied Mathematics at Bloemfontein, Victor Neuburg, who was a 'father poet' to British writers Dylan Thomas and Pamela Hansford Johnson, and Austin Spare, a visionary artist whose talents were so remarkable that he had won a scholarship to the Royal College of Art when he was only sixteen. Crowley also inspired a series of sexual magic societies in the United States.

The voluminous writings of the 'Great Beast' are currently being reissued at a considerable rate under the auspices of Dr Israel Regardie, his former secretary and editor of a four-volume edition of the rites of the Golden Dawn (published 1937-40). However, in his own lifetime his leading disciple and spiritual son was one Frater Achad, otherwise known as Charles Stansfeld Jones whose stated attitudes reveal the particular impression which Crowley made upon his followers. Achad was the author of three books dealing with a modern reinterpretation of the symbolism of the magical paths upon the Tree of Life.

In the introductory pages to his 'Anatomy of the Body of God' Achad notes that Jews have both the wealth of the world, and are also the 'chosen people'. He claims a derivation of Jew from 'Iu, the Ever-Coming Son' and goes on to relate him to 'the Horus of the earliest Egyptian Era'. Beyond this Iu 'extends to all Ages, and of whom are truly typical, God-Men, such as Jesus, have been and are representatives upon earth'.[23]

The Jews, according to Achad, had 'lost sight of their True Will in neglecting the Qabalah ... there has always been a Universal Tradition which when known has led the Nations to the height of civilisation. ...'[24] He then refers to the structure of the Qabalah as an eclectic basis for varied pantheons.[25]

> The Universe is composed of Malkuth and Kether with Tiphareth as the Mediator between them, while in a still greater sense we may consider Nuit and Hadit, the Two Infinites, with the Whole Living manifested Universe of Ra-Hoor-Khuit as their Ever-Coming Son, the Crowned Child and Lord of the Aeon.

Achad's final acknowledgment of Crowley as the Lord of the Aeon occurs on the last page of the book which closes with the central dictum of the 'Book of the Law':[26]

> Take up your places in the Kingdom of the Ever-Coming Son, fulfil yourselves in the fulfilment of the Will of God within you, and show those who are still in darkness without, that there is room for all who are prepared to keep their place, and cease from trying to usurp that of others, for:
> Love is the Law, Love under Will.

It was by such mystico-historical appeal to spiritual authority that Crowley was able to dominate his followers. Jean Overton Fuller, who knew Victor Neuburg personally recalls that 'he really believed Crowley to be the Messiah of the new Age.'[27]

In Crowley's own 'Book of the Law' were the germs of mystical fascism:

> Therefore the Kings of the earth shall be Kings for ever: the slaves shall serve. There is none that shall be cast down or lifted up: all is ever as it was: Yet there are masked ones my servants – it may be that yonder beggar is a King. A King may choose his garment as he will ... but a beggar cannot hide his poverty.

Crowley's 'Comment', appended to the 'Book of the Law' concludes with a statement as autocratic as Mathers's letter to rebellious Annie Horniman: 'All questions of the Law are to be decided, only by appeal to my writings. . . . There is no law beyond Do What thou Wilt. . . .'

Crowley was the Law incarnate. As Gerald Yorke has written, 'The Golden Dawn had given birth to its first pseudo-Messiah.'[28]

CHAPTER 9
Whence the Magician?

The various members of the Golden Dawn and the Argentinum Astrum seem to have joined for quite different reasons. While it is true, as Ellic Howe observes, that few members left any public record of their experiences in the Order, they appeared to have found in the Golden Dawn the following inducements.

The Golden Dawn offered:

1 a substitute religion, notably in opposition to Christianity;
2 a more profound, esoteric explanation of Christianity while challenging its outward form in the Church;
3 a means for charting levels of consciousness and inspiration;
4 a rationale for unusual sexual behaviour;
5 a systematic scientific and psychological model of the mind.

Aleister Crowley, the proclaimed Anti-Christ and Lord of the New Aeon, and his gullible follower Frater Achad have already been cited as belonging to the 'substitute religion' category. The latter appears to have had a messianic outlook, fearing that the Great War spelled the dissolution of earlier civilization, heralding at the same time 'the New Age'.[1]

> We are living in strange times [he wrote]. Civilisation seems rapidly to be breaking up, while yet some inner urge is at work towards a better and more balanced construction in many departments of life.
>
> One of the results of the Great War has been to turn the minds of many people from some of the narrower conceptions of life into wider channels. A Spirit of enquiry has become apparent on the part of those who had previously been content to accept statements in regard to life's deeper issues on mere belief or hearsay. Many new movements have arisen under the guidance of people who have obtained at least a partial glimpse of man's wide heritage, and there has been a corresponding falling away from what may be termed the orthodox or established order of things in the Churches and elsewhere.

For Achad the Great War was proof that man's orthodox forms – his culture and civilization – had failed. The Qabalistic Tree of Life, the symbolism for which Achad had also offered a 'revised' explanation, was primarily a symbol of balance and harmony. Its outer pillars were balanced in polarity, its central column being an equilibrator of extremes. Even the colours of the visions ascribed to each of the stages of consciousness upon the Tree, were balanced diametrically into 'complementary colours'. Hope, for man, lay in raising himself mystically from his abode at the bottom of the Tree to the level of spiritual purity beyond the Abyss. The Jews had 'lost sight of their True Will in neglecting the Qabalah', traditionally their most secret and highly prized mystery teaching.

Men like Crowley (and for *his* followers, Mathers), had attained a rapport with the 'Secret Chiefs' above the Abyss. On such a basis they claimed illumination and authority. Eventually Achad, too, claimed the Ipsissimus grade of the pinnacle of the Tree, implying that his every action had significance for the entire Cosmos. His magical career ended in severe mental confusion.

In the same way that Crowley had arranged a vast system of comparing deities from different pantheons, by allocating them to 'slots' in the Tree of Life categories, so too was Mathers an eclectic. He loved ritual for its theatric qualities and wrote all of the major rituals of the Golden Dawn and R.R. et A.C. using a variety of sources. He turned naturally to Egypt because of the parallel in mystical thinking between the experience of higher states of consciousness and the after-death state. It may well be that Mathers was not only inclined towards ancient Egypt and wrote all of the major rituals of the Golden Dawn because of his 'temperament' and tendency towards a 'pagan Egyptian twist' of thought, as Yorke suggests, but because, as Brandon points out, the Egyptians had a most elaborate eschatology: 'The Egyptians, however, were not only unique in being the first to conceive the idea, but with them it also attained a far greater degree of elaboration than with any other people of the Ancient World.'[2] After-death beliefs, as we have seen, parallel levels of the mind.

One of Mathers's central invocations is taken from Papyrus XLVI in the British Museum:

Thee I invoke, the Headless One. Thee that didst create the Earth and the Heavens. . . . I am he, the Bornless Spirit. . . . I am the Grace of the World. The Heart girt with the Serpent is my name. . . . All Spirits of heaven, earth, air and water and every spell and scourge of God are obedient unto me. . . .

A magician possessed of such a spiritual force could clearly apply his authority to his subservient followers. Mathers clearly believed that in such an initiatory function he was continuing the tradition of the Mystery Schools of antiquity. In the introduction by Mathers's wife to the 1926 edition of 'The Kabbalah Unveiled', published after his death, she wrote:

The general constitution of the teaching, the skeleton of the work, was handed to him by his occult teachers together with a vast amount of oral instruction. The object of the establishment of this school was similar to that of the foundation in ancient times of centres for the celebration of the Mysteries. The literature of this school (i.e. the G∴ D∴), with few exceptions, was written by my husband under the direction of these teachers, based upon the ancient mysteries, chiefly those of Egypt, Caldea [sic] and Greece, and brought up to date to suit the needs of our modern mentalities.

Westcott, Mathers's peer as an original Chief of the Second Order presiding over the Golden Dawn, 'aided in the administrative side of this School' according to Mathers's wife. He was the editor of a series of Hermetic translations published in the 1890s and wrote short, explanatory works on the Qabalah and the Chaldean Oracles. He was not however as creative as Mathers, and was drawn to the newly formed ritual practices of the G∴ D∴ largely because of their resemblance to the earlier, Masonic, Societas Rosicrucianis in Anglia on which they were based. As mentioned earlier, he was in direct rivalry with the esoteric section of the Theosophical Society and had been invited by one of its leaders, G.R.S. Mead, to join. Theosophy was more Eastern than Westcott's horizon allowed, and since he was obliged under the rules to choose one Society or the other, he stayed with the one he had helped create. He did claim for it, an ancient spiritual heritage, if not an historical connection. In a justificatory preamble, Westcott wrote:[3]

The Order of the G∴ D∴ in the Outer is an Hermetic

Society whose members are taught the principles of Occult Science and the Magic of Hermes. . . . Several eminent Adepts in England and France, among them Eliphas Levi and Kenneth Mackenzie, who 'received their knowledge and power from predecessors of equal and even greater eminence'. They received, indeed, and have handed down to us this Doctrine and System of Theosophy and Hermetic Science, and the Highest Alchemy from a long series of practical investigators, whose origin is traced to the Fratres Rosae Crucis of Germany, which association was founded by one Christian Rosenkreuz about the year 1398.

Arthur Edward Waite, the noted occult scholar of the period, recalls in his autobiographical 'Shadows of Life and Thought' that the Golden Dawn first began to acquire a reputation in 'Theosophical and Kindred Circles'. As a learned commentator on Rosicrucian, Judaic and Egyptian thought he was suspicious of all claims to antiquity in the lineal or 'apostolic' sense although he conceded of course that ancient sources were being referred to and included in the rituals. Egyptian hieroglyphics had only been accessible in translation since 1822, and the link between the ten Qabalistic Sephiroth and the twenty-two Major Tarot card trumps whose symbolism was ascribed to the linking 'paths' was an innovation of Eliphas Levi and thus within living memory.

Waite was a major Christian influence in the Golden Dawn and when he came to head it, he rewrote its rituals accordingly, completely changing its earlier emphasis. He 'hated' Blavatsky's 'Isis Unveiled' because of its 'anti-Christian bias', but was impressed by Dr Annie Besant, another Theosophical leader, and was a member of the London Lodge of the Theosophical Society at the time of her conversion to it, in the 1890s.

Much as he loathed the arrogance of Mathers and Westcott, he hoped that their Qabalistic-Rosicrucian teachings might be the veneer of a genuinely spiritual revelation:[4]

> I knew them sufficiently well to loathe their false pretences, their buskind struttings and their abysmal ignorance of the suppositions arcana which they claimed to guard. It happened, however, that I was nourishing still a forlorn hope that there might be something behind the occult pseudo-Temple, some Holy of Holies undreamed of by the so-called Supreme Magus and the High Council of the Soc

∴ Ros ∴ – God mend it – much as in other regions I had heard from very far away the rumours and portents of a church behind the church.

Waite seems to have enjoyed destroying occult myths of 'antiquity' and he ventured to destroy the concept of Rosicrucianism reaching back into all ages past, which Hargrave Jennings had promoted in 'The Rosicrucians, their Rites and Mysteries'. His critical 'The Real History of the Rosicrucians' was the result. He was evidently impressed though by the Masonic structuring of the Golden Dawn. 'It could not be denied that the culminating grade (i.e. Tiphareth, $5° = 6°$), as the system was then developed, had the root-matter of a greater scheme than had ever dawned in the consciousness of any maker of Masonic Degrees under any Grand Lodge or Chapter, Conclave or Preceptory, in the whole wide world.' Waite hoped to meet holy people in the higher grades, whose identity was, needs be, hidden to members of the Outer, 'to whom Symbolism spoke a language, and Ritual opened a realm of grace'. He was seeking a spiritual reality, too, beyond the frameworks of the Christian Church:[5]

> I believe to this day that it is a pregnant illustration of truth in the Spiritual world; that there is a Church behind the Church on a more inward plane of being, and that it is formed of those who have opened the iridescent shell of external doctrine and have found that which abides within it. It is a Church of more worlds than one, for some of the Community are among us here and now and some are in a stage beyond the threshold of the physical senses.

Waite accepted the existence of a spiritual hierarchy, far evolved beyond the level of ordinary mortal men.

The leading female occultist Dion Fortune, whose views on the psychological validity of the Golden Dawn rituals are dealt with later, held a similar notion to Waite, on the question of the 'hidden side of the Church'.

She believed that the disillusionment with Christianity from the late nineteenth century onwards was due to the fact that Christianity had lost its esoteric aspect (Gnosticism)[6]

> which owed so much to Greek and Egyptian thought. . . .
> The exoteric state-organised section of the Christian Church persecuted and stamped out the esoteric section, destroying

every trace of its literature upon which it could lay hands in striving to eradicate the very memory of a gnosis from human history. Very little remains to us of our spiritual heritage in the ancient wisdom.

One of the certain appeals of the Golden Dawn, particularly to its artistic and creative members, was its claim to access to higher levels of consciousness, most explicitly in terms expressed by the emanationary structure of the Tree of Life. The rituals which Mathers had concocted for the Outer Order, and the Portal and the Tiphareth-rebirth stages were designed to focus the attention, and more importantly the will, of the magician, in a given trancendent direction. This aspect undoubtedly influenced W.B. Yeats. In his 'Autobiographies' (1926) he recalls that in Mathers's rituals there was 'much I thought beautiful and profound',[7] and Yorke notes that Yeats recalled that it was mainly through Mathers that he began certain studies and experiences that were to convince him that 'images well up before the mind's eye from a deeper source than conscious or subconscious memory.'[8] For Yeats the Tree of Life was a symbol of inspiration and resurrection. He envisaged, poetically, that the Tree of Life was planted in the heart of his beloved, Maude Gonne, who for a short time was also a member of the G∴ D∴. In his poem 'The Two Trees' he writes:

> Beloved, gaze in thine own heart,
> The holy tree is growing there
> From joy the holy branches start.

In Qabalistic theory, the source of living Inspiration is said to descend through the emanations of the Tree in the same way as the original surge of the Godhead which originated them in the Creation. The magician imagines he has become a god affiliated with each stage of consciousness; he is literally possessed:

> Surely some revelation is at hand,
> Surely the Second Coming is at hand,
> The Second Coming! Hardly are those words out
> When a vast image out of *Spiritus Mundi*
> Troubles my sight: somewhere is sands of the desert
> A shape with lion body and the head of a man,
> A gaze blank and pitiless as the sun,
> Is moving its slow thigh.

In his 'Rose Alchemica', Yeats draws directly on his knowledge of the $5° = 6°$ ritual for Initiation within the tomb of Christian Rosencruetz.

Michael Robertes, entering the 'temple of the Alchemical Rose'

> opened it with a Key, on which I saw the rust of salt winds. Those 'beyond the bronze door' bid the poet 'join three times in a magical dance', and as I turned from the pillars towards the dancers I saw that the floor was of green stone, and that a pale Christ on a pale cross was wrought in the midst.

> ... thus in the tomb of the Adepti do we tread down the Evil Powers of the Red Dragon and so tread thou upon the evil powers of thy nature. For there is traced within the evil triangle the Rescuing Symbol of the Golden Cross united to the Red Rose of seven times Seven Petals ... the triangle represents the three Supernal Sephiroth ... the Rose represents the twenty-two paths of the Serpent of Wisdom.

For Yeats, with his poetic imagination inflamed by ritual, each Petal seemed to be transformed 'into the likeness of Living Beings of extraordinary beauty'. When turning to the pillars of Horus, each appeared to be 'a column of confused shapes, divinities, it seemed of the wind, who in a whirling dance of more than human vehemence, rose playing upon pipes and symbols; and from among these shapes were thrust out hands, and in these hands were censers. I was bid place my censer also in a hand and take my place and dance.'

In a less significant way, Algernon Blackwood, Arthur Machen and Dion Fortune based their occult mystery stories partly on the atmosphere evoked at the ritual meetings. More significantly, Austin Osman Spare who was a member of Crowley's derivative Argentinum Astrum C.1910 used ritual and trance methods as an inspirational technique for producing his remarkable paintings. His theory was based solidly on the magical emphasis on will. Spare had evolved a system whereby he meditated on a visual symbol similar to an anagram, which 'condensed' into a single device the effect he wished to cause in his subconscious. Thus if he wished to concentrate on the lunar imagery of archetypes of his subconscious, he would initially meditate upon the device which contained the letters M, O, O and N. Spare believed that the act of meditation implanted the 'sigil' in the seedbed of the mind, and it had to be, in the same action, 'forgotten' or rendered 'subconscious' by an act of will.

We are fortunate that a painting exists which is a direct visual representation of a specific trance ritual for which there is also a written account. The painting shows Spare himself with the sigil written on his forehead. A piece of paper lies near by identifying the sigil with a sketch of a tiger. Meanwhile behind the head of the trance artist, the menacing shape of a tiger is welling out of the darkness of the mind.[9]

The invocatory sentence was: 'This is my wish, to obtain the strength of a tiger'. The anagramatic method was as follows:

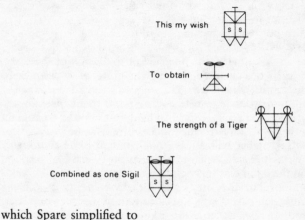

which Spare simplified to

Kenneth Grant who knew Spare well and has recorded the incident, writes:[10]

Spare closed his eyes for a while and visualised a picture which symbolised a wish for the strength of tigers [i.e. the sigil above]. Almost immediately he sensed an inner response. He then felt a tremendous upsurge of energy sweep through his body. For a moment he felt like a sapling bent by the onslaught of a mighty wind. With a great effort of will, he steadied himself and directed the force.

Spare used images obtained in this way as central themes in his paintings. He also believed that trance methods could awaken 'atavistic memories' of earlier incarnations as animals. If one could identify with, and retrace one's identity through these images, one could retrace one's origin back to the Godhead.

Spare's method is heterodox within the framework of ritual magic, but it did evolve initially from a more traditional Qabalistic basis. He and Yeats, then, represent notable examples of magicians of the period who used ritual techniques to trigger the imagination in creative endeavours.

Spare also falls within the domain of those magicians who used ritual magic as a rationale for 'unusual sexual behaviour'. Spare had learnt from Crowley, the doctrine of the fusion of the sexes, explained earlier. For them the highest state of consciousness transcended both sexes.

'Man implies woman', wrote Spare. 'I transcend these by the Hermaphrodite.'[11] However, he also held that in order to implant a sigil in the mind through meditation it had to be 'isolated' or made 'solitary' under will. One's thoughts had to be *thoroughly focused* upon it. Spare believed that during a state of physical exhaustion the mind was less bombarded sensorily, and this was a good condition for the ritual exercise. One means of causing exhaustion which particularly appealed to him was the sexual act; Spare identified his partner as Malkuth, the Divine Maiden, who is symbolically the 'entrance' (upon the Tree of Life) to the subconscious. During the act of orgasm, and the ensuing 'vacuity' caused by physical exhaustion, Spare would will his sigils to cause an influx of transcendental imagery. This was a variation on his trance technique in which his body was of course immobile.

Another of Crowley's followers, Victor Neuburg, also accepted the concept of the union of sexual polarities which was an integral part of the new doctrine of the Aeon of Horus. Man was moving into a new phase of evolution. Both the Qabalah and Madame Blavatsky's 'Secret Doctrine', the Theosophical bible, suggested that man prior to the Fall was androgynous, that is he was really a combination of male and female. Jean Overton Fuller writes that in Neuburg's view androgyny was 'destined to be recaptured in the far future when physical transformations [had] made possible the reproduction of the species in a manner different from that known at present ... [he] thought that anything conducive to a hermaphrodite state of consciousness, must be in line with the ultimate purpose.'[12]

Crowley wrote that his relationship with Neuburg 'was that ideal intimacy which the Greeks considered the greatest glory of manhood and the most precious pride of life',[13] and Symonds mentions that the so called Paris working in which both men took part in an O.T.O. 11° homosexual rite as 'Crowley's first systematic attempt at sexual magic'. Crowley assumed the male role, Neuburg the feminine.[14]

As a leader of the O.T.O. he felt obliged to practise sex magically. And he began with a man instead of a woman (which is contrary to the spirit of Maithuna[15]) because he happened to be living in Paris with a brother of the Order, and he had promised to initiate him into these higher mysteries. The deities to be invoked [i.e. Jupiter and Hermes representing Chesed and Hod respectively on the Tree of Life] were the same as those he had previously worshipped in the Golden Dawn with rituals of a purely ceremonial type; he now wished to find out if this new sexual method was more efficacious.

The full working took six weeks and cannot be described in detail here. However, using the hallucinogen *anhalonium lewinii* and the potency of sexual orgasm itself, Crowley and Neuburg recorded a series of visions during which they believed that they were possessed by Hermes and Jupiter, and the female deities Luna and Venus, both of whom have sexual ascriptions on the Tree of Life.

The union of these transcendent polarities in the sexual act was said to incarnate the new Absolute Consciousness, since in its highest sense it derived its visionary content from a state of consciousness above the Abyss. The magicians were simulating the Creative Act which actually gave rise to the Cosmos.

Finally the Golden Dawn claimed during its existence, and with some validity, to provide a valid, scientific and psychological model of the mind. This explains its appeal for men like William Peck, the Astronomer Royal of Scotland, and Sir William

Crookes, who was already a famous scientist (discoverer of thallium) and prominent member of the Society for Psychical Research when he took the Neophyte grade in the London Temple of Isis – Urania in June 1890.

Two of the other leading figures of the late Golden Dawn (renamed the Stella Matutina after the break with Mathers) also regarded the magical conceptions held within the Society as a basis for a psychological model of the mind.

The first of these was Violet Mary Firth, who under the pseudonym of Dion Fortune compiled the definitive magical interpretation of the new Qabalism in her 'Mystical Qabalah', first published in 1935. During the years after the First World War she studied psychology and psychoanalysis at the University of London, and in 1918 became a lay psychotherapist at the East London Clinic. Influenced by Freud, Adler and especially Carl Jung, she noticed the connection between psychosomatic states and those described by the ritual practitioners of Eastern tantricism and Western Qabalism with which she was also acquainted.

Kenneth Grant writes: 'She realised that Woman, considered in the West to be the negative or passive aspect of the Creative Energy, was, on the contrary, the dynamic awakener of the solar-phallic current, and as such the factor that made the male positive.'[16] Dion Fortune attempted to put this into practice in the Fraternity of Inner Light, which she established to re-institute the worship of Isis, and she established herself as a less spectacular female counterpart of Aleister Crowley, although they were not associated in any way.

In her magico-psychological system she considered that the union in ritual of the dynamic Woman (Isis) with her male partner was capable 'of effecting profound transformations in human consciousness, Black[17] Isis destroys all that is inessential and obstructive to the soul's development. She is the power that liberates the spirit of man from the confines of limited experience.'[18]

Dion Fortune believed that one's being took form in layers, or 'vehicles' which equated with the emanations on the Tree of Life, each progressively more material decending the Tree. Man's mystical task was to operate through a higher vehicle of consciousness. For a system of Qabalistic magic, or yoga (which she equated as Western and Eastern versions of the same technique) to 'stimulate the development of the higher aspects of consciousness', it had to be 'sufficiently powerful and concentrated to penetrate the relatively dense vehicles of the average Westerner, who makes nothing whatever of subtle vibrations.'[19] Dion Fortune believed that Qabalism was especially relevant to the 'psycho-physical make-up' of the 'European city dweller' which she regarded as a type.[20]

> The normal Western temperament demands 'life, more life' – it is not escapist. It is this concentration of life-force that the Western occultist seeks in his operations. He does not try to escape from matter into spirit, leaving an unconquered country behind him to get on as best it may: he wants to bring the Godhead down into manhood.

The second G∴ D∴ practitioner with a psychological orientation was Dr Israel Regardie.

In 'The Art and Meaning of Magic', Regardie wrote:[21]

> Magic is a scientific method. It is a valid technique. Its approach to the universe and the secret of life's meaning is a legitimate one. If it assists us to become more familiar with what we *really* are, it is a Science – and a most important one. And to the scientist, whether he be psychologist or physicist it will open up an entirely new universe of tremendous extent.

On the basis that the documented Golden Dawn accounts of visions and other systematic alterations to consciousness provided data upon the mind, Regardie rightly argued that modern ritual magic is very much a science. Elsewhere, he writes:[22]

> Science is a word meaning knowledge. Hence any body of Knowledge, regardless of its character – whether ancient, medieval or modern – is a science. Technically, however, the word is reserved primarily to imply that kind of knowledge reduced to systematic order. This order is encompassed by means of accurate observation experimentally carried out over a period of time, the classification of the behaviour of natural phenomena alone, and the deduction of general laws to explain and to account for that behaviour. If this be the case, then Magic must likewise claim inclusion within the scope of the same term. For the content of Magic has been observed, recorded and described in no uncertain terms over a

great period of time. And though its phenomena are other than physical, being almost exclusively psychological in their effect, they are of course natural. General laws, too, have been evolved to account for and explain its phenomena.

In Regardie's view Qabalistic magic could provide a psychotherapeutic technique by allowing its practitioners to acquire insights 'structurally' by means of the Tree of Life. They would arrive at the state of mind which Jung calls individuation (harmony with the conflicting energies of the subconscious). Broadly speaking this equates with the Sephirah Tiphareth on the Tree, and the $5° = 6°$ rebirth ritual of the R.R. et A.C.[23]

> If, in the face of some bodily ill or disfunction, we could literally *tell* the Unconscious what we want done, these results could occur in answer to our concentrated wish. . . . A barrier of inhibition is built up between the unconscious and the conscious thinking self – a barrier of prejudices, false moral concepts, infantile notions, pride and egotism. So profound is this armoured barrier that our best attempts to get past it, or through it are utterly impotent. . . .
>
> It was the ancient theory that the unconscious or the deeper levels of the psyche could be reached principally by two methods. These were intense concentration, and intensity of emotion. . . . Ceremonial (Magic) is probably the most ideal of all methods for spiritual development since it entails the analysis and subsequent stimulation of every individual faculty and power. Its results are genius and spiritual illumination.

To summarize Regardie in his own words: 'Magic concerns itself in the main with that self-same world as does modern psychology . . . it deals with that sphere of the psyche of which normally we are not conscious but which exerts an enormous influence upon our lives.'

On its relationship to religion:[24]

> it may be said that Magic deals with the same problems as Religion. It does not waste time with futile speculations with regard to the existence or nature of God. It affirms dogmatically that there is an omnipresent and eternal life principle – and thereupon in true scientific fashion, lays down a host of methods for proving it for oneself.

CHAPTER 10
A Path in the West

We have covered a lot of varied ground, encompassing shamanism, hallucinogens and magic, and a number of approaches to inner space. However, returning to more recent developments, we find, on close inspection, that Carlos Castaneda, Timothy Leary and John Lilly, despite certain differences, all seem to be venturing in the same direction. All seek ways of discovering new inroads to consciousness and understanding them pragmatically as a means to greater knowledge of the mind and new ways of action. In Castaneda's instance, everything depended on the discovery of the *separate reality*. Magical influences and perceptions merged with the normal world. He had achieved the 'breakthrough in plane' and had managed to 'stop the world'. His certainty about 'reality' had been shattered . . . initially by hallucinogenic drugs, and later by his ability to *see*. It is clear though that the techniques which don Juan taught Castaneda hinge initially upon what others have called astral projection. The sorcerer has access to the astral plane of images. He can project his consciousness into the form of a crow or into a bubble flowing with the stream. His modes of perception alter. He sees the aura around living things, he understands that there are tentacles of force which a shaman may use to maintain his 'balance', ways of seeing his environment so that he may act like a 'warrior'. Once a person has witnessed these events, he is a changed man. He is in command of aspects of his psychic potential which he had never conceived of before. Returning to his own world – and interestingly don Juan told Castaneda to be a shaman in Los Angeles rather than Mexico – the sorcerer perceives with 'dual' vision. The planes of reality coincide. He is both awed and mentally reinforced by his understanding of wider realms of being.

It seems to me that Leary's drug consciousness also points towards the same goal. The hallucinogenic sacrament allows insights and encounters with the holy images of the higher unconscious mind. Perception finds itself outside time, on a

133

dizzying journey into the basic life forms, energies and vortexes of existence itself. The danger in Leary's method is that one may experience difficulty in deciphering the flow of subconscious imagery. This can and often does lead to damaging schizophrenic states. However Leary and his colleagues proposed a framework in the form of 'The Tibetan Book of the Dead', for structuring these transcendental experiences. The journey would be representative of order rather than chaos, providing illumination rather than schizoid possession.

It may be argued that Leary's lot has not turned out as well as might be expected. The politics of the pursuit of ecstasy, as he well shows, meant that Leary came face to face with the Establishment. The shaman after all proposes a model of the world which is not in keeping with the corporation-middle-class aspiration ethic. He finds himself chasing different goals, different perceptions from those found in the normal routines of daily life. Precipitated into continuous legal battles and antagonistic confrontations with politicians and others in power, Leary began to espouse revolutionary political ideas, and allied himself for a while with the Black Panthers. This may have been a negative step in the sense that it meant battles had to be fought in the field of normal consciousness with people who had not been on the inward journey and therefore didn't know the territory.

Be that as it may, Baba Ram Dass and Ralph Metzner have found themselves pursuing new spiritual frameworks in order to interpret mystical reality meaningfully in Western society. And it is in this aspect, that what was begun at Harvard, and in another way what was begun in Sonora, Mexico, come to join hands.

John Lilly too has attempted this type of fusion. He has brought his scientific knowledge to bear in proposing empirical models for understanding the psychology of inner space. He has termed the various mystical states 'spaces' and sought to understand the programmes of the subconscious which are activated and are appropriate to these spaces. In his work, sensory deprivation states, hallucinatory states and mystical frameworks are all adjuncts to understanding the workings of consciousness in its most profound and transcendental capacity.

As we have seen, the magicians of the Golden Dawn also sought inroads into the mind by means of a framework, theirs being based on the complex symbol of the Qabalistic Tree of Life. But, as I have mentioned earlier, all did not go well. Aleister Crowley quarrelled, as others did, with Mathers and tried to establish his own source of spiritual authority. He found in Aiwaz his own Secret Chief. Meanwhile the Order was rent by schisms; new subsects were formed, and jealousies and rivalries were wide-spread. Few of the Golden Dawn magicians embodied the type of spirituality or sensitivity found for example in certain ashrams of India.

Yeats, who translated the symbolism from his Tarot-Path Visions into his poetry, and A.E. Waite who was a devotional mystic are perhaps figures within the more introspective spiritual mould. But on the whole the Golden Dawn was dominated by personalities intent on the status of hierarchical grades and either exaggerated notions of spiritual power or exclusiveness. We think of Dr Westcott with his love of Masonic splendour and his ambition to head an occult fraternity whose roots lay in the mists of the ancient past. Of Mathers with his elitist power claims, and Crowley's intense jealousy of Yeats's poetic gift and those above him in the Order.

And yet when all this is said and done, there remain certain fundamental issues of great importance, and a spiritual framework of immense value. Never before had there been a group undertaking such systematic magical and meditative trance work in the West. Never before had there existed a group with ceremonial rituals as extensively or as beautifully constructed.

Perhaps one major source of concern lies in the nature of ritual itself. In the Golden Dawn the grades upon the Tree, each associated with its attendant deity-archetypes, were designed to fortify the psyche in a certain way. One imagined oneself caught up in a cosmic drama, where the truths one learned came direct from the gods themselves. The personifications of the gods were of course the members of the G∴ D∴ in their ceremonial regalia, each partaking of a role appropriate to his spiritual grade. However, the key to the whole working was that by an act of imitation one became the reality. One recited the mythological utterances of Thoth or Osiris and felt the flow of transcendental energy coursing through one's body. The gods were re-awakened and once again embodied in human form.

This of course has serious adverse connotations as well as its positive side. A person identifying with the image of a deity may very well suffer delusions of grandeur. Also if he is successful in activating the Kundalini energies of the Middle Pillar he may precipitate subconscious imagery of such force and impact as to leave his psyche in shreds.

As I mentioned in the Introduction to this book it seems to me that in the study of ritual magic we find two polarities emerging. One is the tendency towards *possession*, and this is what occurs in an act of ceremonial identification. The spiritual force descends into the vehicle of the magus and he is uplifted by it. If he exercises his will appropriately, it will be *possession subject to definite controls*, allowing the magician to integrate the very profound spiritual lessons into the fabric of his own being. He will benefit from the knowledge associated with the transformation of the ritual group into a pantheon of deities. He feels awe rather than power.

The other polarity is what I call the direction towards *ecstasy*. This occurs when the magician, like a shaman, wills to leave his body and 'rises on the planes'. Rather than the gods possessing his consciousness he rises to meet them. He climbs the Sephiroth of the Tree of Life. His astral environment is subject to the controls of his imagination. His invocations bring forth transcendental beings who personify the higher reaches of the spiritual mind. Gradually the magician learns more of his higher nature and becomes transformed. He is making use essentially of the same trance techniques that we have encountered among shamans in Siberia and South America. Like don Juan he finds his Allies within the unconscious realm, and reaches them by 'breaking through in plane'.

In both of these methods we find dangers and pitfalls. The first polarity may produce the type of power-based personality that insists on spiritual sanction for its authority. The magician comes to believe that he has superior quality of inspiration and is able to justify autocratic behaviour on the basis of it. He subjects his fellows as minions. He demands unbridled respect and subservience. Another danger is that one imagines oneself to have incorporated a level of spiritual attainment when one has merely skirted its periphery. Frater Achad, who became mentally deranged after taking the Ippsissimus vow of Kether (at the very top of the Tree), is perhaps an example in point.[1]

In the second method, that of encountering the archetypes, on the astral plane, we may find a tendency to enhance the aspects of escapism and fantasy. The magician returns from his journey in the trance state and is unable to act in the world of normality. He becomes enchanted with the visionary scenery of his subconscious, trapped by his failure to distinguish meaning from its symbolic representations.

Having said this, there remains a worth-while course of action which like the lessons of don Juan, follows closely the methods of the shamans:

> One operates within a Cosmic framework, whereby one is able to encounter the deities of one's own culture since these are most meaningful to the Western psyche.
>
> The method involves the ability to project consciousness into specific areas of the mind at will.
>
> There are certain defences one may use in order to pursue the Way of the Warrior. One fortifies oneself, and allows only the spiritual influx to occur. The magician is armed against the demonic forces of his subconscious.

On the inward journey our framework is the Qabalistic Tree of Life, which like a graph, may be used for 'plotting' and encompassing all the deities which reside in the Western subconscious mind. Unlike the shamanistic societies of the Americas our culture is not, relatively speaking, 'closed' or self-contained. Our literature abounds with many classical references. Our art incorporates the styles and symbols of many other cultures, thus drawing on quite varied sources for its inspiration. The Tree of Life has the function of providing means for comparing the universals underlying these varied sources of inspiration. Our pantheon, unlike that of don Juan's, is a *complex* unity. The path to be followed winds through a maze of imagery many thousands of years old, and incorporates a myriad possibilities.

This brings us to the universals themselves, and at this stage we begin to see that in its highest form, Transcendental Magic is very much the Yoga of the West.

1 The highest principle in the universe is formless, absolute, all-encompassing. No image can describe it. No word can capture the awe felt in union with the source of all-being.
2 Below this level of totality are gods and goddesses who personify levels of spiritual attainment, the higher side of man, since man contains potentially within his mind the whole universe. These are the holy images.

3   The essential concept underlying levels of spirituality and the hierarchy of god-energies is *vibration*. The universe depends on sound, on the great, holy mantras. 'In the Beginning was the Word. . . .' To recite the mantra, to enter into its rhythm, is to become god-like, for the sound will transport us beyond ourselves. These are the sacred names.

4   Man begins to feel the influx of god-energy when his mind is suitably disposed for the current to flow. His will is directed towards emulating the gods, by learning the great lessons which they represent, by imitating their actions in the transcendental mythology, and in the final liberation, by realizing they they too are an aspect only of the greater – all-encompassing totality. Man's initial task is to perform the holy actions, which symbolize the motions of the universe.

In yoga *Nirvana* is the word to connote the highest union with Godhead, and the *chakras* are the spiritual energy levels which represent the path to enlightenment. The yogi chants his *mantras* as he meditates in certain, appropriate *asanas*, or postures. These postures may include certain *mudras* or ritual gestures which symbolize certain mystical ideas.

In magic, we find the same patterns. The highest levels upon the Tree of Life are those above the Abyss. These are the levels which were not affected in the Fall; the Trinity of the Great Father, and the Great Mother which find their origin in the *Crown*, or Monad. Beyond them is the unknown, formless *Ain Soph Aur*, the Limitless Light.

Below the Abyss are the deities of man's immediate aspirations: gods which have ascribed meanings and symbolic attributes in our mythology. These are contained in the 'higher' more spiritual reaches of the unconscious mind. The gods have certain holy names and man may come to know them if he has these names or mantras within his grasp. Among these gods are the Demiurge, the fashioner of the immediate world, the Father of our own limited universe of forms. Also the divine Son, the Saviour of man, who represents the transition from human consciousness to god-consciousness. Here too the female deities representing fertility, beauty and nature.

Beneath them, on the first rung of the mystical ascent, is man. And 'below' him the lower less-evolved aspects of his personality, which he has in some measure overcome; the animalian forces of his character which constitute metaphorically an obverse or 'black' Tree of Life with its branches spanning out far below the Earth.

The Qabalistic framework for inner space has ten stages or *Sephiroth* in all; three within the Trinity, and seven below the Abyss. As previously mentioned, within a monotheistic religion such as Judaism it is not possible to refer to different gods so much as different aspects of the *One*. Thus the following mantras and 'levels' are appropriate to different manifestations of God in the Universe. However, as we will see, it is possible to correlate the deities of other pantheons on specific levels and Paths upon the Tree, because in these instances – Greek, Roman, Egyptian and so on – the deities were regarded as more individual in their own right.

FIRST LEVEL

Malkuth

Associated with the earth, crops, the immediate environment, living things. This sphere of consciousness represents the last stage of descent in the 'Lightning Flash' of creative energy which has zig-zagged its way down through descending formative levels to the physical basis as we know it. Ideas have their materialization here; all inward journeys begin here. In Roman mythology the entrance to the underworld was through a cave near Naples, and symbolically Malkuth is the entrance through earth, (the totality of the four elements), to the subconscious. Malkuth is immediate consciousness. The higher Sephiroth represent the territory upon which mystical man may encroach.

Mantra: *Aaa-doh-naiii Haaa Aaaretz*

Mythological images: Persephone (Greek), Proserpine (Roman), Geb (Egyptian).

SECOND LEVEL

Yesod

Associated with the moon, Yesod, like Malkuth is a predominantly female sphere. It is both the recipient of impulses and fluxes from the higher astral plane and the transmitter of these energies into a more tangible physical form in Malkuth. Consequently it abounds in an ocean of astral imagery, and is appropriately associated with water. It is also the seat of the sexual instinct, corresponding with the genitals chakra of the microcosmic man. Yesod is thus a sphere of subconscious activity immediately entered through transcendental sexual magic, and is the level of awareness activated in witchcraft. The ancient rites of Wicca were a form of lunar worship; the traditional dance around the maypole derived from the worship in a witch-coven of an enlarged artificial phallus worn by the coven leader who assumed the role of the Goat-headed god. Yesod thus takes man through his animal karma on the way to rebirth as god-man.

Mantra: *Sha Dai El Haii*
Mythological images: Hecate, Artemis, Luna, Diana, Bast.

THIRD LEVEL

Hod

Associated with the planet Mercury, representing intellect and rational thinking, Hod is a lower aspect of the Great Father (Wisdom) for Mercury is the messenger of the gods. As the next stage beyond Yesod it represents in some measure the conquest of the animal instincts albeit at an intellectual rather than an emotional level. Hod is the structuring principle in our immediate universe; a levelling and balancing *Sephirah* which embodies order. It is in this capacity that we perceive God the Architect manifesting in a world of myriad forms and structures.

Mantra: *Eloheeem Tzaabayoth*
Mythological images: Hermes, Mercury, Anubis.

FOURTH LEVEL

Netzach

Associated with the planet Venus, Netzach complements Hod for whereas Hod is to some extent clinical and rational, this Sephirah represents the arts, creativity, subjectivity and the emotions. In the same way that Hod lies on the Pillar of Form on the Tree of Life, Netzach resides on the Pillar of Force. It is outward-going in its emphasis, with an element of instinctual drive as opposed to intellect. It is the sphere of love and spiritual passion, again a higher form of the orgiastic indulgent frenzy associated with the witch Sabbath. Within the scope of nature a fine balance exists between Hod and Netzach as the process of creation weaves a fine web of love energy between the polarities of Force and Form. These potencies flow through the uniting Sephiroth of the moon and are channelled through to earth where they are perceived as the beauty resident in natural living forms.

Mantra: *Ye-ho-waaa-Tzaabayoth*

Mythological images: Aphrodite, Venus, Hathor.

FIFTH LEVEL

Tiphareth

Just as Hod and Netzach are opposites, so too are Yesod and Tiphareth, embodiments of the moon and sun, or feminine and masculine polarities. If Yesod represents the animal instincts, Tiphareth is the mediating stage between man and Godhead on the mystical ascent. It is here that man experiences spiritual rebirth. His personality harmonizes; his rational and emotional sides are balanced, his aspirations are towards higher being. Tiphareth is associated with deities of rebirth and resurrection, and in a planetary sense with the Sun as giver of Life and Light. Man catches for the first time a glimpse of the Dawn Light of the Father beyond the Abyss, above form and imagery. The first rays of god-awareness are aroused in him. Tiphareth is also the sphere of sacrifice, for the old restricted human personality is offered in place of new universal understanding and insight. Man begins to operate through a spiritual vehicle.

Mantra: *Ye-ho-waa Aloaaa Vaaa Daaath*

Mythological images: Dionysus, Apollo, Osiris.

SIXTH LEVEL

Geburah

Associated with Mars, traditionally a god of war, Geburah represents severity and justice. The energies of Geburah are absolutely impartial, since there can be no flaw of self-pity or sentiment in the eye of a wise ruler. The destructive forces of this sphere are intended as a purging, cleansing force and are positive in their application. Thus it embodies a spiritual vision of power operating in the universe to destroy unwanted and unnecessary elements after their usefulness has passed. As an aspect of the Ruler or Father of the Gods below the Abyss Geburah is once again one half of the dual-aspected just Creator. He shows discipline and precision in his destructiveness. His mission in the battlefield of the cosmos is to inculcate a rational economy of form which in a lower aspect is reflected in Hod.

Mantra: *Eloheeem Giiborrr*

Mythological images: Ares, Mars, Horus.

SEVENTH LEVEL

Chesed

Associated with Jupiter, Chesed is the other face of the destructive Ruler, representing Divine Mercy and Majesty. In the same way that Geburah breaks down forms, Chesed is protective and tends to reinforce and consolidate. It maintains the potency of the Great Father Wisdom beyond the Abyss, which it reflects on a lower, if exalted, scale. Whereas Mars rides in his chariot, Chesed is seated on the throne, overviewing his kingdom which is the entire manifested universe originating from the energy life-force of the Trinity. Through his stabilizing influence, formerly abstract Mind precipitates a myriad of latencies and potentialities which will eventually sift downwards into forms. In him are all archetypal ideas; he is the highest point in the Collective Unconscious for beyond him no images are really appropriate. (However within the Tarot, for the sake of uniformity, the language of symbols is extended to the Trinity.)

Mantra: *El*

Mythological images: Zeus, Jupiter, Ra.

EIGHTH LEVEL

Binah

At the first of the levels associated with the Trinity we find the Great Mother in all her forms. She is the womb of forthcoming, the source of all the great images and forms which will enter the manifested universe as archetypes. She is also the supreme female principle in the process of Creation, and as such is invariably the mother of the god-man or messiah who intervenes between man and the gods. Binah is thus associated with the Virgin Mary, mother of Christ in Tiphareth, but also with Rhea and Isis. In a more tangible form she is the wife of the ruler of the archetypal world too, and we thus find Demeter, mother of Persephone, as Zeus' spouse, also.

Mantra: *Ye-ho-waa Eloheeem*
Mythological images: Rhea, Demeter, Isis.

NINTH LEVEL

Chokmah

The next of the Trinitarian god-images is the Great Father, the giver of the seminal spark of life which is potency only until it enters the receptive female vehicle. From the union of Father and Mother come forth all the images of Creation. Associated with the ancient gods beyond the universe itself, Chokmah is represented by images like Kronos and Thoth, who sustain existence itself. They are the unswerving absolute principles within Being which are unaffected by the tides of time and mankind. In Judaic thought, the levels of the Trinity were not affected by the Fall.

Mantra: *Ye-ho-waa*
Mythological images: Kronos, Saturn, Thoth-Atum-Ra, Ptah.

TENTH LEVEL

Kether

This stage of consciousness represents the first dawning of

Creation from beyond the veils of non-Existence (Ain Soph Aur – the Limitless Light). Upon the Tree of Life, Kether lies on the Middle Pillar and is therefore at a level beyond the duality of sexual polarity itself. Transcending the Great Father and the Great Mother, it takes the form the Heavenly Androgyne, union of male and female in one. It represents a level both of neutral sublimity and also transcendental potency for being, since from Kether comes the first outpourings on the Tree of Life which will only subsequently engage themselves in the zig-zagging flow from male to female across and down the Tree. Kether has few appropriate representations in paternal or maternal pantheons, and is far removed from the world of mankind in Malkuth.

Mantra: *Eee-Heee-Yeh*

Mythological images: Aion, Abraxas.

These then are the major levels of consciousness according to the Qabalah, each with its divine name or mantra. They correlate with yoga, and represent a progression from animal-man to god-man. However, as John Lilly has pointed out it is wise to view such frameworks as 'programmes' or profound, symbolic metaphors. They allow the mystical ascent to be orderly and gradual. Just as the yogi gradually learns the disciplines associated with raising the Kundalini, so too does the magician proceed carefully, by stages. He is all the time assimilating new information about mystical consciousness. He is undergoing a steady transformation of the personality. The Tree of Life has three Pillars representing positive, negative and neutral, and these are the building blocks of the psyche. According to the Qabalah the very essence of manifestation is the interplay between force and form. The universe begins in an abstract way, with the pure energy of creation. Gradually images and ideas take form. The universe multiplies its contents in the great cosmic love dance between male and female polarities. Gradually the world as we know it, the culmination of descending creative impulses, comes to be. These levels of being, however, are only accessible to man when he retraces the inward journey. He must first of all overcome the lower, more material side of his personality – its limitations and narrow horizons. His aim is to universalize his consciousness. His aspirations become less parochial and less self-centred. New levels of unity are discovered both within the mind, and with others sharing the same 'psychic spaces'.

The Qabalah rests on a tenfold division of the mind. But the Tree is in itself a whole. Each level of consciousness reflects in some measure every other. The mystic and magician achieves full realization only when he has travelled betwen all of the levels of consciousness, for they are all interconnected in the maze-way of the subconscious.

Modern occultism uses the Major Trumps, the twenty-two cards, of the Tarot pack for its doorways to greater consciousness. Each card contains symbolism relating to a certain portion of the psyche. Each mirrors aspects of consciousness resulting from the 'influences' of levels of consciousness in a given 'area' upon the Tree. The Tree is a living, vibrant thing. It is a type of multi-vortex energy framework. Each Sephirah flows into another. The magician too, must flow along the tides of consciousness.

As he does so, he encounters the mythological figures that reside in the subconscious. His meditation upon one card rather than another, takes him astrally onto certain paths. He selects a doorway appropriate to where he wishes to go. The Tarot is thus an instruction to the mind to re-activate certain innate subconscious imagery which in turn produces certain spiritual experiences. New paths of inspiration are opened, new access to the mind created. The magician travels from one polarity to another, from force to form, from the realms of outward destructive deity-energies like Mars, god of war, to those like the warm and passive Venus, goddess of love and nature. He comes to gain increasing rapport with what was formerly his truly *unconscious* mind. Eventually he will achieve a total integration. Then he rises above imagery itself. He encroaches upon the pure energy behind creation itself. The reality above images.

There are ten Sephiroth – major levels of consciousness – and twenty-two Tarot Paths joining them. I have indicated in the following pages their position on the Tree, and as far as I am able, the mythological experiences associated with each of them.

We begin at the lowest levels, at the first doorway.

THE PATHS OF THE TAROT

The World
(Malkuth-Yesod)

This card represents the descent into the underworld of subconscious. In Greek mythology this theme is personified by the descent of Persephone into the Land of the Dead. However as we have seen, death is the obverse side of life, and Persephone symbolizes the wheat grain which grows and dies, and yet undergoes a perpetual cycle of harvests. She dies to live again: her existence is manifest both in the realm of the living and the dead.

In *The World*, she is androgynous, representing both male and female polarities despite her apparent femininity. She dances within a wreath of wheat grains, and around her are the Kerubimic Man, Eagle Ox and Lion, symbolic of resurrection. Her path is the first on the journey towards cosmic consciousness for she is a reflection of her Father in Kether. She embodies the spiritual rebirth themes of the Eleusinian mysteries.

Judgment
(Malkuth-Hod)

A new personality has to be formed and integrated from the diverse and unharmonized aspects of the unenlightened man. Hephaestos, the cosmic blacksmith, is one deity ascribed to this path and we find a similar legend, already mentioned, of the Great Shaman who forges a new identity for his candidates in trance. The path leads to Hod, representing intelligence, and the spiritual direction is towards mastering the more irrational, animal instincts. Figures are shown gesturing with their arms to form L.V.X. – 'light', as they rise in triumph from the grave of ignorance. Above them, Gabriel, Angel of Divine Breath, revivifies them. On his trumpet he heralds *new being*.

The Moon
(Malkuth-Netzach)

This too points towards a new evolutionary phase. The lobster, representing an early form of life, is seen to emerge from the waters; the aggressiveness of the wolf has been modified to the form of a dog, as both look upwards towards Hecate, the Moon, to whom the dog is sacred. Water is the predominant element. Aphrodite, a goddess of the Netzach sphere, was said to have been born in the foam, and represents the White Isis, the resplendent beauty of love and nature. The Moon too symbolizes water, and the ebb and flow of tides; the cycles affecting man in his environment.

The Sun
(Yesod-Hod)

Beneath the Sun in a magical ring dance the young naked twins; boy and girl holding hands. They represent both a type of innocence, and the synthesis of opposite polarities, a common theme in the Tarot. They are clearly ruled by the Sun, representing unity and vitality, and represent a path of enlightenment. Yesod incorporates the workings and fluxes of the lower subconscious; Hod the splendour of the cosmic design.

The wanderer on this path will undergo rigid self-scrutiny. Michael, the Angel of Fire, harshly disperses darkness, and there is no scope for self-delusion. However, the most rigorous trials of Karma will occur further up the Tree in regions associated with the Dark Night of the Soul.

The Star
(Yesod-Netzach)

This card is associated with intuition, meditation and the hidden qualities of nature, represented by Netzach. The beautiful naked White Isis kneels by a pool pouring water from flasks held in both hands. She is Hathor and Mother Nature, a less transcendent aspect of the Great Mother Binah, and she looks thoughtfully upon the waters of universal consciousness towards which the magician slowly takes his way. In his quest for the Grail of Enlightenment, he will gradually have to modify his own vessel of perception to allow it to be filled with the waters of higher consciousness.

The Tower
(Hod-Netzach)

The Tower of Babel was an arrogant attempt by man to scale the heights of Heaven. However, it is clear from this card that potentially the Tower reaches up to Kether, the Crown of all Being, if man can overcome his pride. This path reinforces and consolidates by implication, the opposites Hod and Netzach. According to Gareth Knight, the Tower is also the body, and the influx of divine energy, like the Kundalini occupying the human vehicle, will produce a devastating and harmful effect unless the personality is well-balanced. *The Tower* is ruled by Mars, who ruthlessly destroys ignorance and limited, vain conceptions.

The Devil
(Hod-Tiphareth)

We see demonic forms of man and woman bound by chains to a pedestal upon which sits a gloating, torch-bearing Devil. At this stage, the wanderer in inner space must take stock of his weaknesses, particularly those relating to worldly possessions and security concepts because he is on the verge of his first spiritual transformation. Capricorn, the Goat, represents darkness and bestiality. He has the legs of eagles parodying the union of opposites air (transcendent) and earth, and upon his brow rests an inverted pentagram indicating reverence of illusion rather than essence. However, he really indicates the plight of man within his limited frameworks, and thus offers a definite lesson towards the gaining of inner unity.

Death
(Netzach-Tiphareth)

Like *The Devil*, *Death* indicated man's shortcomings, and the limited, temporal nature of his personality. But death is also the herald of new life, and behind the scythe-wielding skeleton figure we see new light appearing on the horizon. The scythe is associated with the Kronos, the Greek founder-deity, transcendent above time, and the path is called *Nun*, meaning a fish. Christ was often symbolized by a fish ('I am a fisher of men . . .') and *Nun* leads into Tiphareth, a sphere of spiritual awakening and rebirth appropriate to the Christos consciousness. The path through death thus finds its way towards regeneration.

Temperance
(Yesod-Tiphareth)

This card represents the line of direct mystical ascent from the level of the enclosed and limited personality to the more illuminated spiritual man. Raphael stands in the desert, representing the arid toil of the Dark Night of the Soul prior to spiritual fulfilment, and pours the waters of life from a Sun vessel into a Moon vessel. This constitutes a tempering, or union of opposites, of male (Solar) and female (Lunar) energies. All the aspects of the lower subconscious find their unity on this path. All the elements are synchronized: Raphael stands over both earth and water. He bestows grace and unites air (the Eagle) and fire (the Lion). Above him arches the rainbow symbolizing God's covenant with man, and new light is dawning over a distant mountain peak. One of the visions of *Temperance* is that of Sagittarius, a symbol of aspiration. In his own being he represents man and animal. However, his goal is upwards, following the path of his arrow. He incorporates transition. Tiphareth, the level of god-man is within reach.

The Hermit
(Tiphareth-Chesed)

Like the Ancient of Days we see a bearded, patriarchal figure, although his splendour is shielded by the anonymity of a hooded cloak. Having reached Tiphareth, the magician must find his way now towards the source in Kether. This path is ruled by Mercury, who in a higher form is personified in the Wisdom of Chokmah and Thoth, the Great Father archetypes of the Qabalah and Egyptian mysteries. The path is also called Yod, ascribed to Virgo, showing that in some measure a unison of the sexual polarities has been achieved. The Hermit will wend his way upwards, towards the hazards and loneliness of the Abyss, but he has achieved the harmony of Tiphareth and his final goal is firmly in his mind. A lamp held aloft illumines his pathway.

Justice
(Tiphareth-Geburah)

This is a Karmic path demanding balance, adjustment and total impartiality. Ruled by Venus, it leads to the sphere of her lover Mars, and is appropriately designated by the figure of Venus holding scales and the sword of justice. She resembles Maat, the Egyptian goddess of Truth, who resided in the Osirian Hall of Judgment, and weighed the heart of the deceased against a feather. Thoth, the Great Scribe, would record the verdict.

The shaman on this path will have to encounter and integrate visions of his own Karma, the accumulated wrongdoing in present and former incarnations which thrive in the subconscious as images based upon negative power. Since in the Hall of Judgment only the truth can be admitted, all of these Karmic images represent imperfections, and the magician will not be able to proceed higher until he had made retribution. Knight writes:[2]

> the ability to face up to the true situation within oneself coupled with the willingness to change it . . . is a lot easier to say than it is to do, for it requires ruthless honesty, considerable powers of discernment, and not a little courage, but prolonged intention and aspiration.

We find at this stage a more advanced process of transformation of the personality occurring. Karma is built up during incarnation by the personality, and as the magician proceeds towards integration with his higher spiritual self, he must overcome the lesser, more worldly qualities of the finite, earth-bound identity. These have always been his security, and now he finds himself having to obliterate pretence and outward semblances to rediscover the true, inner man. Mars, god of war, characterizes the assault upon and destruction of these imperfections, as barriers to true realization.

The Hanged Man
(Hod-Geburah)

This path, like that of *Justice*, leads to Geburah, the sphere of action. The Hanged Man swings by his foot, symbolizing sacrifice, but because of his position he also seems like a reflection in water, the element ascribed to the path. His head is aglow and he seems to be reflecting light at lower levels of manifestation. The waters flow from Binah, the Great Mother, and the female symbol associated with this is the cup. Man must become the vessel for the influx of higher, spiritual energies, and allow them to fill his being. If this is done he will begin to reflect the transcendental purity beyond the Abyss.

The Wheel of Fortune
(Netzach-Chesed)

Appropriately this card symbolizes the forces of fate and destiny. In the Qabalah words composed of similar letters have related meanings and TARO or ROTA, the word upon the wheel, reads ATOR in reverse. This is a variant spelling of the White Goddess Hathor, showing her influence, and Paul Foster Case writes:[3] 'The Wheel of Tarot speaks the Law of Hathor'. However, the path leads to Chesed and understandably comes under the jurisdiction of Jupiter. Chesed is the region of pure archetypes, the realm of being which of all those below the Abyss reflects the Holy Trinity of Spirit in the most pristine form. Since Kether is androgynous, we would expect both polarities to feature on this path for the ultimate destiny of man is fusion of opposites: mastery over duality.

Strength
(Geburah-Chesed)

This card, resting horizontally upon the Tree occupies an equivalent position to *The Tower*. Whereas *The Tower* lies just below the so-called Veil of Paroketh and separates the terrestrial personality and the true spiritual self, *Strength* lies just below the Abyss, the gulf between individuality and universality. We observe a woman, traditionally in chauvinistic terms a symbol of weakness, nevertheless able to prise open the jaws of a lion. This symbolizes complete mastery over any vestiges of the animal soul (Nephesch) that may have remained, and the ability to endure the Karma of earlier stages of one's growth during the lessons of incarnation.

The Chariot
(Geburah-Binah)

The Chariot is a vehicle of motion and carries the king in his active aspect through his realm, while on the opposite side of the Tree, in Chesed he views his kingdom from his stationary throne. He is empowered on this path to bring down the watery potencies of Binah into archetypal manifestation. He is a mediator as we must ourselves become receptors or carriers of light. This is indicated by the central symbolism of the card which is of the king bearing the Holy Grail. Aleister Crowley writes: 'It is of pure amethyst, of the colour of Jupiter, but its shape suggests the full moon and the Great Sea of Binah . . . spiritual life is inferred; light in the darkness.'[4]

The Lovers
(Tiphareth-Binah)

The Twins (Gemini) stand naked in the innocence of Eden regained, the Holy Guardian Angel towering above them bestowing Grace. As male and female representations of Tiphareth and Binah, we are reminded of the love of the Great Mother (Mary) for her Son (Christ). Greek mythology records a legend showing a similar bond in the form of the half-brothers Castor and Polydeuces (Pollux); one mortal and the other immortal. In love and compassion, Zeus allowed both of them a common destiny, placing them in the sky as Sun and Moon, thus indicating their complementarity as Solar (Male) and Lunar (Female) equivalents. This path, flowing upwards from Tiphareth (Harmony) thus shows the happy and enduring union of opposites.

The Hierophant
(Chesed-Chokmah)

This path is that of the 'triumphant intelligence'. The paternal, merciful qualities of Chokmah/Chesed are enhanced by the love and feminine grace of Venus who rules this card. We find here an enduring bond of wisdom and mercy; the inspiration of the Spirit manifest as an archetype of enlightened intuition in the transcendent reaches of the cosmos. Divine authority owes its inspirational origin to this region.

The Emperor
(Tiphareth-Chokmah)

The Emperor faces towards Chokmah, the unmanifested Great Father above the Abyss, and draws upon his abstract, purified energy for a basis of all authority and order in the universe below. He transforms the lightning bolt by giving it archetypal potential. He is paternal, wise and vigilant: the 'Ancient of Days'. In him we find also the qualities of divine mercy, for although he has the strength and vitality of his other aggressive aspect in Geburah, he is also the father of the manifested universe. Looking out upon his kingdom, he has compassion for his subjects, for they owe their being to his union with the Empress, *the Womb of All Becoming*.

The Empress
(Binah-Chokmah)

Along this path we encroach upon the realm of pure illumination for we combine the great archetypal opposites, the Mother and Father. The Empress is warm and beneficent. Laden with child, she is also symbolically the Mother of All, since from her womb will flow all the potential images and forms capable of existence in the entire cosmos. Mythologically she is Hathor, the greater form of Venus, and she epitomizes love and nature on the universal scale. She sits among the wheat grains, the trees and the River of Manifestation, for she is the feminine side of the God-force which sustains these forms. Potentially this path is the highest form of *balance* upon the Tree. Above her lie two paths, male (*The Magician*) and female (*The High Priestess*) which have not yet been counterbalanced by an opposite force. They are not paternal or maternal but have only the *potential* for further development. And *The Fool* symbolizes the border-dimension of manifestation itself. Thus, in *The Empress* we have a very high degree of illumination indeed, a full integration of polarities upon a path which looks down upon the whole of subsequent manifestation.

The High Priestess
(Tiphareth-Kether)

This path, unlike *The Empress* reaches to the very height of creation, Kether *The Crown*. It incorporates in essence the path beyond opposite archetypes, for Kether is androgynous, the potency behind sexual duality. Correspondingly the High Priestess, the goddess upon this path on the Tree, has an element of untaintedness about her. She is of Kether, she reaches up beyond the Abyss, she is unsullied and virginal. As Case has said,[5] if the Empress is Mother Venus (Hathor) then the High Priestess is a transcendental aspect of Diana, the cold and pristine Lunar goddess who has had no union with a male deity. In her aloof condition she has the potential for motherhood but she has not yet realized the possibility of giving birth to a myriad of forms. In this sense she is very much above the Abyss. Those who follow her path, however, undergo a final transformation. They begin to rise above form itself, returning to the virginal, undifferentiated state of being. They transcend duality. They approach the crowning glory of Kether, the all-encompassing Nirvanic unity. In such a state of ecstasy they no longer retain individuality but merge with the ocean of spirit.

The Magus
(Binah-Kether)

Linked to Mercury, the cosmic intelligence, the Magus represents the pure, masculine capacity for force and potency which is yet unrealized through union with the female polarity. Lying above the Abyss, this path deals with a type of male purity which equates with the virginity of the High Priestess. The Magus stands above Creation in the archetypal sense. However, one hand is raised aloft to bring down the energy of Kether, which he may then transmit further down the Tree. Around him is the Garden of Paradise, indicating that he has his being in a dimension which seeks further manifestation in nature. He has access to the divine mysteries, since his knowledge reaches Kether. Mythologically he is Thoth, the logos of the universe. He embodies the Will of the Godhead to be manifest: 'In the Beginning was the Word. . . .' We note that Thoth is the presiding deity in the Egyptian underworld who overviews at the court of Osiris. It is he whose word sustains the universe, and all men have their final identity in their *name*. Thoth, as the Magus, is thus the Divine Vibration or Utterance which makes accessible, and transmits, the Light of Kether downwards towards form.

The Fool
(Chokmah-Kether)

The Fool is a symbol for him who knows nothing, and upon this path one draws near to the veil of no-thing, that which is unmanifest, beyond the scope of creation. Of this realm nothing can be said for no qualities or attributes may be ascribed. The Fool is about to plunge into the Abyss of manifestation and form. Eventually his energies will descend to the depths of the kingdom which lies in the chasm at the bottom of the Tree of Life. The Fool precipitates the cosmic process, and the reverberations which follow, like lightning from the mountain top, wend their way down, coursing from male polarity to female, and back again. Finally what has been previously unmanifest, comes *to Be*, and the interplay of force and form produces 'reality' in the world as we know it.

In the preceding pages I have attempted to demonstrate the scope of the journey undertaken by the Qabalistic shaman in the West. But the symbolic, mythological universe I have described is in only one half of a twofold division into good and evil. These qualities I take to represent aspiration, rather than absolute values, as such. There is a white Tree and a black Tree. My own interest lies with the transcendental aspects of magic which parallel yoga in showing a path towards union with the Godhead. However all Qabalists recognize the presence of the Qlippoth, or negative mirror-images of the gods upon the Tree. Just as there is transcendental good, so too is there transcendental evil. Just as there is sacred order, there is also demonic chaos.

A magician upon the shamanistic journey thus needs to arm himself against the negative characteristics of his psyche. Like don Juan, he must be prepared for anything. He must always be on the alert, in a dimension of ever-changing images, for that which could destroy or confuse his mystical intent.

We have seen in earlier chapters that the will has a paramount role to play once we venture onto the astral planes. The will literally determines what we shall perceive, which 'space' we find ourselves in. Thus, in making his venture as orderly as possible, in a region where certain transcendental energies could theoretically knock him off balance, the magician begins with *himself*. He must find initial peace with himself. He must fortify his frame of mind.

He must initially 'clear the air' of doubts and worries. To repeat don Juan's admirable phrase, he must go to knowledge as he goes to war, with 'absolute confidence' in himself.

I referred earlier to the magical circle, which is used as an imaginative device differentiating negative and positive thoughts. The magician stands *inside* the circle, and directs his will towards mystical knowledge and realization. All of the thought forms and images which are contrary and thus 'negative' are forced similarly under will, to remain *outside* the circle.

This is not an easy process because the mind resists efforts to focus the attention on a single thought or symbol. The magician must thus surround himself with an imagined circular force-field to act as a 'protection' against the intrusions of unwanted ideas. This becomes highly relevant, because as we saw in the early chapters on shamanism and astral projection, *one perceives what one imagines* on the astral planes. If the magician has a strong will he will be able to proceed through the Tarot doorways because when he visualizes them, they will become a reality. However, there will always be Qlippoth – negative thought forces – lurking around to trick him. If the shaman moves everywhere within his force field, or as some occultists say, his 'astral shell', he will have an in-built protection against undesired imagery. Thus, just as don Juan chose to travel in the 'appropriate' form of a crow – watchful and anonymous – and just as he had to beware of being trapped by the spirit of the water-hole, so too does the Qabalist have to keep his wits about him. Like don Juan he can assume a form appropriate to his environment. His environment is an area of mythological inner space, so he often imagines himself in the form of the god whose sphere he is approaching. He will be familiar with the characteristics of these deities from the classical mythologies. The visualization will help him to be united with a certain symbolic region of his psyche. If he approaches Hod he will imagine himself filled with the illuminating intelligence of Mercury. If he approaches Geburah, he will imagine that he is destructively and aggressively routing the negative and unwanted attributes of his personality.

He will need certain protections. According to both yoga and the Qabalah, the universe is maintained by *vibration*: the great mantras, the God-names. The magician utters these as he enters each sphere. His invocation literally means that he is appealing to the highest type of spiritual authority. He wishes to acquire knowledge and understanding at transcendental levels of aware-ness. In so doing he is able to use these mantras both to reinforce what is 'positive' and also to 'banish' imagery on the astral plane that is either confusing or unnerving. If he does not do this he will enter a 'space' that, so to speak, is off the path.

The most basic form of 'banishing by mantra' in Qabalistic magic is the so-called Ritual of the Lesser Pentagram.

In this 'purifying' ritual the magician, just like don Juan, is really isolating a certain area of 'holy ground'; free from malign influences. He uses a symbol – the Pentagram – to represent the totality of earth, fire, water, air and spirit.

His first action is to perform the so-called Qabalistic Cross. He imagines light descending from his *forehead* (mantra: *Ateh*), down to his breast (mantra: *Malkuth*), then from his right shoulder (mantra: *ve Geburah*) to his left (mantra: *ve Gedulah*). He holds his hands over his chest (mantra: *le Olahm*). This is an activating exercise similar to that of the Middle Pillar described earlier.

He now begins to create the magical circle which will be his mental 'protection'.

He faces east and describes with his outstretched arm a large pentagram, commencing at the lower left-hand corner and moving clockwise. He imagines that it is made of a luminous pervasive fire. He utters the great mantra *Ye-ho-waaa*, the God-name for air.

Now he faces south, imagining as he turns that a barrier of flame-energy extends from the eastern pentagram round to his new position. He makes the pentagram and utters the mantra *AaaDohnaiii* representing fire.

Facing west, continuing the circle as before, he makes the pentagram for *Eee-Hee-Yeh*, symbolic of water.

Completing the protective circle and the final pentagram in the north, he vibrates the mantra *Aaa-Glaa* for earth.

In this sequence the magician has placed four protective pentagrams of fire at each of the cardinal points, and he has contained himself within a circle of luminous energy. This reinforces his notions of self-unity and security. The four elements are a medieval rendition for totality, and as Jung has shown, the number four represents stability and order.

The next procedure involves visualizations of the archangels of the elements, which like don Juan's Mescalito may be said to act as protectors.

The magician holds his arms outstretched like a cross and imagines before him, in the east, Raphael. A force of wind is felt across his face. A column of yellow and violet light, appropriate to Raphael, rises into the sky.

Remaining in position – for the east symbolizes spiritual knowledge – the magician calls the Archangel Gabriel. Water, representative of purity, flows down his back, and he visualizes Gabriel's colours – blue and orange – shining upwards in the west.

Concentrating now on his right arm, he visualizes the Archangel of Fire, Michael, and the vibrant colours of the complementaries red and green. It seems to him that his body is lit from this side with an illuminating warmth.

Finally he calls Uriel, the Archangel of Earth, and imagines the moisture and tangibility of earth on this side. The colours that are normally ascribed to this quarter are russet, citrine, olive and black.

Once again we find that the visualizations are designed to enhance the sense of balance, and induce in the magician a type of awe. He finds that he is able to will the images and colours to remain. They add a new strength to his already existing magical circle. He feels as if he is about to undertake a monumental inner journey. He imagines the radiance of the pentagrams held in his mind, and blazing in a circle around him. Above his head he now gives added concentration to the crown chakra, the dazzling white light of Kether. This represents his aspiration and his goal.

I think we can see from this exercise that what may initially appear to be a rather pagan, superstitious exercise, actually has considerable value. Such visualization allows the Magician to enter the astral plane through sacred territory. He enters like a warrior, in a position of strength. His protection consists of imagery which within his own framework for inner space is meaningful and well balanced. He has already induced a frame of mind which puts him well on the way to the first pathways of the psyche. He will be able to perceive from within his circular 'shell' the astral imagery which the Tarot doorways will open for him. Like don Juan, he will remain always in control.

He may now commence his astral exploration of the pathways which lead to higher consciousness. As subconscious imagery arises before him he will recognize the appropriate Tarot symbols of the path on which he is travelling. In addition, by again using a pentagram visualization, he may enhance the quality of his vision or he may 'banish' additional negative images by a reverse process.

The Tarot path on which he is journeying will be ascribed to an element (see Appendix B). In performing the pentagram, the shaman begins his movement with the point on the pentagram which is appropriate to the element, and then completes the figure. This has the effect of *enhancing*. To remove the image he 'banishes' in the opposite direction:

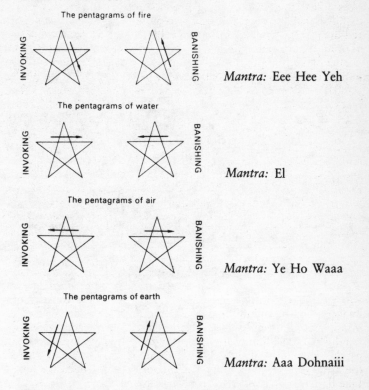

The pentagrams of fire

INVOKING   BANISHING

Mantra: Eee Hee Yeh

The pentagrams of water

INVOKING   BANISHING

Mantra: El

The pentagrams of air

INVOKING   BANISHING

Mantra: Ye Ho Waaa

The pentagrams of earth

INVOKING   BANISHING

Mantra: Aaa Dohnaiii

The magician is now armed to go where he will on the pathways of the psyche. He has within his grasp a knowledge of the various planes of consciousness, and he may expect certain mythological and magical events to occur. In Castaneda's

accounts we have some of the finest descriptions of magical
consciousness extant. However the Qabalistic magicians invariably kept personal records of their inner journeys, and they
provide an interesting comparison with the universe of don Juan.
The following is an account by Aleister Crowley of one of his
astral journeys along certain of the Tarot paths. As with the
sorcery of don Juan, the psyche is shown to be perhaps the most
fascinating field of all enquiry, the source of a living mythology.

> I was carried up above the circle which I had drawn, through
> a heavy and foggy atmosphere. Soon, however, the air grew
> purer, and after a little I found myself in a beautifully clear
> sky.
>
> On gazing up into the depths of the blue, I saw dawn
> immediately above me a great circle; then of a sudden, as I
> looked away from its centre, there swept out towards me at
> intolerable speed the form of a shepherd; trembling and not
> knowing what to say, with faltering voice I asked, 'Why
> speed ye?' Whereupon the answer came: 'There is haste!'
> Then a great gloom closed mine eyes, and a horror of
> defilement encompassed me, and all melted in twilight and
> became cloaked in the uttermost darkness. And out of the
> darkness there came a man clothed in blue, whose skin was
> of the colour of sapphire, and around him glowed a
> phosphor light, and in his hand he held a sword.
>
> And on seeing him approach I fell down and besought
> him to guide me, which without further word he did.

At this point Crowley accepted his guide, who equates in the
account of Castaneda with the Ally. Crowley appeared to run a
risk of not questioning the spirit form in order to discover his true
identity. In the astral journey of Soror Vestigia quoted earlier we
see that the guide was tested symbolically according to the sphere
from which he had come. Don Juan too warns of the dangers
associated with encountering the Ally, and the necessity of
maintaining firm control within the visionary experience.

Crowley appears to have been precipitated initially into a
'space' related to Chesed. The colour blue and the form of the
shepherd are traditionally ascribed to Jupiter. As it turned out, the
guide proved to be of invaluable assistance:[6]

> On turning to the left I saw that near me was a rock door,

and then for the first time I became aware that I was clothed in my robes of white. Passing through the door, I found myself on the face of a high cliff that sank away in the abyss of space below me; and my foot slipping on the slippery stone, I stumbled forward, and would of a certainty have been dashed into that endless gulf, had not the shepherd caught me and held me back.

Then wings were given me, and diving off from that great rocky cliff like a sea-bird, I winged my course through the still air and was filled with a great joy.

Now, I had travelled thus but for a short time, when in the distance there appeared before me a silver-moss rugged hill.

And on its summit was there built a circular temple, fashioned of burnished silver, domed and surmounted with a crescent. And for some reason unknown to me, the sight of the crescent made me tremble so that I durst not enter; and when my guide, who was still with me, saw that I was seized with a great fear, he comforted me, bidding me be of good courage, so with him I entered. Before us in the very centre of the temple there sat a woman whose countenance was bright as the essence of many moons; and as I beheld her, fear left me, so I stepped towards her and knelt reverently at her feet.

Then as I knelt before her, she gave me a branch of olive and myrtle, which I folded to my heart; and as I did so, of a sudden a great pillar of smoke rose from the ground before me and carried her away through the dome of the temple.

Slowly, the pillar loosened itself, and spiral puffs of smoke, creeping away from the mighty column, began to circle around me, at which I stepped back to where my guide was still standing. Then he advanced, and beckoning me to follow him, we entered the great pillar of smoke and were carried through the bright dome of the temple.

On, on, we soared, through regions of cloud and air; on, on, past the stars and many myriads of burning specks of fire, till at length our journey led us to a vast blue sea, upon which was resting like a white swan a ship of silver. And without staying our flight, we made towards the ship, and descending upon it, rested awhile.

On awaking, we found that we had arrived at a fair island, upon which stood a vast temple built of blocks of silver, square in form, and surrounded by a mighty colonnade. Outside it was there set up an altar upon which a branch had been sacrificed.

On seeing the altar, I stepped towards it and climbed upon it, and there I sacrificed myself, and the blood that had been my life bubbled from my breast, and trickling over the rough stone, was sucked up by the parched lips of the white sand. . . . And behold, as I rose from that altar, I was alone standing upon the flat top of the square temple, and those who had been with me, the shepherd and my guide, had vanished – I was alone . . . alone.

And as I stood there, the east became as an amethyst clasped in the arms of the sard, and a great thrill rushed through me; and as I watched, the sard became as a fawn; and as I watched again, the east quivered and the great lion of day crept over the horizon, and seizing the fawn betwixt his gleaming teeth, shook him till the fleecy clouds above were as a ram's skin flecked with blood.

Then thrill upon thrill rushed through me, and I fell down and knelt upon the flat roof of the temple. And presently as I knelt, I perceived other suns rising around me, one in the North, and one in the South, and one in the West. And the one in the North was as a great bull blowing blood and flame from its nostrils; and the one in the South was as an eagle plucking forth the entrails of a Nubian slave; and the one in the West was as a man swallowing the ocean.

And whilst I watched these suns rising around me, behold, though I knew it not, a fifth sun had arisen beneath where I was standing, and it was as a great wheel of revolving lightnings. And gazing at the Wonder that flamed at my feet, I partook of its glory and became brilliantly golden, and great wings of flame descended upon me, and as they enrolled me I grew thirty cubits in height – perhaps more.

Then the sun upon which I was standing rose above the four other suns, and as it did so I found myself standing before an ancient man with snow-white beard, whose countenance was a-fired with benevolence. And as I looked upon him, a great desire possessed me to stretch forth my hand and touch his beard; and as the desire grew strong, a voice said unto me, 'Touch, it is granted thee'.

So I stretched forth my hand and gently placed my fingers

upon the venerable beard. And as I did so, the ancient man bent forward, and placing his lips to my forehead kissed me. And so sweet was that kiss that I would have lingered; but I was dismissed, for the other four suns had risen to a height equal to mine own.

And seeing this I stretched out my wings and flew, sinking through innumerable sheets of blinding silver. And presently I opened mine eyes, and all around me was as a dense fog; thus I returned into my body.

For don Juan the realm of sorcery similarly involved entry into the 'separate reality' of magic portents, and the ability to manipulate and understand these so that one could become a man of knowledge.

In taking Carlos Castaneda for his apprentice don Juan hoped to show him that parallel universes – the normal and the mysterious – exist as equally valid dimensions. From our discussion of astral projection, trance visions and out-of-the-body experiences we see that reality is a condition which is determined by our state of consciousness at the time. We have the option to enhance our perceptive faculties, and enlarge our scope of vision. This is what don Juan meant when he told Castaneda that he must *see* rather than *look*. The universe is full of possibilities from which we are blinded unless we first challenge the basic premises upon which our concepts are built.

As Castaneda says, we agree upon our description of the world when we learn and communicate within a language. We tend to forget that other cultures and societies distinguish different categories of meaning and stress different ways of interpreting what occurs.

Don Juan had access to the magical universe, and for several years endeavoured to break down Castaneda's certainty about his normal Western modes of perception. Initially the breakthrough came with hallucinogenic drugs, which are a common feature of shamanism in many cultures. Castaneda insists now that the drugs are not integral but merely assisted in the fracturing of his limited view of the world. From the point of view of Western magic, Castaneda had been given access to the plane of astral imagery where he found different laws operating. He found, for example that will and imagination played a key role. That the essence of sorcery was in fact *transformation* and that this was not merely an occurrence in folk-myth but an unquestionable fact.

The viewpoint and the actual character of a person changes when he has access to this type of expanded perceptive universe. He is unable to retain his old ideas. He is unable to view the world as a constant, for it is always revealing new mysterious facets and qualities according to the way one is trained to see it. As don Juan says, the world of the *brujo* is 'awesome'.

We found in don Juan's techniques certain ritual expressions, certain attitudes, certain types of explanation which we might have expected to exist outside the Western way of thinking.

However, it is true, I think, that the magical view of the world has always been an available option. There have always been ways open to man to allow him to change his mode of consciousness. In our Western history alone there have been a number of initiatory mystery traditions which have held out this alternative. Neither were these groups so far removed. The mysteries of Eleusis centred around the rebirth symbolism of Persephone, who represents, as we have seen, the first phase of the inner journey. There is some thought too, that just like the psychedelic pioneers of the early 1960s, the candidates at Eleusis may have drunk an hallucinatory beverage.

Since these early times, Gnosticism, Mithraism, Alchemy, Rosicrucianism and Qabalism have existed in the West in one form or another, allowing man to take upon himself the transformation of consciousness.

Like the shamans of the Americas these mystics have had different frameworks for the inner journey of the spirit. Some were devotional, others like Qabalism produced in the Golden Dawn, rituals, trance workings and mythological ceremonial. Unlike shamanism in general, these mystical schools have not generally used hallucinogens although where they have it has been to assist in the 'flight of the soul'. What does unite them, and this is true whether or not such substances are used as sacraments, is that the mystic or magician has access to other planes of causality. He explores beyond where he has been before. He encounters the forces and potencies deep in the psyche which inspire and awe him. And in order to convey this knowledge to those who have not experienced it, he devises a framework or hierarchy personifying all the energies, gods and demons that he has experienced in the alternative universe.

In this book we have discussed such frameworks as the 'Tibetan

Book of the Dead', the magical realms of don Juan, the Gurdjieff models adopted by John Lilly, Agni Yoga, and the Tarot-Qabalah of the Golden Dawn. All of these have merit, and in a very profound sense they mirror each other. Their main value, it seems to me, is in their capacity to portray symbolically certain regions of consciousness appropriate for those commencing the inward journey. It has been termed variously the flight of the soul, the out-of-the-body experience, the shamanistic journey. Essentially it is the pathway through to higher realization. An encounter with the mysterious and illuminating energies of inner space.

PART THREE

The Book of Visions

The Tarot cards are doorways of the mind, and represent the paths which the magician follows on his inward journey. However, the cards also represent living forces rather than abstract symbols, and it is my intention in the following pages to describe these paths as a three-dimensional phantasy voyage into inner space. The shamanistic purpose is to follow paths which, once imagined, become real. The magician goes forth on his venture knowing the archetypal milestones along the way. As he remembers them they come into the scope of his vision. And from them, he learns the lessons of his higher self.

THE WORLD

I found myself in a field of grass, with the wind blowing gently and birds whistling in the distance. It seemed to me that I had found a profound peace with my environment. I felt a unity with nature, and her life forces flowed through me. I experienced what it is like to live and feel. And then I reflected sadly that what is living must also die. Nature has her cycles of birth and re-birth. The plants grow from seed, attain maturity and then wither into dust.

As I walked onwards it seemed to me that I was journeying simultaneously towards my own death and a new life. I had come now to a rocky cliff-face, hard and worn with time. I looked upon the granite textures as a symbol of permanence, as something that would continue. I detected in the rock-face small rifts and channels, lines like wrinkles upon the visage of an old man. Suddenly these fissures in the rock appeared to open, becoming a doorway. I was passing into the rock, through the space that leads down between the worlds into the land outside time itself.

Beyond the rock-entrance it was dark and moist. And yet the earth seemed to welcome me. It seemed that all around, forces and powers were at work, sustaining living things growing in the soil, and in the water, and in the sun-filled air above.

As I continued I detected an ethereal glow at the end of my path. A misty, greeny-brown light played on the walls of the cave and I saw for the first time that in the flecks of light energy, a figure was dancing.

She was naked and youthful in appearance and yet, as I watched, her body seemed to take different forms. As if in a mirror, I saw in her the fields of ripened wheat, and a golden light shone from her face. Then she darkened, hardening into rock. Waters now seemed to flow over her form, dissolving her hardness, and she resembled the currents and eddies of a country stream carrying the grains of sand in their flow. Wind rustled through her golden hair.

As she danced, she called out to me, saying that she was both death and life, and that she could teach me through her movements the motions of the world itself. Streams of energy flowed from one hand to the other.

I noticed that everything about her very being related to motion. There was no constancy, no sense of being able to stand back and watch.

She called me again embracing me in her currents of life force. I rose and fell. Elated and despairing, joyous and sad, I realized the two sides of my own being. I danced with her too, for I could do nothing else. Then a circle of misty light came up around us, and it seemed that we were dancing in the dawn of the first days of the world. I knew then that she and I were one, and I had forgotten her all these days past. I called out, exhuberant with joy, but then the mists subsided and I was left alone. She had disappeared completely. I stood upon a rocky crag looking around, wondering where she had gone. Then a light breeze swept my face and I heard her voice again: 'I am in the world but I am also beyond the sky. Follow the path. We will again meet, in this region which is yet another. We will again dance together, but you will have first travelled an entire Universe.'

JUDGEMENT

As I walked on it seemed that I was approaching the end of a tunnel. A radiant light enticed me onwards and then for the first time I heard the sudden blast of a trumpet, rich and full, which seemed to herald an awakening. Pure waves of all-encompassing music flowed over me and I was drawn along towards the new day at the edge of the kingdom of the earth. Vortexes of fire coursed by beside my path, and a revivifying breath of life, like a wind gust, lifted me along as if I were a feather.

And then I came into the new land, and there were others here too. They were naked like I was, and were holding their hands in the sky as if a marvellous portent was imminent. Men, women and children were here, side by side, awaiting.

As we stood, I saw that I was stationary not upon dry land, but upon an unusual terrain which seemed to undulate like ground becoming liquid, and then transforming into vapour. We had all arisen from the realm of the earth, and I spoke with others who said that the naked dancing goddess had brought them here too.

Suddenly the entire universe was ablaze with sound, and the waves of music which I had heard before resounded again, a hundredfold. I was awed by the grandeur and regality of those noble harmonies. A new life-force flowed from them, filling my body with vibrant energy. Every particle of my being seemed enhanced, revitalized.

As I watched, new forms emerged from below, swirling upwards on the musical current. This sea of life took on a sheen of vivid deep blue, and mounted high into the air carrying all of us with it. Again I heard the sound of the trumpet hearkening new awareness, and I knew now that I was flowing towards the source of all being.

Then it seemed that I was high up in the air, embraced by a mass of swirling orange clouds. A new sense of exultation and awe swept over me and I heard the voice of the clouds and the sky, welcoming me. 'Part of you has been left behind. But another part lies ahead: When you find that forgotten portion of your being, you will know that your living has been like death, and you must now regain what was yours a long time ago.'

XVIIII

THE SUN

The path ahead leads onwards to the foot of a verdant grassy mountain. Halfway up the slope a rocky wall encircles the peak, dividing off the sacred territory which unpurified man may not approach.

High in the sky glows the indescribably glorious cosmic sun, vibrantly illuminating the universe. Twelve rays of life-energy reach outwards into the galaxies of the night, and the whole zodiac appears, with its chain of constellations slowly gyrating like the clock which measures that which is beyond time.

As I approached I saw two young children, dancing naked in a circle upon the grass of the lower slopes. They held hands and seemed to bring down into their dance motions the life force of the sun itself. I had seen them before, when they were old and in need of replenishment. But they had now begun a new journey. New understanding lay before them.

There were certain lessons inscribed upon the wall beyond, and these were five in number. The first lesson was that of seeing the world as it really is. The next was of hearing, and then followed the lessons of the other senses, touch, smell and taste. And the wall seemed to proclaim that beyond this sensory barrier there lay a new measure of perception and illumination, a universe not to be profaned.

I saw that the children grasped this instinctively and that their joy arose from an awareness that one day they would pass by onto the higher slopes of the holy mountain, and be reunited once again with their father and mother, gods of the highest heavens.

I noted too, that the wall was of firm stone and that no one could pass who wished to bring darkness onto the slopes illuminated by the sun even if he wished. Meanwhile the solar orb blazed down from the sky, filling the world with the radiance of life and hope. I knew that I had danced before in this magic ring with the white goddess of the earth, and that my task was to find her beyond the barrier of human understanding.

Somewhere beyond the wall of night and the day, beyond darkness and light, beyond youth and old age.

THE MOON

Before me I watched the rippling waves upon the waters of being and possibility. There came forth a crustacean, with his ancient armour and his fierce claws: an early, primeval form of life. Then I saw two animals upon the bank. One of these was a wolf, his fur shaggy and his expression hostile and aggressive. Beside him stood his domestic counterpart; tame and mild in his manner, no longer dependent on prey for his survival, but instead a friend of man, who sustained him. Beyond them in the distance stood the walls of the castle, man's domain. Their turrets, symbolic of aspiration, stretched upwards into the night sky. They seemed to rend the darkness and merge with its texture.

It seemed clear to me then that man evolves by transcending his primitive animal nature in favour of spiritual awareness. The darker side of his being remains as a remnant of his primeval heritage.

High in the heavens I observed the silvery face of the moon lit by the illumination of the sun. I remembered that the sun casts away the shadows of the dark and that they may take refuge with the moon, guardian of Hecate's demons.

As I stood there, the tides ebbed and flowed. The waters coursed up and down the banks in cyclic rhythms. The dogs assumed a myriad variety of representative shapes from the animal kingdom. Man strode around his turrets, fortifying himself for the assault on the heavens, at odds with the demonic forces outside.

I came to know that man forges the armory of his own advancement. Like the lobster with his protective coverings, the ascent to the all-encompassing sea of forms must be carefully made. The turrets of the castle then seemed again like the gateposts of the underworld through which I had already begun to make my way.

Eventually, beyond the moon, I would reach the central sun, herald of the light of new day. Again I heard the call of the white goddess, urging me to continue on my journey.

It then seemed that I had found her, for coming towards the domain of the land beneath the stars, I saw a beautiful naked woman, kneeling beside a stream. She held two vessels, one of gold and the other of silver, which reflected the ethereal light of the stars above. From her right hand she poured the waters of life into the stream and I saw that the vessel could never be emptied for she was the priestess of the waters and these were her sacred domain. In her was entrusted the secret that all life flows from an eternal beginning which knows no beginning and no end. From her left hand she poured fluids rejuvenating the earth, and I saw that her whole body was of water, and her flowing hair was like the current of the stream. Her skin was pale and silvery, and I knew that she was not the goddess of the cosmic dance, but her sister from the sky. She told me that she guarded the elixirs of nature by night, while her sister was able to bring them into fruition by day, and I saw that there was no abundance of wheat here, but only a solitary tree. In this tree I noticed the scarlet feathers of the magical ibis, and the star goddess told me that this bird was her companion in truth. I saw his feathers light up like flames controlling the fickle shadows and the steady gaze of his watchful eye upon the stream of life near by.

In the night sky shone eight stars, one of them golden and brighter than the others. The lady of the moon told me she would reveal her most prized secret, and reaching up into the sky she caught in her golden cup the solar brilliance of the brightest star. Then she knelt, pouring its fluids from her vessel, and it seemed that the whole world was alive with life while man yet slept.

She told me too that the other stars were the pools of light in the body of man and he must find and capture their rejuvenating power on his journey to the sky.

Then it seemed that she poured her fluids from the gold and silver vessels into my own being, and I swam for a moment in the ocean of infinity from which I had myself, in times past, come forth. I saw the pure moonlight in her eyes and heard her words flowing like the stream. I knew I must make and purify my own vessel and that it would hold the waters of truth and life itself.

I continued on my way, uplifted by the waters of life which had been bestowed upon me by the lady of the stream. I felt the energies of the sun and moon in my body and yet was not, I felt, a worthy custodian of these profound secrets.

The night sky, with its radiant stars now clouded over and I sensed an impending storm. A threatening darkness engulfed me, and the whole universe, it seemed, had taken on a hostile aspect.

Ahead in the grey light I saw a tall and weathered stone tower reaching up into the sky, and momentarily a vision of those vain men who had eagerly built the monument of Babel in defiance of their gods came into my mind. But now the tower was threatened by the storm, a puny artifice at the mercy of the heavens.

Without warning, the sky appeared to heave wide open and a

molten torrent of thunder and lightning hurled itself wrathfully upon the vulnerable tower. Huge segments of stone masonry crashed to the ground; battlements collapsed meekly before the onslaught, and the whole edifice was consumed by an enormous tongue of flame.

From the battlecry of the thunder god I learnt the lesson behind what I had seen.

There are forces and powers far in excess of man's minor achievements. If he will build an edifice reaching to the heavens he must drawn upon inspirational knowledge of the structure and being of the highest spheres.

The lady of the stream had warned that man must perfect his own vessel if he is to receive the inflowing waters of truth. The path and construction of a spiritual identity are only gradually and painstakingly achieved. He who challenges the gods on high when he is unready for the encounter can only face destruction in the Kundalini flame.

THE DEVIL

Continuing in the murky blackness of the night, I found myself at the entrance of a poorly illumined cave. A great torrent of frenzied human voices issued up out of the opening, followed by penetrating, hollow, rumbling noises which vibrated through the ground with an eerie resonance. I felt drawn along by a vortex of sound, and seemed to slide along a narrowing passage in the musty darkness. I had the impression that I was descending into the bowels of the earth, and was overcome by a sense of despair. My path was no longer clear. It seemed that I had wandered too far from the path in the night's blackness.

I now sensed other human presences although the shapes were hard to discern. Then my attention focused upon a crude splinter torch, whose flame caused monstrous exaggerated shadows to play in macabre pantomime upon the wall.

I saw that the torch was held by a grotesque bestial figure whose head had the form of a tattered and weather-worn goat. Threatening, misshapen horns protruded from his skull and an expression of abject apathy and innate evil had permanently etched their scars in his distorted, leathery face. A few strands of fur hung down from his drooling, twisted lips, and his eyes were like burning coals without a pupil. His right hand he held aloft, while with his left he swept his torch through the air with dizzying movements, apparently designed to disorientate the onlooker. An inverted white pentagram was ingrained upon his forehead.

From his back extended crumpled, bat-like wings, in contrast with his fleshy thick-set body. This creature appeared to combine both male and female attributes, for on his left side a drooping breast confirmed that his form was androgynous. His legs resembled those of an eagle with heavy plumage and menacingly sharp claws took the place of feet.

Standing before him were two semi-human figures, one male and the other female, clad only in chains. Horns had developed like growths from their heads, and the lower half of their bodies was thick-set and bovine. They seemed bound by enduring self-pity and ignorance to the dark throne on which the goat deity sat.

I found it difficult to breathe in the putrid atmosphere, and envisaged that it would be impossible to find my way out of the cave. It was then that the dark god spoke to me. He said that his domain was the last outpost of physical man, and that it was his pleasure to allay and encourage those who found indulgent satisfaction in sensory delights.

He offered me a place in his kingdom, pretending that his minions were in no way bound to remain in his service. I refused, demanding passage from his cave. He smiled benignly, disbelieving my determination as I repeated my request. Then extending his arm, he held his torch aloft so that I could draw near to see his face. 'Be not afraid', he said, 'For even the Devil is another form of Light.' I drew closer to his distorted visage, and he grasped me with his fleshy hands. I observed his dark, bottomless eyes, and his strange, misshapen skull, and then it seemed that beyond his ugliness and degradation lay an undoubted transcendent spiritual reality. From within the depths of his being there came forth rays of white light, increasing in intensity. Soon his head was ablaze with luminosity. His outline was no longer discernible, his grasp no longer apparent. I travelled through his effulgent head as if it were a doorway, and looking backwards as I passed it seemed to me that his bizarre, grossly exaggerated form was nothing other than a monstrous pretence, a joke of cosmic magnitude. His very being seemed one-sided, like a stage dance his very existence seemed founded in illusion. I looked again, and now no demonic shapes whatever could be seen, only a granular rocky surface without access to a subterranean cave. A feeling of triumph mingled with joy overtook me and I no longer felt alone. The darkness had subsided, and new light was dawning.

I came to a sparkling stream, and followed it towards the direction of new light. And then I saw that on one side of the stream was darkness and on the other the luminosity of the new day, and they seemed to meet and mingle in the flowing water.

It appeared that I was pursuing a path of delicate and profound balance. I had brought some of the vestiges of darkness from the cave of the beast and needed to be cleansed of these impurities. Fibres of light exerted a pressure upon my body, drawing me along. I became increasingly one with the stream.

And then I saw that the stream had a guardian, and he had a most imposing form. An enormous winged figure with trailing orange and vivid blue drapes stood majestically before me. In his right hand he held a water vessel, and in his left a glowing torch similar to that which I had seen in the cave. At first I could not see his face. It appeared that he wished me to observe his form, and for a moment it seemed that the whole fabric of the heavens was alive upon his breast. A bright vibrant sun shone forth, and circling around it I observed the motion of all the planets and constellations. He said to me then, 'You see that the bringer of light, and his companion stars in the dark night of the universe, are brothers and sisters of the heavens.'

Then the golden luminosity moved up to his head, and suddenly it was ablaze with light. I could see details of my surroundings more clearly now. The guardian of the waters had one foot in the stream and one upon dry land. He was the overlord of two creatures as well.

One of these was a ruddy lion which lay angrily scowling near his foot. The other was a silver eagle on his left, whose wings whipped ferociously in the air in an act of defiance. But the guardian had both under sway for he told me he would show me how to control their tenacious qualities. Uplifting his water vessel from the stream he poured its silvery glistening waters upon the head of the lion. The crystal fluids seemed to pour right through him and he was instantly transformed, and subservient to his master. Then the robed figure lowered his torch above the head of the eagle, which seemed then to be of glass, reflecting the glowing embers of the torch. A spark of flame fell down into the eagle's heart and filled its entire translucent body with an orange-red glow. And the eagle ceased any longer to menace his master.

Then the guardian spoke again: 'I am Raphael, and I guard here the secrets of the stream of night and day, and the rainbow of the sky above. He who comes here is transformed beyond what he was before. You have seen the waters fill the lion of fire, and the flame fall upon the eagle of water. Know this for the mystery which it is.'

Then he beckoned me onwards to his domain, and I followed the stream towards a mountain cleft into two commanding peaks. Beyond this mountain I could see the pinky golden rays of the rising sun lighting the mountainside and heralding the new day.

It appeared to me that I should soon have full vision of the cosmic sun, but the landscape took on a strange and menacing aspect. The sun, indeed, still glowed radiantly and had risen higher above the horizon, but the sky seemed to be ablaze with blood, and the fields in the foreground were strewn with carnage.

A vile and monstrous skeleton god strode up and down across the terrain with a commanding and persevering air. In his hand he held a large sickle, the sharp metallic blade of which glinted in the sun.

I saw that his crop was of human heads and hands which emerged through the grass in a macabre harvest. Now the time had come for him to reap the grain, and as the angry blade sang through the air heads of kings and commoners alike toppled and rolled along the ground. The skeleton god seemed impervious to the rights or wrongs of his vengeful task and continued in his downsweeping motions, wielding his terrible weapon.

Lying in the amber light the fractured heads and limbs mocked the passive dignity of the nearby river which flowed turgidly in the direction of the rising sun. And still the reaper continued upon his never-ending task.

There was nevertheless a presence in his being, for the light of the sun cast strange shadows upon the indented and hollow areas of his skull. Then a voice came out of the dry harsh fissure that had once been a mouth, and its tone was not at all as I expected it. Whereas his actions seemed consumingly cruel and wanton, his voice was gentle, like the air itself. 'Only one thing lives here', he told me, 'And that is the solitary white rose which grows beside the stream of light as a beacon for the wise.' I looked, and saw that a single rose flowered upon a thorny bush, the only living thing, it seemed, that had resisted the fatal sweeping motion of the reaper's blade.

'I am Death the first', he continued, 'but not Death the last. Once men have come here they need not their old worn-out personalities. It matters not whether they were princes or poor men when they began their journey, for all must assume a new bearing if they will dwell in the sun.'

As I stood there it seemed that a curious transformation occurred and part of me, fragile and brittle, fell to pieces. I felt like a shell which had fractured and yet I knew that I continued to live in the space within. Looking down to the ground I saw my arms and legs and my crumpled body and head, which now seemed like masks, lying upon the field of death. But I was curiously detached from my former being and understood that part of me must forever remain upon the field. The skeleton motioned to me then to make my way towards the river, and as I did so, I saw that the stream was golden and filled with light. I knew that I must go with the current, and that the direction was of light journeying towards light.

THE HANGED MAN

Around me the air seemed tenuous and moist. I appeared to be entering a pervasive watery domain illumined by a light which filtered down from above me providing an ethereal misty effect. Ripples of pale blue light filled my vision.

Then before me I observed a curious effect. A cloud had formed in the heavens and seemed pregnant with light. Suspended from it in precarious balance was an Egyptian ankh. Its loop faced downwards supporting the bound foot of a man hanging upside down.

But this man was no ordinary human, for his gesture implied a profound symbolic mystery. One leg was crossed over the other, and his arms were held behind his back.

As I stood there a stream of light illumined the cross-formation of his legs and they glowed with red, burning flame seeming for a moment to consume him in fire. Then the potent light descended to his head, sending out in all directions a penetrating but diffuse glow. I saw a torrent of transforming, ever-varying images of what had been, and all that ever could be, coursing down through his body, as if it were a funnel, then welling up within the triangle formed by his head and arms. For a moment the sea of light in which I found myself, thronged with possibility. Shapes and images seemed suspended in fluid readiness, about to burst into a more discernible form from behind the misty veil which shielded them from full vision.

I knew then the figure was a bridge between the lights of heaven and the subliminal oceans of being, and that I myself had come forth from beyond the barrier of mist in this way. I knew that if I could venture upwards beyond the watery confines I would arrive at the ocean beyond all oceans, the form beyond all forms.

The hanging man now seemed ancient beyond all time. His fair, flowing hair grew hoary with age, his fine handsome face became weathered by the currents and tides of the passing years. Wrinkles lined his face and his eyes glowed with an alert all-encompassing wisdom. I knew him for the Ancient of Days.

It seemed then that I was on the threshold of the domain of the gods. Pointing to a silver button upon his jacket he told me that his duty in this realm was to ensure the well-being of the moon for in her reflection we discern a glimpse of the mighty sun beyond. His life-blood was the sun, and his body was the moon. He told me he was a beacon reflecting in the waters of being so that all dwellers in the ocean of form could find their way forth.

From his face came forth a mighty radiance, and there was no longer darkness in the texture of the waters.

But I came now into another royal chamber, and saw before me once again a face I remembered. It was the lady of the wheat field with whom I had danced at the commencement of my journey. Now, however, her face was stern and impassive. She seemed to have forgotten our former acquaintance and she looked down upon me unsmilingly, her eyes searching my soul.

In her cloak I saw once again the colours of the grass swaying in the fields. In her draped and flowing robe I discerned a molten fire which was both the heat of warmth and destruction. I knew that her role was to judge my progress upon the journey so far, and that my fate, as from the beginning, lay solely with her.

In her right hand, uplifted in a solemn and threatening gesture, she held a sturdy steel sword, in her left, a pair of golden scales.

'I guard the secret of the sacred song which sounds throughout the Universe', she told me, 'and only a few may prove worthy to hear it. This is the song through which all things live and breathe. The song which tells all forms and beings that they too will one day come home. But only some may hear it. Only some may know from which direction it comes.'

As I watched, her eyes grew hard like the glistening steel of her sword and her body seemed close-knit like stone. There was no longer any spontaneity in her form, but an enduring impartiality and sternness which overwhelmed me with awe.

Beyond her throne, a rich, purple curtain lay draped across an archway, and it seemed to me, as its folds moved now and then, that beyond it lay a great light, and that there the great gods were afoot in their kingdom teaching their songs to their people, lifting up the universe with the sounds beyond time.

The goddess now held out her sword and it rested upon my head, menacing in its presence, yet light and true in its touch. I saw my image reflected in one of the golden scales and watched tremulously as she placed a feather in the other. And I knew that either I would be permitted to pass or else her sword would take full vengeance for my profane assault upon the sacred domain of the heavens.

I heard a rustling in the curtains, and saw once again in her cloak the grass beckoning graciously in the meadows of the first journey. And there was a warmth in her presence and her form was once again the goddess of life rather than the harbinger of death and despair. I knew that I had been spared her wrath, and that I would be given a song.

I heard it then. A reverberating murmur which gradually quickened in pace and force until it became a mounting wall of thundering sound. Waterfalls of music coursed through my body. I swam in the life-song of the gods, echoing down through the pathways of the universe. Its splendour was overwhelming, its conception rich and overflowing with grace. And yet it narrowed, scaling itself down in complexity and where before I had heard a symphony of harmonics, I now heard a single musical note uplifted by the wind. And now the gods were calling me, and I could go on, continuing my journey towards the land of great ones. They were asking me to return to their kingdom and I was welcome.

THE WHEEL OF FORTUNE

I stood before the gateway to the land of the great gods, and on this gateway was portrayed a regal motif, a mighty wheel which turned with the destiny of the universe implicit in its motion. The wheel itself seemed fashioned out of cosmic fire and as it revolved great pulses of energy which would make the stars and the planets and the home of man, coursed off into the purple darkness.

No hand, it seemed, moved the wheel, and yet its rhythm was profound. Eight golden spokes supported the rim like foundations of the very cosmos itself. And there were guardians within its precincts.

In the four cardinal points I saw the great ruddy lion, and the silver eagle, the tawny bull and the face of the first and last man. And, holding the wheel upon its axis and guiding its rotation, I saw the form of the vermillion jackal god whom the Egyptians called Anubis and whom the Greeks knew as a form of Hermes, messenger of the gods, vehicle of wisdom.

Beneath his gaze, nations and peoples were born and rose only to die and fade from memory with the turn of the wheel. Continents and cultures assumed prominence and then were no more. Ideas once valued were lost or neglected. But always man went on, discovering new things and forgetting others. In time he would discover that all these thoughts lay merely as inscriptions upon the wheel of the mighty ones from whom all ideas and creative impulses were given.

As I watched it seemed then that Hermanubis, the jackal-headed man, transformed his own being and became suddenly the lofty sphinx, the lion with human face, seated upon the crest of the wheel.

And he was man fulfilled, master of paradox, with an eye towards the land beyond time. He moved not with the wheel but sat above it, oblivious of its rotations and tides of destiny.

I remembered that the lady of the hall of judgment had observed my being, and that here too my own future, and that of the entire universe, was in evidence.

But above the wheel, lay a symbol of hope; I knew now there was a stationary point beyond all finite movement. A central and infinite certainty beyond the cycles of nature; beyond life and death. It was to this region that I wished to be taken.

As I stood watching, the gate was no more, and the wheel was without bounds. The pathway, it seemed, was by way of the central hub which supported the very spokes of the wheel itself. I continued on my way.

But I came again into darkness, and I remembered that I was entering the land of Hermes and Anubis, and that Anubis was the guardian of the night-land whose other face is light. Once again I felt the solitude, the isolation of the journey to the land of the gods. It seemed for a moment that I stood in the shadow of the wheel whose splendour and magnificence I had just passed, and that the motion of this wheel though measuring only a fraction of a moment for the great ones, was for a mortal trapped in time, an aeon in length.

I felt that the darkness would endure beyond all respite, and that once again I had been deluded by my vanity in an effort to enter the land beyond time.

And yet as I gazed fearfully around me in the velvet darkness, I saw that faint wisps of light were finding their way before my vision; I could discern in part that the terrain here was mountainous and barren.

I had no choice but to continue onwards although I was now unaware of my direction. Nevertheless I felt reassurance, for in greater measure than before, I felt new being within myself. I knew that in my own fabric I had to find the light to counteract the pervasive darkness of the mountain slopes.

It was at this point that I no longer felt alone. Some of the inherently threatening qualities of the darkness seemed to disappear. And quite suddenly, I saw that once again I had a guide. The gods had seen my approach through what I supposed to be the mountainous outer regions of the great kingdom itself.

My guide was robed in the grey of half-light, and stood high up upon a mountainous ridge. He looked down towards me, holding in his right hand a lantern, illumined by a star from the night-sky. In his left hand he carried a trusty wooden staff, with which he maintained his balance upon the ledge. Drawing closer, I could see the age etched upon the partially concealed face, and his beard and hair were as white as parched rock. It seemed to me that I had seen him before.

He called to me, asking me to come to him, and his voice was rich and deep. The sound was in the valleys, and in the mountains and in the sky, when he spoke.

I climbed warily up to where he stood, my pathway increasingly illumined by the rays of the star in his lantern. And when I grew near he asked me to tell him who he was, and I saw that the face beneath his hood was also the ocean beyond time. I saw the clear reflections of the waters of becoming in his fine, majestic features. Then there was no image but only my own reflection and I saw my own eyes in his, and my own face where his had been.

'I am your father and you are my son, but also, we are each other', he told me. 'You had forgotten, and I have brought you here so that you may remember.' The light from his beacon poured into me like warmth. 'This', he said pointing to it, 'is your lantern too, and you have been guiding yourself. And soon you will meet with yourself, and it will not be in the darkness of the mountain path, but in a place of light beyond light. And then you will know who you are, and also who you are not.'

FORCE

There was a secret that my guide wanted to show me, which he said was a mighty paradox. As we walked together, we came down from the rocky mountain path, and the path widened onto a grassy plain. Once again it was light and the sky was a golden yellow. We had left the dark and threatening rock ledges behind.

And the paradox, he told me, was that in my understanding strong and brute force usually controlled the gentle and mild, but that the two were really like brother and sister in the family of nature's forces.

As he explained this to me I watched as two shapes appeared in contrast against the trees in the distance, and as we drew nearer I saw them more clearly.

One was the maiden of my first journey, but again she did not acknowledge me. Her hair had the same golden hue of the ripe wheat grain, and around her forehead were strands of wild flowers.

The other shape I saw, to my amazement, to be the ruddy lion familiar from earlier ventures upon my journey. But his roar and temper had diminished completely, his eye was no longer ferocious, his tail no longer whipped through the air in defiance.

The maiden had placed a wreath of white roses around the lion's neck, and he was calm and peaceful, constrained by her hands which gently caressed his cheek.

And then a song came forth from the lion's mouth and it was the song of the world of animals and their domain. It told sadly how man had once strode through the jungles in the first days as a mighty rival, but now he had gone from the fray into distant parts and the animals were left alone except when by devious tricks he returned on the hunt. Man was no longer dominant by the rule of might.

The maiden, hearing his song, whispered to him, her white robe lapping around his burnished coat of fur. Her voice was the rustle of the leaves of the wild rose itself, and it fell upon the lion like the descent of calm. And she told him how man had found a new and potent way to master the mighty force and rage of the lion, and that in such a manner she could presume to place the rose chain around his neck. And where the lion fought his competitors in an open battle, she had found a new song within herself, and this had given her a new kind of all-consuming strength. The song was the song of the mountains which was not only in the mountains, and the song was of the stream and yet was not the stream. It was in the air, and in the earth, in the leaves and in the rocks, and it was greater than all the forces of the animal kingdom.

This secret, my guide told me, was a mighty and enduring truth, and I would come to discern its value more clearly as my journey continued. With a white rose, he told me, I could quell the lion of fire.

THE CHARIOT

I knew now I was within the outer regions of the domain of the great ones, who dwelt beyond time. Yet, I had been told by my guide that I had first to penetrate a veil of mist which surrounded the holy precincts in ineffable mystery.

I walked along the paths of the grassy plain, and presently the golden light of the sky began to transform into a regal blue. And yet the air became heavy with droplets of exquisite dew which hung precipitated like a sheen of crystal. And although it was still day it had the quality of night.

I began to perceive that I was entering a region of mist and I wondered who dwelt in this region as the guardian of the sanctuary beyond. A golden light now appeared from within the swirling mists, and its pervasive illumination grew stronger in intensity. It seemed metallic in hue, and soon acquired such a vivid radiance that I was dazzled by its glare.

A voice now came rumbling like ancient thunder through the clouds of crystal: 'I am the guardian of the mighty sky chariot that will take you to the land of the holy ones. But it is a journey in which great mysteries will be shown to you, and they are not for the profane. If you are unworthy, beware the ravages of the sphinx of the night.'

I felt both awe and total apprehension, as if I were entirely at the mercy of a mighty warrior. And yet I knew that in this region I could depend forthrightly upon his strength and direction, if my intent was true. He was the guardian of the star-mist.

Now it seemed that I was better able to discern his form, and I saw that he was indeed a great warrior king, for he was adorned in golden armour and wore an orange crown with the motif of a sea crab. His hair was like pale, shimmering fire and reached down to his shoulders which were decorated with the insignia of the moon. Around his waist was a mighty band inscribed with the legends of time and the stars.

His hands held golden reins which harnessed two sphinxes: one white the other black, and I perceived that these creatures were the sky horses which bore his cosmic throne through the starry clouds of vapour.

The chariot itself was less distinct in shape and seemed to merge with its surroundings. A canopy shimmering with silver stars covered the chariot and was supported by four columns of golden crystal. It seemed to me that the chariot was born along on wheels which were also zodiacs, and that inherent in his flight was the very motion of the planetary constellations themselves.

He spoke again to me, telling me that on his sky-borne journeys he took light to the darkest regions of the universe, and that he was a messenger of mysteries. As his words echoed around me, the crystal droplets of misty dew seemed to light up like little torches, and I knew I was in the presence of a very great being.

At his request I entered his chariot and watched tremulously as we ascended into the banks of vapour in the sky. His sphinx horses mounted their speed, and I felt caught up in the very motion of the universe itself. It seemed to me that the chariot carried tidings of great import, and that as we passed by, and bubbles of crystal brilliance were broken in the sky, new universes and life forms came into being.

We were flying towards the land of the first ones. Those who had fashioned time itself, and knew its secrets.

THE LOVER

We came down through the mist and alighted upon the grassy verges of a great mountain. And I knew that I had been to this mountain slope before, but that in times past I had been prohibited from entering its sacred enclaves. Mist came up around the ledge on which I was standing and I knew that the warrior guardian had fulfilled his task and would soon leave me. There was a rush of hooves, and a spray of crystal mist which sent a shiver of vibrancy through my entire being. A mighty torrent of wind passed by and he was gone.

Looking down the slopes into the valley below I saw again the rocky wall dividing man from the heavens, and I remembered that this was the place where I had seen the dance of the children of the gods when they were yet young.

But now new ground had been opened to me, and I followed a path which seemed to open out into a wider space upon the hilltop. Suddenly the vapour around the slopes was filled with a glowing incandescence and the sun once again came forth, filling the sky with orange light.

A great radiance fell upon me and energy surged through my body and I knew I was in the presence of the holy ones.

Suddenly I saw two naked figures, one man, the other woman, and they were standing, welcoming the light of new day upon the mountain of Anubis. The man was strong and well built, and the wisdom of the first days shone from his face. He was the guardian of twelve fires which glowed like orbs in the air behind him, and these were the fires of the zodiac.

His partner had a delicate form, reflecting the golden orange light of day. She had in her domain the tree of knowledge and a coiled serpent was entwined upon the tree, yet in abeyance. I knew she was Eve and her lover was Adam Kadmon, the first man.

As I watched them in the dawn of the first day, a mighty gust of air came up and a great force dwelt above them. It glimmered with a violet-purple haze, and it seemed that from this force came forth the breath of new life upon the mountain. The grass shone with new light, and the fire-orbs in the air were enhanced tenfold in brilliance. Eve and Adam joined hands and a life current of love and tenderness entwined them in sublime union.

And from within the purple haze, and the eddies and streams of life-breath which filled the air, there appeared a radiant face of transcendental beauty. It spoke, saying, 'I am Gabriel, and these children are in my care. This land is holy ground and they are the creation prized above all by those who first built this mountain and who placed living beings upon its slopes. The gods of the first day watch you too as you approach.

THE POPE

Now I came before the first of the mighty ones, seated upon a throne carved from stone out of the earth. He sat between two pillars, one called wisdom and the other beauty, and his role was to guard the mysteries of the mighty word and tell it only to those who were worthy to hear.

I dared not look upon his face at first, but saw that his robe, which flowed down to the ground before me, was flame-red like molten lava, and that written along its border in the blue of the sky and the green of the fields were the legends of those who had been given a name. And the name was their bond and their being, and it was inviolate.

Upon his chest shone a mighty silver pentagram, and within its points was inscribed the figure of the first man, whom I knew now to be my brother.

In his left hand the great one held a golden staff and in his right, the keys of the sun and moon. He sat, majestically upon a square dais within an area of red velvet, and I knew that in him were secrets of my own being which he would tell me if I were able to receive them.

Looking up, I beheld his face which shone with white light, illumining his beard and highlighting points of splendour upon his golden, triple-layered crown.

As I stood before him he began to sing, and from its rich, undulating tones I knew it to be a secret song from the first days of the world. And all of the words of the song were both alike and different for they fell in layers of music one upon the other like stratas of earth upholding the universe. As I stood there it seemed that new forms and structures came into being, but I knew that they had always in truth existed, and that they came forth again when he sang.

He was lord of the earth, and in him were all the secrets of the word made manifest. He gestured towards the pentagram upon his chest, and again I saw the silver star and the figure of the first man.

Then I saw in its place my own face, and I knew that I too had a name from the earliest times, and that for this reason I had come forth into the world, later to return. But I had forgotten my name and had come again to learn.

As I stood there he held out his golden staff and placed it lightly upon my head. The music fashioned by the gods beyond time flowed into my ears and through my being. And through that cascade of lilting sound I detected that one minute particle within that fine and overwhelming music was my own. As I listened forms and shapes gathered around it in a vortex and I saw myself as I had travelled, down through the ages from death to birth to life.

A torrent of faces passed before my eyes and I knew that these were vestiges of myself but that they had been taken back like shadows by the lord of the earth when no longer needed.

He spoke to me then, telling me that my name was my most precious possession and that I must guard and remember it always. And then it seemed to me that I had been given my own pentagram and that it was inscribed as a birthmark from the gods upon my chest. Looking down upon it, I saw its silver radiance, the light of life, and in its centre was written my innermost and most prized secret, *my true and sacred name*.

Continuing my journey, I came now to a range of wondrous and awe-inspiring mountains which seemed carved by time itself from crystal fire, currents of flame, caught like thunderbolts in ice.

I discerned that these bold, timeless mountains had a ruler, but at first I did not perceive his form for he too was ancient as the rock disguised in its folds, and as unchanging as time. But he sat there, emperor of the axis of the universe, upon his throne carved as a cube from the red rock itself.

His crown flashed blazingly, dispersing beams of ruddy golden light. His armour, embossed with symbols of the sun and time had been given as a gift from Mars, his warring brother who rules his quarter of the cosmos with vengeful hand.

But the Emperor here sat watchfully, calmly awaiting news

from his realm, writing new laws and maintaining peace in a world of force and flux. In his grasp he held the lights of the rays from the rising sun and these he passed on as a gift to his kingdom. His valleys were filled with a mighty radiance, and seemed to glow with an inner fire, like smouldering embers.

And yet the Emperor remained as monarch of a quiet land. There was no abundance of vegetation here but instead the glinting jagged cliffs and the ancient river below, etched like a scar upon the rock-face.

There was no goddess in his kingdom and I knew that he yearned for the silver face of the moon over his fiery landscape. A face of stars with eyes of mist: a mirror of images, in which to discern the forms of things to be, emergent worlds and beings to come forth as progeny.

I felt a sadness in his form, and I knew that the lord of the mighty ones was in this corner of his kingdom, without his queen, the goddess of night. I knew that beyond the mountains there was yet another time and place, and here they too would be united.

THE EMPRESS

I seemed transposed, and suddenly before me stretched the domain of the great mother of the gods. Whereas the rocks of flame had been inhewn upon a barren earth, I saw here fields of golden wavering wheat and forests of regal and luxuriant trees. Rich and nourished grass sprang up, watered by the stream which is Life itself.

And beside the stream upon a throne of flowers sat the lady of the new day herself.

In her cloak of green were the hues and colours of the leaves and in her hair danced beams of light and life forthcoming. The brocade of her train was formed from roses growing at her feet, and in her sway were the flowing colours of the seasons, fashioned like stories upon the fabric of her gown.

But it had been given to her to rule also as queen of the night, and above her head were twelve stars like cohorts of the darkness. And beneath her foot, as a symbol of her domain, lay a crescent moon, a scythe for the ripe wheat by day, but a blade of silver in the night.

I knew that she had two faces, and that like my lady, she was both the night and day, darkness and life, mother to the world, and wielder of the tides of death.

As I looked upon her pale, awesome face I saw again my partner from the dance of the dawn of the first time. But here she took another form for she was in one aspect the mother of us both. This seemed to me a great mystery, but in the stream and in the grass I heard her words, softly. And she was telling me, singing me a song which told how all men had once walked in the land of the first dawn, and how all had once been as gods. Now, I had returned and I myself would be the king among the mountains of the red flame and earth, and she would be my queen.

Yet in her was all being, and from her womb I had myself come forth. And when I asked her concerning this, I saw that she was also a mighty sea, and on the waves and in the foam danced all that was and could ever be. Upon the crest of every swirl of spray were a thousand universes, and the tides of water were also the motions of suns and planets which come forth and fall to grains of sand upon the shores of time.

My lessons were not yet learned; my journey not yet complete.

THE HIGH PRIESTESS

And yet there was a time when the lady of the fields and mother of forthcoming had herself been young, when she herself had been the light beyond the moon, the pale beauty beyond the land of new day born.

I came to the temple of her younger days when she was not yet queen with the king of the red mountains. In this place she sat enthroned as a princess between two pillars of night and day. In her hair I saw the motion of the cycles of the moon, and all around her was a haze of shimmering silver light.

Her skin was white, like milk, but her eyes and mouth were hard like steel, untempered by the warmth of embers. From her shoulders flowed a cloak of water, deep blue like the depths of the ocean which even beams of sunlight have not reached. And her throne was made of salt from the sea.

Upon her lap lay unfurled the scroll of memory, the book of deeds forgotten by men but remembered by the gods like pictures in a mirror. And I knew that in her scroll my being was written by name, that there was the name which had been given to me as my most prized possession. But she seemed not to heed me when I entered her court, and I felt that a veil of mist came between us, through which only her lunar light diffused.

But her light was not yet of the sun and seemed to come up out of the valley beyond all forms and time. There was a newness in her presence, for she was the first daughter of the gods.

I felt deserted by her coldness, chilled by her foreboding air. And yet in this place, indeed, it seemed there was a freshness, and I walked upon the sacred ground of the first times. In this sanctuary, even before the sun had made his kingdom in the mountains of the sky, his moon queen had not yet come forth. Still she abided in the temple, veiled beyond the twilight of the first dawn.

I

THE MAGICIAN

Again, beyond the veil of mist, I came to the realm of the great magus, sovereign of the great ones, and builder of earth, fire, air and water. It seemed to me that he was force and creativity itself for as I entered his domain, I approached the centre of a great vortex which poured forth like portents all that I had seen and heard already upon my journey.

He was a noble figure. His eyes were ablaze like lightning and thunder roared in his hair. His uplifted arm brought down from the sky mighty waves of energy, and with his downpointed arm he guided this force into worlds constrained within the bounds of time. But he was himself a guardian beyond the veil of past and present. In him thoughts were still new, and had not yet taken form. And I saw that his strengths were infinity and wisdom and that his own being channelled their ever-ceasing possibilities into universes of lesser worlds governed by lesser gods below. I felt awed in his presence. A profound humility swept through my being. I knew that I was entering the very mystery of the first things.

The lord of magic had four symbols which were his language. And when he spoke his first words to me I saw that they were of fire, and I beheld the flame beyond flame, the luminosity behind all blazing suns. And this was the light beyond light which illumined universes as yet undreamed of by man. Yet, there were more songs to be sung in the coming forth of worlds. His next words were of water, and the cosmos was afloat with an ocean of images, and all thoughts that could ever fill the mind of man came to shine like facets in a crystal wave of spray.

But then his words were of air, and the breath of life; the winds which blow above the world urging all below to grow and thrive. This too came forth, and then his last words were of earth and of all the mountains and the armoured rock which are the backbone and the strength of the universe.

And I saw that all his words were the story of a marvellous and beautiful song and that the song of coming forth was itself a hymn for all to hear. All directions were one direction, all beauty one beauty. There was no division, but a mighty and stupendous harmony.

The magus showed me his treasured and sacred allies, which were the messengers of his will: the sword which was the father and the wand which was the son. The cup which was the mother of forthcoming, and the pentacle, the five-pointed star of daughter earth.

In these was a great mystery for I saw that they were themselves the tools by which the world was formed. Through them, like all other beings and forms, I had myself come to be. I now went forth, in quest of my first being.

THE FOOL

I know I have come upon the last pathway in the mazeway of the gods. I look around and I perceive myself to be upon the edge of an awesome cliff beyond which lies the ocean of all that is not. I feel I stand upon the brink of infinity.

And yet I am at peace. This is my home and I have been here before. All around me I feel a great warmth and love. The warmth is in the air and in the openness and in the ground below my feet.

I feel young again, renewed. My clothes are gay and brightly coloured. I wear an inner jacket as white as snow, and my outer garb is embroidered with the sigils of the sun. Upon my shoulder is the emblem of the silver moon, and around my waist I wear a belt inscribed with the legends of the zodiac.

In my right hand I bear a wand of great mystery and force. And yet I feel I mimic all its powers for I dangle from its end my wallet, containing all that is mine within the world. These possessions I have treasured on my journey and yet I do not know the value of their worth. They are shadows of myself which I have saved like coinage, and which in fond memory I carry with me now as curios of former times.

I take them from my wallet to esteem my wealth. But the sun has caught them, and demands its spoils. My memories dissolve within the haze: And yet a new treasure is mine. The light has grown brighter now and looking down upon the rocks of the cliff edge, I perceive a solitary rose, glimmering like the deep fire in the eyes of the all-seeing gods. I stoop to pick it up.

And all the time I feel the lure of the enticing ocean of no-being which embraces me from all sides upon the ledge.

She is calling me. I hear the sweet voice of my lady of the fields in the sky beyond. She is telling me that at last I have returned to her and she is happy I have come. And yet I cannot see her face or form. I feel she is around me, all around me. I sense her love within me. I hear her voice. We are together already. She is me and I am her.

We float out beyond the mountain into the great sky of all being. And looking back I see another figure in imitation of myself, draped in gay colours. A Fool sitting upon the cliff edge. But I cannot see his face.

His staff has been discarded and his wallet has fallen upon the rocks. Its contents are scattered forth in merry disarray and dance carefree in the air.

APPENDIX A
Drugs and Mysticism
A personal account

There has never been such intense and widespread interest in so many varied types of religious or 'semi-religious' expression as we find today. Even in Sydney, Guru Maharaj ji, Meha Baba, Moses David (leader of the Children of God), Aleister Crowley, Tolkien, Baba Ram Dass, the Korean prophet Sun Moon, and others, have a devoted 'evangelical' following apart from the major orthodox religions.

To some extent this fragmentation of appeal hearkens back to the United States in the early 1960s when young people in particular, who had had certain profound spiritual experiences under hallucinogens – LSD and marijuana especially – were searching for religious frameworks which would provide relevant insights into what had happened personally to them. In those days some of the above-named sects and groups were not so prevalent. More important perhaps were the various branches of Buddhism – Zen and Mahayana especially – which had developed an intellectual and literary following in California. Names like Allen Ginsburg, Aldous Huxley and Gerald Heard spring to mind as part of a mystical coterie which in a sense provided a boost for both the popular understanding of Oriental religion (Buddhism as mentioned, also Vedanta) and psychedelia.

Aldous Huxley who had documented his experiments under mescalin in the 1950s, and who had become a Mahayana Buddhist, is perhaps the one man to whom the debate about the validity of the drug-induced mystical experience can be appropriately traced. As he lay dying in November 1963 his wife gave him a dose of LSD which was designed to lift his consciousness into the more positive and spiritual realms of visionary experience. His study of the 'Tibetan Book of the Dead' had made it clear that there was an art to dying which would allow the deific rather than demonic recesses of the mind to appear first in the after-death vision. Huxley's wife wanted to assist him in relieving any pain, and in helping him to ride his life out on the wave of a transcendental experience.

One of Huxley's greatest admirers was Timothy Leary, the Harvard PhD who was to be dismissed from the Faculty of Psychology for his experiments with hallucinogens and his alleged use of 'human guinea pigs'. Three months before Huxley's death, Leary related before a meeting of mostly Lutheran psychologists gathered in Philadelphia how in 1960 he, like Huxley, had eaten 'the flesh of the gods'. A scientist had given him 'seven sacred mushrooms' (the type regarded as sacred by the Aztecs) and for five hours Leary had been 'whirled through an experience' which was in his own words 'above all and without question, the deepest religious experience of my life'.

A person who takes a psychedelic drug will not necessarily have a religious experience. Walter Pahnke, whose famous experiment relating to drugs and mysticism I want to refer to later, writes:

> Positive mystical experience with psychedelic drugs is by no means automatic. It would seem that the 'drug effect' is a delicate combination of psychological set and setting in which the drug is itself the *trigger*. . . .'

It is known that there are people on whom drugs even of the potency of LSD have no effect whatever, and others who can have an LSD-type 'high' without taking any drug. The mental attitudes of the people involved, their expectancies and the surroundings in which drugs are taken all have an extremely important bearing on the end result.

I can vouch for this personally. In 1968 I had what could be called a 'mystical illumination' under the influence of LSD. In March 1973 my father experienced a spontaneous rebirth-initiation which was more extensive in its effects than what happened to me, but nevertheless shared some important characteristics. The question of whether what I experienced was 'artificial' and whether the other was 'more natural' is obviously relevant. My father, who was raised along the lines of Theosophy and who had been profoundly influenced by Buddhism since his days in the Indian army during the war, had always insisted in discussions with me that any experience induced by partaking of some 'external' substance had to be artificial. As any mystic will tell you who is worth his salt, the answer to all lies within.

Some friends and I took 200 micrograms of LSD in the early hours of the evening. As I recall we were listening to records by groups like Jefferson Airplane and Vanilla Fudge and it was a quite typical party. Someone had a mango and at about the same time we all decided that it was appropriate to sit down in a circle together. No one in particular had decided. We were all in good spirits and had gone through preliminary laughter and idiocy behaviour. The mango suddenly acquired super-natural qualities. Its fleshy qualities seemed to endow it with life: we were handling and eating in turn from a *living thing*. This seemed to me to alternate between being cannibalistic and being sacramental. At the same time, the passing of the mango seemed to reinforce the idea of the circle of friends. We all had the eating of the mango in common. We were all one. I remember that I seemed to read others' thoughts, and anticipate what they were going to say. It doesn't really matter whether this effect was due to erroneous perception of sequences of events and time. While we were all there it had a reinforcing effect on the idea that we were all *one*.

There was an armchair behind where I was sitting on the ground and I lent back against it while remaining cross-legged. One of my friends wanted to see whether I could ascend the 'Middle Pillar', a reference to the Qabalistic equivalent of the Kundalini. This is a mental journey which in effect takes one through archetypal experiences in the subconscious mind. In the Qabalah one begins at the level of consciousness represented by Malkuth, the Maiden (= the Earth) before venturing towards Yesod, the Moon and Tiphareth, the Sun (and archetype of rebirth and life). My friend began reading to me certain passages from a very remarkable book called 'The Most Holy Trinosophia' by Comte de St-Germain, which in essence is a series of alchemystical visions. I began to experience visually what he was relating to me; the descent through a volcano into the underground of the unconscious mind.

> It was night. The moon veiled by dark clouds, cast but an uncertain light on the crags of lava that hemmed in the Solfatara. My head covered with the linen veil, holding in my hands the golden bough, I advanced without fear towards the spot where I had been ordered to pass the night. I was groping over hot sand which I felt give way under my every step. The clouds gathered overhead. Lightning flashed through the night and gave the flames of the volcano a bloodlike appearance. At last I arrived and found an iron altar where I placed the mysterious bough ... I pronounced the formidable words ... instantly the earth trembles under my feet, thunder peals ... Vesuvius roars in answer to the repeated strokes; its fires join the fires of lightning. ... The choirs of the genii rise into the air and make the echoes repeat the praises of the Creator.

I passed into an underground cavern and began to have visions of strange sub-human creatures of the earth. They did not particularly encroach and were not especially worrying. Some of them looked like the gnomes of fairy tales. At that stage the girl who had been sitting next to me on the floor went behind me to sit in the armchair. I felt both her feet beside me and she placed her hands on my forehead. Then she put them over my closed eyes and the sense of darkness was enhanced. At the same time I experienced what seems to me now to have been a tantric flow of energy through our bodies. My holding her ankles closed a circuit, and I began to rise on a wave of force. I began to soar away from the Earth towards the Moon, while my friend continued to read from St Germain. Genuinely stupid creatures with silvery bodies and inane expressions began to appear which I found very amusing. Some had heads attached directly to their legs with no abdomen in between.

Suddenly I began to experience a very pronounced soaring effect. I had no awareness of my body and seemed to be a dislocated mind. I was being sucked upwards into a white-golden light. At first there were only particles of light but these seemed to converge into a point. I followed them to their source and was enveloped by an increasing sense of transcendental bliss and well-being. An overwhelmingly sacred personage then appeared and held out his hand towards me. It was a Christ-figure in the centre of a vividly illumined cross.

I began to fall away from the vision because I could not sustain it. It was too profoundly overwhelming to bear. Gradually I gained the sense of my body and fell back 'to earth'. I was unable to think rationally for days afterwards. It had never occurred to me that I would experience a Christian vision the first time I had taken LSD. I had never regarded myself as especially Christian, and most of my theological inclinations were in the direction of Gnosticism, which had been condemned in the early Christian centuries as heretical.

Ever since this occurrence I have felt that anyone who claims that the drug experience is *necessarily* 'artificial' is uninformed. The intake of LSD, coupled with the 'tantric' flow of energy had taken me to a 'peak experience' which I can recall quite vividly now, even after eight years. Sidney Cohen makes an apt comment in his book 'Drugs of Hallucination':

> LSD is like a trigger not only in the way it releases chemical activities that proceed long after the drug has been eliminated. It also seems to trigger a depth charge into the unconscious processes. The direction that the explosion will take is the result of factors *other than the drug*.

I am quite sure that thousands of people have had spiritual experiences under hallucinogenic influence. If Pahnke is right they were probably in conducive surroundings, and in a peaceful state of mind that could only be enhanced by the effects of the drug. Undoubtedly the drug itself is an aid, but as William Braden writes in 'The Private Sea':

> The point is often made that religious ascetics traditionally have promoted their mystical states of consciousness by employing techniques that rival LSD in their probable impact on biochemical balance. These include fasting, yogic breathing exercises, sleep deprivation, dervish dances, self-flagellation, and monastic isolation. Even in the pews of the pious, religious contemplation may be supported by such trance-inducing aids as organ music, stained glass windows, repetitive chants and prayers, incense and flickering candles.

It is interesting that LSD is structurally similar to the substance serotonin which is stored in the pineal gland in the brain, traditionally the location of the 'third eye'. LSD is believed to act in the serotonin receptor site in the brain, causing an overaction of psycho-physiological stimulation which a person may or may not be able to cope with. Yogic preparations enable the devotee to perfect the physical vehicle of his body, through which the Kundalini energies will flow. However yogic *asanas* are not necessarily the only means of inducing a mystical experience.

Since the days of William James's 'The Varieties of Religious Experience', the mystical experience in its myriad of cultural settings, has been widely documented and analysed. Some writers, particularly those with a Theosophical bent, have sought to examine the universals, the common experiences underlying religious and mystical expression and illumination everywhere. Others, like Professor Zaehner who took mescalin in order to differentiate drug-precipitated and natural mystical experiences, have been motivated by their own allegiances (Zaehner was a devout Catholic) to seek for differences.

Walter Pahnke, who was Director of Clinical Sciences Research in the Maryland State Psychiatric Research Centre in Baltimore, before his death in 1971 undertook to test the nature of the religious-drug experience. He used as his framework a list of common mystical attributes drawn up by W.T. Stace, a leading scholar in the field of comparative religion. These attributes or qualities fall under nine headings which represent the most commonly reported aspects of the mystical experience:

Unity   both within, and without in the external world. A profound sense of 'one-ness'.
Transcendence of time and space   the mystical experience is not contained within three-dimensional space. It is often described as 'eternal' and 'infinite'.
Deeply felt positive mood   Joy, blessedness and peace impart to the person the sense that his experience has been of incalculable value.
The sense of sacredness   something is beheld which has the quality of being able to be profaned. There is a profound sense of awe.
Objectivity and reality   knowledge and illumination: the experience seems to be overwhelmingly authoritative. No 'proof' is necessary, 'ultimate reality carries its own sense of certainty'.
Paradoxicality   Rational interpretations following the illumination seem to be logically contradictory. An all-encompassing unity devoid of specific attributes is also in another sense an emptiness, and so on.
Alleged ineffability   Words fail to express adequately the mystical experience.
Transiency   Mystical consciousness is not sustained indefinitely; it is more of a 'peak experience'.
Persisting positive changes in attitude and behaviour   Lasting psychological changes are experienced which affect the quality of interaction with others, and with life itself. The mystical experience itself is held in awe, and one is more at peace with oneself.

Pahnke gathered together twenty Christian theological students in a private chapel. Ten had been given the hallucinogenic agent psilocybin, the active principle in psychotropic mushrooms. The others were given nicotinic acid, a vitamin which causes 'transient feelings of warmth and tingling of the skin'. The participants listened to a $2\frac{1}{2}$-hour religious service consisting of organ music, four solos, readings, prayers and personal meditation. During the weeks before the experiment, special care had been taken to reduce fear and maximize expectancy, and during the session none knew the nature of the substance he had taken.

Pahnke collected data for up to six months afterwards, and each subject had prepared by this time an account of his own personal experiences. The following are Pahnke's statistics, which condensed as percentages are admittedly clinical. They do however prove a point.

Of those who had taken psilocybin, 70 per cent experienced *inner* unity, and 38 per cent *external*. Eighty-four per cent had a sense of transcendence of time and space, 57 per cent the positive mood, 53 per cent a feeling of sacredness, 63 per cent the sense of objectivity and reality, 61 per cent the element of paradoxicality, 66 per cent ineffability, 79 per cent transiency, and an average of 50 per cent were substantially changed in psychological attitudes, along the lines of Stace's framework.

The control group, that is, those who had not taken the hallucinogenic drug, for the most part had much less intense religious experiences. The most pronounced sentiment was the feeling of love (positive mood) which was felt by 33 per cent. Otherwise the figures were: unity (7 per cent); time and space (6 per cent); positive mood (23 per cent); sacredness (28 per cent); objectivity and reality (18 per cent); paradoxicality (13 per cent); ineffability (18 per cent); transiency (8 per cent) and psychological changes (8 per cent).

Pahnke's experiment went a long way in showing the value of hallucinogens in intensifying what would normally be a mild and rare religious experience. The degree of enhancement is most marked in all categories and shows that *within congenial surroundings, people can experience transcendental illumination of the type reported universally, under the impact of a hallucinogenic catalyst.*

What I have called earlier my father's 'spontaneous rebirth initiation' occurred entirely without the use of drugs. As I have indicated, he is quite opposed to them. However, my father's experiences, which occurred over the passage of a few weeks, could be said in some measure to have come at a time when he was summing up his whole life: its successes, failures and possible future direction. I was present only towards the end of the cycle, at my mother's request since she thought he was going mad. This is important because much of what happened is focused upon the family unit, and I no longer live with my parents.

My father was walking along a beach in Perth with my mother. He quite suddenly experienced extreme paranoia, feeling that he was surrounded by others on the beach who were antagonists. Suddenly he made a gesture which was to characterize the whole cycle: *he stared steadfastly at the sun.* He then rushed into the sea, submerging himself as if in an act of baptism and stared again at the sun as if by command. A voice, which my father has insisted was mine, told him to behold the Rosy Cross, and the colours blue, green and gold which would follow in sequence. He should then avert his eyes. He was assured by the voice that his eyes would not be harmed by this practice. (At this stage I would like to make it clear that I was somewhat embarrassed when my father told me that he had heard my voice in the sun. I think that the relevance of his experience has since become clearer, but it was not my intention to speak to, or 'initiate' my father. There was certainly no conscious telepathy from one side of Australia to the other.)

Over a sequence of visits to the beach the voice continued to instruct and to comment upon the range of psychic colours which became visible as my father looked upwards to the sun. Father became aware at this time, of the auras of the whole family, and the latter acquired a sacred significance expressed in biblical terms. He saw himself symbolically as Joseph, and my mother as Mary. My younger brother appeared as the *companion*, John the Baptist, and my youngest brother, who has very fair, golden hair, took the role of the divine Christ child. The voice speaking from the sun identified itself as the 'Lord of the World'. When walking along the beach my father seemed surrounded by portents. Gulls flew by in symbolic number groups; he spoke with friendly animals; he again saw 'adversaries' clothed in 'hostile' colours.

During the same period he had a number of Shiva visions, and was also 'told' on one occasion to stand on an excrutiatingly hot metal grid which upon so doing, became as cold as a normal floor.

More recently my father began to speak with the sun daily and to await the motion of the wind which accompanied the voice. He was told that anyone who violated the sacred nature of the 'family' would 'reap the whirlwind'.

As a consequence of these encounters with the voice of the sun, my father became physically renewed. He gave up his habit of very heavy smoking and was able, when focusing on the human outline, to see the auric colours vibrating in an energy field. He had never been able to do this before, and subsequently painted a picture of my mother and youngest brother in the symbolic blue and gold colours in which they appeared to him. The frustrations, contradictions and paranoia of this earlier personality appeared to have played themselves out to an extent where he felt for the first time at peace with himself. It is not surprising that the family had special significance in these events because my father is essentially nomadic, and with few possessions, has taken the family 'band' from England to Australia three times in a type of career frustration which is now unlikely to continue.

There is a hazy line as many have indicated, between madness and illumination. Perhaps the only valid criterion of assessment is the way in which the individual can see the world after these insights (or delusions) have occurred. In my father's case I felt that he had acquired a degree of integration and harmony with himself which had not previously been present. There did not appear to be any mystical schizophrenia, or desire to escape from the real world. Instead, in a sense, the profane and sacred had met on common ground. Through the voice of the sun he had had contact and rapport with a transcendental dimension which was able over a time to reshape his life.

The only way I have found of understanding aspects of both my own and my father's experiences, has been through the symbolism of the Qabalistic Tree of Life and the Middle Pillar. As if on a mythological journey, my LSD visions had taken me through archetypal imagery so that after an overwhelming and blissful 'ascent' I had encountered the Christ as a giver of life and light within the centre of the Rosy Cross. Within Pahnke's framework, I had had ideal circumstances, being together with friends in a 'ritual' context. The sun archetype in the Qabalah, which is typified by the heart chakras, the colour gold, and the spiritual experience of rebirth and transformation, is called Tiphareth. It is the home, in mythology (and the Collective Unconscious, to use Jung's term), of the sun gods, whether Apollo or Helios. Also, of deities of rebirth and resurrection – Osiris and Christ. My father had encountered these factors in different circumstances whereby his immediate context, the family, acquired sacred, transformational characteristics. I was at great pains to point out to my mother that she had not really given birth to the new Messiah but that my father's outlook was purely symbolic of the regenerative processes which were happening in him at the time!

Finally, on the question of the validity of the drug-initiated mystical experience; it appears that if a hallucinogen can trigger an out-of-the-body experience, and if the person concerned then uses a *spiritual framework such as the Tree of Life* as a guide to his expansion of consciousness, then some type of 'transcendental illumination' may occur. John Lilly describes another framework, based on Gurdjieff, in his book 'The Centre of the Cyclone', and of course the celebrated 'Tibetan Book of the Dead' with its central theme of birth and rebirth, is the focus of Leary's 'The Psychedelic Experience'. Drugs, according to their potency, unleash unconscious imagery from the recesses of the mind. Whether the 'trip' will be into heaven or hell is for the candidate to determine.

APPENDIX B
Elements appropriate to the Tarot Paths

The Fool	Air
The Magician	Fire
The High Priestess	Water
The Empress	Earth
The Emperor	Fire
The Hierophant	Earth
The Lovers	Air
The Chariot	Water
Strength	Fire
The Hermit	Earth
The Wheel of Fortune	Water
Justice	Air
The Hanged Man	Water
Death	Water
Temperance	Fire
The Devil	Earth
The Tower	Fire
The Star	Water
The Moon	Water
The Sun	Fire
Judgment	Fire
The World	Earth

Notes

CHAPTER 1 THE SHAMAN AND HIS UNIVERSE

1 The account of Father Trilles's experience is related in a number of books, among them E. de Martino's 'Magic, Primitive and Modern', 1972, pp. 148 ff.
2 M. Harner, 'The Jivaro', 1972, p. 134.
3 R.E. Schultes, in G.M. Weil et al., 'The Psychedelic Reader', 1971, p. 105.
4 H. Munn, in M. Harner (ed.), 'Hallucinogens and Shamanism', 1973, p. 101.
5 R.E. Schultes, op. cit., p. 97.
6 M. Harner, 'Hallucinogens and Shamanism', 1973, p. 161.
7 C. Castaneda, 'The Teachings of Don Juan', 1973, p. 60.
8 Ibid., p. 114.
9 A. Huxley, 'The Doors of Perception/Heaven and Hell', 1963, p. 18.
10 M. Harner, 'Hallucinogens and Shamanism', 1973, p. 16.
11 Ibid., p. 166.
12 E. de Martino, op. cit., p. 74.
13 Ibid., p. 82.

CHAPTER 2 ASTRAL PROJECTION: THE PIONEERS

1 D. Sharon, 'The San Pedro Cactus in Peruvian Folk Healing', in P. Furst (ed.), 'Flesh of the Gods: The Ritual Use of Hallucinogens', 1972, pp. 114 ff.
2 S. Muldoon and H. Carrington, 'The Projection of the Astral Body', 1971, p. 52.
3 Ibid., p. 91.
4 Ibid., p. 49.
5 S. Ostrander and L. Shroeder, 'Psychic Discoveries Behind the Iron Curtain', 1971.
6 S. Muldoon and H. Carrington, op. cit., p. 125.
7 O. Fox, 'Astral Projection', 1962, pp. 32 ff.
8 Ibid., p. 113.
9 Ibid., p. 50.

224

10 Ibid., p. 66.
11 Ibid., pp. 127-8.
12 Ibid., p. 107.
13 See Dr Tart's Introduction in R.A. Monroe, 'Journeys out of the Body', 1973.
14 R.A. Monroe, op. cit., pp. 60 ff.
15 Ibid., pp. 74 ff.
16 Ibid., pp. 94-5.
17 See Part three: The Book of Visions, in this book.
18 P.F. Case, 'The Tarot', 1948, p. 190.
19 Ibid., p. 192.
20 R.A. Monroe, op. cit., p. 131.

CHAPTER 3   FURTHER CONSIDERATIONS

1 The after-image of normal vision is believed to be the 'complement' or other face of images occurring on the astral plane.
2 Soror Vestigia, in I. Regardie, 'The Golden Dawn', 1940, vol. 4, pp. 43 ff.
3 C. Castaneda, 'The Teachings of Don Juan', 1973, p. 188.
4 Ibid., p. 192.
5 Dr C. Tart, in R.A. Monroe, 'Journeys out of the Body', 1973, p. 4.
6 Yram, in H.F.B. Battersby's 'Man Outside Himself', 1969, p. 87.
7 M. Harner (ed.), 'Hallucinogens and Shamanism', 1973, p. 180.
8 Ibid.
9 D. Ebin, 'The Drug Experience', 1961, p. 332.
10 Ibid., p. 106.
11 Ibid., p. 108.
12 Quoted in N. Drury, 'The Path of the Chameleon', 1973, pp. 112 ff.
13 See commentary in J.D.P. Bolton, 'Aristeas of Proconnesus', Oxford University Press, 1962, p. 3.
14 O. Fox, 'Astral Projection', 1962, p. 68.
15 R. Johnson, 'The Watcher on the Hills', 1959, p. 150.
16 S. Cohen, 'Drugs of Hallucination', 1970, p. 83.
17 R. Johnson, op. cit., pp. 157 ff.
18 O. Fox, op. cit., pp. 106-7.
19 C. Castaneda, 'A Separate Reality', 1971, p. 271.
20 Ibid.

CHAPTER 4   COMPARISONS: TWO SYSTEMS OF MAGIC

1 C. Castaneda, 'Journey to Ixtlan', 1972, p. 30.
2 Choronzon was the demon of Chaos. For an interesting account of

this incident see J.O. Fuller, 'The Magical Dilemma of Victor Neuburg', 1965.
3 Details of this ritual are given in A. Crowley, 'Magick in Theory and Practice', 1973 edn, p. 456.
4 Soror Vestigia, in I. Regardie, 'The Golden Dawn', 1940, vol. 4, p. 43.
5 C. Castaneda, 'The Teachings of Don Juan', 1973, p. 58.
6 Ibid., p. 151.

CHAPTER 5 TOWARDS A FRAMEWORK FOR INNER SPACE

1 C. Castaneda, in 'Psychology Today', 1972, reproduced in Sam Keen's 'Voices and Visions', 1975, Harper and Row, New York.
2 T. Leary, 'High Priest', 1968, pp. 20-1.
3 Ibid., p. 25.
4 T. Leary, 'The Politics of Ecstasy', 1970, p. 112.
5 Ibid., p. 131.
6 Ibid., p. 15.
7 W.Y. Evans-Wentz, 'The Tibetan Book of the Dead', 1960.
8 At the time that this book was being written, Leary had just been transferred from Folsom Prison to a lower security prison confinement. More recently he has been released from prison altogether.
9 R. Metzner, 'Maps of Consciousness', 1971, p. 9.
10 Ibid., p. 38.
11 Ibid., p. 148.
12 See The Circular Ruins, in J.L. Borges's anthology, 'Labyrinths', 1970.

CHAPTER 6 CHRISTIANITY, MAGIC AND SCIENCE

1 O. Chadwick, 'The Victorian Church', 1966, pp. 558-9.
2 Ibid., p. 567.
3 Ibid.
4 P.T. Marsh, 'The Victorian Church in Decline', 1969, pp. 38-9.
5 A.O.J. Cockshut, 'Religious Controversies of the Nineteenth Century', 1966, p. 246.

CHAPTER 7 THE HERMETIC ORDER OF THE GOLDEN DAWN: CEREMONIAL FOR THE GOD-MAN

1 E. Howe, 'The Magicians of the Golden Dawn', 1972, p. 127.
2 Ibid.

3 F. King, 'The Secret Rituals of the O.T.O.', 1970 edn, p. 97.
4 Ibid., p. 57.
5 I. Regardie (ed.), 'The Golden Dawn', vol. 1, 1937, pp. 35-6.
6 This was one of Mathers's magical mottoes intended to incorporate his magical 'will'. This one reflects Mathers's Celtic affiliations and aspirations.
7 The Fool knows nothing, the abstracted transcendent Godhead.
8 N. Drury, 'The Path of the Chameleon', 1973, pp. 142-3.

CHAPTER 8   ALEISTER CROWLEY AND THE AEON OF HORUS

1 A. Crowley, 'Magick in Theory and Practice', 1929 edn, p. xv.
2 Ibid., p. xvi.
3 Ibid., p. xvii.
4 Ibid., p. 4.
5 Ibid.
6 Ibid., p. xvi.
7 S.L. Mathers, 'The Book of the Sacred Magic of Abremelin the Mage', 1932, pp. xxv ff.
8 Ibid.
9 J. Symonds, 'The Great Beast: The Life and Magic of Aleister Crowley', 1972, p. 43.
10 Contained in the Appendix of 'The Magical Record of the Beast 666', ed. J. Symonds and K. Grant, 1972.
11 A. Crowley, op. cit., p. 12.
12 K. Grant, 'The Magical Revival', 1972, p. 20.
13 A. Crowley, op. cit., p. 11.
14 K. Grant, op. cit., p. 45.
15 Ibid., p. 144.
16 Ibid., p. 145.
17 J. Symonds and K. Grant (eds), 'The Confessions of Aleister Crowley', 1969, p. 395.
18 Ibid., p. 396.
19 Ibid., p. 398.
20 Ibid., p. 403.
21 K. Grant, op. cit., p. 9.
22 Ibid., p. 2.
23 Fr. Achad, 'The Anatomy of the Body of God', 1969, p. vi.
24 Ibid.
25 Ibid., p. xv.
26 Ibid., p. 111.
27 J.O. Fuller, 'The Magical Dilemma of Victor Neuburg', 1965, p. 136.
28 E. Howe, 'The Magicians of the Golden Dawn', 1972, p. xix.

CHAPTER 9   WHENCE THE MAGICIAN?

1   Fr. Achad, 'The Anatomy of the Body of God', 1969, p. v.
2   S.G.F. Brandon, 'The Judgment of the Dead', 1967, p. 6.
3   Ellic Howe, 'The Magicians of the Golden Dawn', 1972, p. 6.
4   A.E. Waite, 'Shadows of Life and Thought', 1938, p. 99.
5   Ibid., p. 161.
6   D. Fortune, 'The Mystical Qabalah', 1966, p. 5.
7   W.B. Yeats, 'Autobiographies', 1926, p. 471.
8   Ellic Howe, op. cit., p. xxii.
9   This painting is reproduced in a companion volume to the present
    book, N. Drury and S. Skinner, 'The Search for Abraxas', 1972.
10 Ibid., p. 66.
11 Ibid., p. 63.
12 J.O. Fuller, 'The Magical Dilemma of Victor Neuburg', 1965, p.
    135.
13 J. Symonds, 'The Great Beast: The Life and Magic of Aleister
    Crowley', 1973, p. 177.
14 Ibid., p. 186.
15 A tantric term for mystically directed coition between man and
    woman.
16 K. Grant, 'The Magical Revival', 1972, p. 175.
17 Isis is a member of the Trinity, and when charted on the Tree of Life
    is represented by the colour black.
18 K. Grant, op. cit., p. 177.
19 D. Fortune, op. cit., p. 9.
20 Ibid., p. 10.
21 I. Regardie, 'The Art and Meaning of Magic', 1964, p. 26.
22 Ibid., p. 9.
23 Ibid., pp. 16-17.
24 Ibid., p. 28.

CHAPTER 10   A PATH IN THE WEST

1   J. Symonds, 'The Great Beast: The Life and Magic of Aleister
    Crowley', 1973.
2   G. Knight, 'A Practical Guide to Qabalistic Symbolism', 1965, vol. 2,
    p. 115.
3   P.F. Case, 'The Tarot', 1948, p. 123.
4   A. Crowley, 'The Book of Thoth', 1969, p. 86.
5   P.F. Case, op. cit., p. 59.
6   Quoted from A. Crowley's 'Equinox', vol. 1, no. 2, pp. 302-6. The
    complete set of Crowley's 'Equinox' has been reprinted by Weiser,
    New York, 1975.

APPENDIX A   DRUGS AND MYSTICISM: A PERSONAL ACCOUNT

1   This first appeared in 'Cosmos', (Sydney) vol. 1, no. 8, in a slightly
    different form.

Bibliography

ACHAD, FRATER (1969), 'The Anatomy of the Body of God', Weiser, New York, 2nd ed.

BARDON, FRANZ (1967), 'The Practice of Magical Evocation', Pravica, Graz Puntigam, Austria.

BATTERSBY, H.F.P. (1969), 'Man Outside Himself', University Books, New York.

BORGES, JORGE LUIS (1970), 'Labyrinths', Penguin Books, Harmondsworth.

BRADEN, WILLIAM (1967), 'The Private Sea', Pall Mall, London.

BRANDON, S.G.F. (1967), 'The Judgment of the Dead', Weidenfeld & Nicolson, London.

BUTLER, W.E. (1959), 'The Magician, his Training and Work', Aquarian Press, London.

BUTLER, W.E. (1964), 'Magic and the Qabalah', Aquarian Press, London.

CASE, PAUL F. (1948), 'The Tarot', Macoy, New York.

CASTANEDA, CARLOS (1970), 'The Teachings of Don Juan: A Yaqui Way of Knowledge', Penguin Books, Harmondsworth.

CASTANEDA, CARLOS (1971), 'A Separate Reality', Bodley Head, London.

CASTANEDA, CARLOS (1972), 'Journey to Ixtlan: The Lessons of Don Juan', Simon & Schuster, New York.

CHADWICK, O. (1968), 'The Victorian Church', A&C Black, London.

COCKSHUT, A.O.J. (1966), 'Religious Controversies of the Nineteenth Century', Methuen, London.

COHEN, SIDNEY (1970), 'Drugs of Hallucination', Paladin, London.

CROWLEY, ALEISTER (1929), 'Magick in Theory and Practice', published privately. Published in 1973 by Routledge & Kegan Paul, London.

CROWLEY, ALEISTER (1962), 'The Book of Lies', Hayden Press, Devon.

CROWLEY, ALEISTER (1969), 'The Book of Thoth', Weiser, New York.

CROWLEY, ALEISTER (1972a), 'The Vision and the Voice', Sangreal Foundation, Dallas.

CROWLEY, ALEISTER (1972b), 'Book Four', Sangreal Foundation, Dallas.

DASS, BABA RAM (1973), 'Doing Your Own Being', Spearman, London.

DRURY, NEVILL and SKINNER, STEPHEN (1972), 'The Search For Abraxas', Spearman, London.

DRURY, NEVILL (1973), 'The Path of the Chamelon', Spearman, London.

EBIN, DAVID (1961), 'The Drug Experience', Grove Press, New York.

ELIADE, MIRCEA (1964), 'Shamanism', Routledge & Kegan Paul, London.

EVANS-WENTZ, W.Y. (ed.) (1960), 'The Tibetan Book of the Dead', Oxford University Press, New York.

FORTUNE, DION (1966), 'The Mystical Qabalah', Benn, London.

FOX, OLIVER (1962), 'Astral Projection', University Books, New York.

FULLER, JEAN O. (1965), 'The Magical Dilemma of Victor Neuburg', W.H. Allen, London.

FURST, PETER T. (ed.) (1972), 'Flesh of the Gods: The Ritual Use of Hallucinogens', Allen & Unwin, London.

GRANT, KENNETH (1972), 'The Magical Revival', Muller, London.

GRANT, KENNETH (1973), 'Aleister Crowley and the Hidden God', Muller, London.

GREEN, CELIA (1968), 'Lucid Dreams', Hamish Hamilton, London.

HARNER, MICHAEL (1972), 'The Jivaro', Robert Hale, London.

HARNER, MICHAEL (ed.) (1973), 'Hallucinogens and Shamanism', Oxford University Press, New York.

HOWE, ELLIC (1972), 'The Magicians of the Golden Dawn', Routledge & Kegan Paul, London (Introduction by Gerald Yorke).

HUXLEY, ALDOUS (1963), 'The Doors of Perception/Heaven and Hell', Penguin Books, Harmondsworth.

JOHNSON, RAYNOR (1959), 'The Watcher on the Hills', Hodder & Stoughton, London.

JUNG, C.G. (1968), 'Man and his Symbols', Dell, New York.

KING, FRANCIS (1971), 'Ritual Magic in England', Spearman, London.

KING, FRANCIS (1973), 'The Secret Rituals of the O.T.O.', Daniel, London.

KNIGHT, GARETH (1965), 'A Practical Guide to Qabalistic Symbolism', Helios, Cheltenham.

LEARY, TIMOTHY (1964), 'The Psychedelic Experience', University Books, New York.

LEARY, TIMOTHY (1968), 'High Priest', College Notes and Texts, New York.

LEARY, TIMOTHY (1970), 'The Politics of Ecstasy', Paladin, London.

LEVI, ELIPHAS (1959), 'The Key of the Mysteries', Rider, London.

LILLY, JOHN C. (1973), 'The Centre of the Cyclone', Calder & Boyars, London.

LILLY, JOHN C. (1974), 'The Human Biocomputer', Abacus, London.

MACINTOSH, CHRISTOPHER (1972), 'Eliphas Levi and the French Occult Revival', Rider, London.

MARSH, P.T. (1969), 'The Victorian Church in Decline', Routledge & Kegan Paul, London.

MARTINO, ERNEST DE (1972), 'Magic, Primitive and Modern', Bay Books, Sydney.

MATHERS, S.L. (1932), 'The Book of the Sacred Magic of Abremelin the Mage', De Lawrence, Chicago.

MATHERS, S.L. (1957), 'The Kabbalah Unveiled', Routledge & Kegan Paul, London.

MERRELL-WOLFF, F. (1973), 'Pathways Through to Space', Julian Press, New York.

METZNER, RALPH (1971), 'Maps of Consciousness', Macmillan, New York.

MISHRA, RAMMURTI (1959), 'Fundamentals of Yoga', Julian Press, New York.

MONROE, ROBERT A. (1973), 'Journeys Out of the Body', Anchor/Doubleday, New York.

MULDOON, SYLVAN and CARRINGTON, HEREWARD (1929), 'The Projection of the Astral Body', Rider, London.

OSTRANDER, S. and SHROEDER, L. (1971), 'Psychic Discoveries Behind the Iron Curtain', Bantam Books, New York.

PAHNKE, WALTER (1971), The Psychedelic Mystical Experience, in 'Psychedelic Review', no. 2, San Francisco.

REGARDIE, ISRAEL (1937), 'The Tree of Life', Rider, London.

REGARDIE, ISRAEL (ed.) (1937-40), 'The Golden Dawn', (4 vols), Aries Press, Chicago.

REGARDIE, ISRAEL (1964), 'The Art and Meaning of Magic', Helios, Cheltenham.

SAINT-GERMAIN, COMTE DE (1949), 'The Most Holy Trinosophia', Philosophers Press, Los Angeles.

SANDFORD, JEREMY (1972), 'In Search of the Magic Mushroom', New English Library, London.

SCHAYA, LEO (1971), 'The Universal Meaning of the Kabbalah', University Books, New York.

SCHOLEM, G. (1961), 'Major Trends in Jewish Mysticism', Schocken Books, New York.

SYMONDS, J. (1973), 'The Great Beast: The Life and Magic of Aleister Crowley', Mayflower, London.

SYMONDS, J. and GRANT, K. (eds) (1969), 'The Confessions of Aleister Crowley', Hill & Wang, New York.

SYMONDS, J. and GRANT, K. (eds) (1972), 'The Magical Record of the Beast 666', Duckworth, London.

TART, CHARLES T. (ed.) (1969), 'Altered States of Consciousness', John Wiley, New York.

TORRENS, R.G. (1973), 'The Secret Rituals of the Golden Dawn', Aquarian Press, Northamptonshire.

WAITE, A.E. (1914), 'The Secret Doctrine in Israel', OMTBC, Boston.

WAITE, A.E. (1938), 'Shadows of Life and Thought', Selwyn & Blount, London.

WASSON, R. GORDON (1972), 'Soma: Divine Mushroom of Immortality', Harcourt, Brace, Jovanovich, New York.

WATTS, ALAN W. (1962), 'The Joyous Cosmology', Vintage/Random House, New York.

WEIL, G.M., METZNER, R. and LEARY, T. (1971), 'The Psychedelic Reader', Citadel, New York.

WHITE, JOHN (ed.) (1972), 'The Highest State of Consciousness', Anchor/Doubleday, New York.

YEATS, W.B. (1926), 'Autobiographies', Macmillan, London.

YEATS, W.B. (1959), 'Mythologies', Macmillan, London.

Index

ARKANA

Timeless Wisdom For Today

ARKANA is the new paperback imprint from Routledge & Kegan Paul devoted to books which contribute towards our understanding of ourselves and our place in the universe.

One of the most exciting challenges facing us at the end of the twentieth century is to learn to live harmoniously with ourselves, with each other and with the planet which sustains us.

There are many ways of meeting this challenge: the practice of a spiritual tradition, one of the new psychological techniques of transformation, the esoteric arts, or a greater awareness of the body and its relation to mind and psyche.

ARKANA makes available to a new generation of readers classic works which have been a source of inspiration and guidance from the earliest times to the present day, and new books from the leading edge of contemporary thinking.

A full list of ARKANA paperbacks is available from:

> The Publicity Department
> Routledge & Kegan Paul
> 14 Leicester Square
> London
> WC2P 7PH.

On the following pages you will find a selection of ARKANA titles which you might enjoy.

ARKANA

HOW TO BE HAPPY

John Pepper

How to be Happy is a simple guide to that most complex of tasks, changing your life for the better.

Pointing out that happiness can be no escape into a fantasy world free of misfortune, only a way, first, of coping with adversity, then making something life-enhancing of the result, the author leads us towards the centres of ourselves where the secrets of our happiness lie. He shows us a wellbeing built on compassion, understanding and social conscience which needs neither worldly success nor institutionalized religion to sustain it; one not dependent, either, on our belonging to any group or subscribing to any ideology.

How to be Happy, by a prize-winning British writer, celebrates the possibility of love and renewal for us all.

ARKANA

THE MAGUS OF STROVOLOS
K C Markides

In this vivid account, Kyriacos C Markides introduces us to the rich and intricate world of Daskalos, the Magus of Strovolos. In what appears at first to be an exercise in fantasy, we see the extraordinary Daskalos draw on a seemingly unlimited mixture of esoteric teachings, psychology, reincarnation, demonology, cosmology and mysticism, from both Eastern and Western traditions.

But Daskalos is first and foremost a healer, whose work is firmly rooted in a belief in "Holyspirit", or absolute love. We cannot fail to be impressed by his feats of healing, his immense knowledge-ability, intelligence and wisdom, and eventually we comprehend the logically consistent world-view within his labyrinthine reality.

ARKANA

THE CULT OF THE BLACK VIRGIN

Ean Begg

Why are over 400 of the world's miraculous images of the Madonna black? Why is this fact so little known?

The Cult of the Black Virgin investigates the pagan origins of the phenomenon as well as the heretical Gnostic-Christian underground stream which flowed west with the cult of Mary Magdalene and re-surfaced in Catharism. Many black virgins date from this period and are reputed to have been brought back from Templars from the Crusades. They are a symbol of the Ark of the Covenant and the Holy Grail which are the goal of the quest for the lost feminine wisdom and the search for soul.

THE WESTERN WAY - VOLUME ONE

Foreword by Gareth Knight

Below the surface of Western culture run hidden springs of a secret tradition that has its source in the ancestral past. Its lore is transmitted by guardians of the earth-wisdom and the powerful energies which are called gods. We are each potential guardians of this rich and deep tradition, which is carried within our ancestral bloodlines. Within this book are practical exercises relating traditional wisdom to everyday life: ways to put you in touch with your native roots, to help you discover your personal totem, to take the journey to the Otherworld, and to experience for yourself the ancient earth mysteries.

In this two-volume work on the Western Mystery Tradition, the authors trace the origin and practices of esotericism and the ways in which they have survived or been revived in this century. In the first volume, they deal with the development of the Native Tradition; in the second volume they will discuss the Hermetic Tradition which grew out of and built upon these earlier foundations.

With the experience gained from travelling the Western Way, we can learn to understand the patterns of evolving consciousness, becoming skilful mediators on both inner and outer levels.